AMBEDKAR AND HIS WRITINGS
A Look For The New Generation

AMBEDKAR AND HIS WRITINGS

A Look For The New Generation

DR. RAJ KUMAR

KALPAZ PUBLICATIONS
DELHI-110052

Ambedkar And His Writings : A Look For The New Generation

Rs. 750

ISBN: 81-7835-659-7

Published in 2008 in India by
Kalpaz Publications
C-30, Satyawati Nagar,
Delhi-110052
E-mail: kalpaz@hotmail.com
Phone : 9212729499

Lasser Type Setting by: Rudra Computer Graphics, Delhi
Printed at: Singal Print Media, Delhi

Contents

Preface

The book entitled "*Ambedkar and His Writings, A Look For the New Generation,*" which covers the fascination history behind Dr. B.R. Ambedkar and his career. It is a matter of great pleasure that the book aims to present all the essential information required by the readers who has no previous knowledge about the early career of Dr. B.R. Ambedkar, who he fought with communal forces with the writings of his pen during '*Round Table Conferences*' with practice and experience with scientific methods of the teachings of *Buddh* or *Kabir* which called '*Nam*' or God in this universe. He was born as an '*Untouchable*' had undergone all sorts of humiliation, torture and discrimination at the hands of Caste Hindus and Muslim despite his being the highly educated intellectual in India, and highly appreciated in the world community.

He understood the gravity of the disease which Hindu society was effected that caste system or '*Varnashram* Social System or called Brahminical Hindu Social Order which were based on blind faith called educated society suppressed the Depresses Classes,' those were used to work for the welfare of the man in different professional courses the false propaganda of the Bahmans based on 'ego' as a destructive size of the society as *Gandhi* and *Jinnah* did in the national movement of India and India was partitionized on the 'ego' clash. Dr. B.R. Ambedkar was highly depressed by their attitude and behaviour, they could not understand the logic of the history and political science as the Britishers know to Dr. B.R. Ambedkar. On the basis of the untouchability, he has been degraded by these of the sixty year of independence, the caste system, the blind faith of Brahmins because on his simplicity and pious approach toward Father. There was a full deprivation of *Sudhra* people in the Government job since the period of Dr. Zakir Hussain, even the founding Father of the Constitution has made full privision in Government services. It shows that there was a lot of exploitation, compression, humiliation of the 'Depresses Classes' and who he fought at that time, it again shows that what kind of torturing and humiliation he faced during his life time. Year ago, author has published a book i.e. *'History of the Brahmans'* 2006. But that could not be materialized by the people from the background of Brahmins, because they think that Father was *Schedule Caste* and His spiritual idea of *Lord Buddha* and *Kabir* as the negligible, no need to pay the attention to such book which gives the historical truth of human history. Even, Dr. B.R. Ambedkar made a speech on November 17; 1949 on the floor of the Constituent Assembly, that "*History Will Repeat Itself*" but they could not bother for the *Sudhra Caste*, because they are degraded people of the Father.

As a result, the evil of injecting caste poison into politics, as Gandhi and Jinnah did during the partition of India, they measured the number of people for their leadership which based on 'Religion' as blind faith, tradition, rite and ritual not based on human principle. Major caste began to monopolise political power and corner the social services of the people for their welfare. The work which we have seen after 1947, they did for their own benefit by making the corruption from the different projects and schemes. As a result, the social evils are on the increase to grab the political power for their own benefit and T.A. D.A. Ambedkar gave a top priority in the Constitution for the destruction of such separatist feelings and the evil of intolerability by making Laws in the Constitution of India for the social harmony. But the people from the background of the Brahminical Ideology, they have suppressed the view of untouchable, called Dr. B.R. Ambedkar, who was the maker of modern India by providing certain facilities to the women and employment opportunities by creating a visionary document on that direction, number of institution and employment has be given to the Indian, but thankless Indian forgotten the Father, they hate with him on the basis of caste. It is a matter of fact, that hardly they know the meaning of *Caste.* We must realize, and this is unfortunate that many in public life tend to overlook the historical fact of the history which we already mention about the book, sometimes out of ignorance of the forces of history i.e. *Sudhras* have been deprived from actual right that country like India belong to them. Perhaps now where else in the world has nature or God been so kind and benevolent to people as in Kashmir where the *Sudhra* Class used to rule in number of years in India which have been ignored by the modern politicians as well as by the Brahmins.

They destroyed their history on the basis of their 'ego', it took the benefit of the simplicity of *Sudhras.* From the ancient indigenous poets who compared sweet lyrics in praise of the origin of the coin during Indo-Aryan society that was the *tanner* or *Chamar*, he never dies, he works for the common peoples in hide, as his simplicity, but Kashmir is his homeland, after working the people as a *Cooli* or *Kulli*, he land on earth from the Heavenly world to save his force which distorted by Brahmins under the blind faith without any logic and reason as we take the example of *Ravidas* he defeated the communal forces during medieval period and serve the society by making shoes and sandal. When we go for the study of Dr. B.R. Ambedkar, he used the same concept, but in the modern methods of the evolution of the history defined *'The Problem of Rupee in India'* as a coin has two sides, one has the emblam of Ashoka and other has metric system of measurement as the life has itself God and the man. Man has to see the right track, i.e. humanistic and rational approach because they are the force of the Father. Thus, the *Sudhra* is constructive force and Brahmin is a destructive force of the History, creates Caste, Colour and Creed in the society as barrier for their own benefit else is nothing.

Abbreviations

The following are used standardize Abbreviations:

A.I.C.C.F.N.	All India Congress Committee Files (N.M.M.L.)
A.S.I.	Archaeological Survey of India
E.P.W.	Economic and Political Weekly
FIG.	Figures
Home Public FN	Government of India Home Public/Home Political
Home Public FN	Files (N.A.I.)
I.E.S.H.R	Indian Economic and Social History Review
I.H.R.	Indian Historical Review
I.O.L.,	Indian Office Library, London
M.A.S.	Modern Asian Studies
N.A.I.	National Archives of India, New Delhi
N.M.M.L.	Nehru Memorial Museum and Library, New Delhi
N.W.F.P.	North Western Frontier Provinces
R.T.	Rajatarangini
R.T.C.	Round Table Conference
Tr.	Translation
W.B.S.A.	West Bengal State Archives

Introduction

Dr. B.R. Ambedkar (1891 – 1956 A.D.) has a long and fascinating history behind him. His writings of own literary as well as corresponding to the world community from 1913 to 1956 A.D. played a very historical role in India as well as the world community. The period for his writings, especially when one is not supposed to read and write. He did a wonderful work in his life as a fatherly-figure of the nation like India from the background of a poor family called *'Untouchables'* or *Sudhras.* His phenomenal career is, as if, organically 'interwoven' with the Geography, Sociology, History and Culture of the land which Brahmins could not understand it in which he was born, and which he strove to cleanse and reconstruct the history of the *Sudhras,* which was lost in the myth of the Brahminical Ideology. He was a great man like the Moses of the Jews, he made ceaseless, Herculean task to emancipate the *'Untouchable'* or *Sudhras* of India from the Thraddon of the ages, and form the curse of the evil of the untouchability; like Moses, he gave his people an ideology to unify against the Brahminical forces and lead them onwards. Babasaheb's life and work constitute a glorious chapter in the history of *Sudhra* in India, as did by other rules of the dynasty like, N*andas*, *Chandragupta Maurya, Ashoka, Kushanas, Guptas, Karkotas* called *Chamar* of the

'Kashmir' and ungrateful would be the nation to forget the services of the Father, he rendered in writings that memorable chapter should be included in the history of India.[1]

During the Social and Political Reform Movement was there in India, the gentlemen who presided over the sessions of the Social Conference lamented that the majority of the educated Hindus were for political advancement and indifferent to social reform like *sati* system, child marriage, untouchabilty, etc. That while the number of those who attended the Congress was very large and the number who do not attend but who sympathized with it even larger, the number of those who attended the Social Conference was very much smaller. This indifference, this thinning of its ranks was soon followed by active hostility from the politicians under the leadership of the late. Bal Gangadahar Tilak, the courtesy with which the longers had displayed in *pandal* was withdraw because of their shrewd politic of the Brahmins and the spirit of enmity, they have created against the *untouchable.* Thus in course of time the party in favour of political reforms won and the Social Conference vanished and was forgotten. The speech, delivered by W.C. Bannerji in 1892 at Allahabad as President of the eight session of the Indian Congress, sounds like a funeral oration at the death of the Social Conference and is so typical of the Congress attitude towards the *Dalit* or *Untouchables.* He quoted a statement in his book *Annihilation* of *Caste.* "under the rule of the Peshwas in the Maharath Country. The *untouchable* was not allowed to use the public streets if a Hindu was coming along lest he should pollute the Hindu by his shadow. The untouchable was required to have a black thread either on his wrist or in his neck as a sign or a mark to prevent the Hindus from getting themselves polluted by his touch through mistake. In Poona, the capital of Peshwa, the untouchable was required to carry strung from his waist, a broom to sweep away from behind the dust he treaded on lest a Hindu walking on the same should be polluted. In Poona, the untouchable was required to carry an earthen pot, hung in his neck wherever he went, for holding his spit lest his spit falling on earth should pollute a Hindu[2] which has no history. But really and scientific speaking is truth who is better and more worthy of our respect '*Chamar*' or '*Nam*' the Mohammadans and Christians who attempted to thrust down the throats of unwilling persons what they regarded as necessary for their salvation in History, whether the Hindu religion was or was not a missionary religion in the interest of trade for the development of society, because it has no logic and reasoning which *Buddha* or *'Nam'* has. Assuming the theory of *Chaturvarnya* of Gandhi is practicable,' I contend that it is the most vicious system which different shade the man to man that *Brahmins* should cultivate knowledge, that the *Kshatriya* should bear arms, that the *Vaishya*, should trade and that the *Sudhra* should serve *'Sounds'* or *'Nam'* as though it was a system of division of labour. Whether the theory of *Sudhra* was intended to state of mind to the Brahmin in the history of India, is an interesting question in *History*. Where the term *History* bears such *'sounds'* to the historians of *Sudhra* families which they have enough literature in the worlds which became difficult for the upper class historian, to find out the *'Reality'*. So far as the Gandhi's theory is concerned, which is based on *Varna* system bare on caste factor. It makes clear from the study that Ambedkar's theory was based on *Buddha* and *Kabir* unless and until, one cannot obtain the bliss of the God or *'Nam'*, *Varna* system could not understand. He says 'there is no code of law's more in famous regarding social rights in the history of Brahmins equivalent to law's of Manu.' Any instance from anywhere of social injustice have been took place due to their reason, because the theory of *Manu* or *Mana* can not justify except God or *'Nam'*. Therefore, Dr. B.R. Ambedkar could have done the great harm to the socio-political fabric of this country by establishing Law in India. He did not embrace the *Christianity*, Sikhism, *Islam*," but Dr. B.R. Ambedkar, as a constitutionalist, a champion of peaceful change, never visualized a bloody revolution in India by plunging the *Untouchables* into a grim fight against either the conservative Hindus or the Capitalists. The foremost question during pre-independence era was how to a waken these neglected people and make them realize their legitimate rights which were hitherto denied to them. It was Dr. Ambedkar alone who awakened the *Untouchables* from their centuries old slumber for demanding the human rights as independently as they could[4]".

According to the *Communal Award* declared by the British Government in Act of 1935, where there were the rules of India, the Depressed Classes were granted separate electorate 'Reserves Seats' in nature in India within the Hindu fold. Simultaneously on the basis of this Act, *Communal Award* were granted as '*Separate Electorate*' to the Muslims, Sikhs, European, and Christians. Gandhiji never objected their electorate system, but when ever the talk of *untouchable* was there, he raised issue that their solution is lying in the Hindu fold. Ambedkar was very right at that time that Hindu possess no history as Kalhana mentions in his *Rajatarangini*. Infact, Gandhiji wanted to save the Hinduism not the *Sudhras* and to embarrass Dr. B.R. Ambedkar that communal forces were not in the favour of the *Sudhras*. He frustrated Gandhiji attempt and Gandhi was hell bent to defeat the natural leaders of *untouchables*. Dr. B.R. Ambedkar was, at that time was under tremendous pressure by the caste Hindus to agree the demand of Gandhi to protect his life for the sake of his own people. Whatever historical or political rights were secured by him, he deprived the *untouchable* of their bright future. To sum up, in the words of Dr. B.R. Ambedkar "To and this long and sad story of the Congress sucked the juice out of the Poon Pact by Reserve the seats for Untouchables"[5] Ambedkar was of the view that "The outcaste is a by-product of the caste system. There will be outcastes as long as there are castes. Nothing can emancipate the outcastes except the destruction of caste system which has been created by Brahmins. Nothing can help the Hindu and their survival incoming struggle the purging the Hindu Faith of this odios and vicious dogma. It shows that Gandhi was undoubtedly a strong believer in the sanctity of *Varnashrama* social system, which has destroyed the whole life of the *untouchables.* How can a person from the millions people, it again shows, that who a biased man or destructive of society inspire the people of the world, one who has no knowledge of *History* i.e. God and man, Dr. Ambedkar was alone a leader from India who could not adored as the real inspiration for the struggling people world over for securing their dignified status, self-respect and honourable life[6] under the subject title '*History of the Chamar Dynasty*', of the same author.

Dr. B.R. Ambedkar was also the greatest champion of the Women Right for equality. He says "under the Hindu law i.e. *Manusmriti* (A Symbol of inequality and injustice), the code of the Manu are not safe, because, their theory believe in rite and ritual as a pollution for society as well as women's though Hindu Code Bill could not be passed as a whole the same was the split and later on passed in four different Acts. He was as an Architect of the Indian Constitution, through the Articles 14, 15, 16, 39 and 325, all together, have often the Indian women all opportunities of equality before law, equal protection of law, equal opportunities in the matter of employment and there shall be no discrimination on the ground of sex or religion. Thus, restrictions imposed upon their freedom by *Manusmriti* and other religious Hindu scriptures, were totally removed. Shackles of bondage of rituals, slavery of customs and traditions were totally blown-up into pieces through the Indian Constitution. Now, Indian women can join police, administration, army, navy and air force. Thus, she could join any service of the state or centre government[7] even in the world community.

Traditionally, *Shri Krishna* is imperishable legacy of Indian Culture and Civilization is in the sources of inspiration to so many different people of different persuasions, and which for Mahatma Gandhi and many others has been the 'solace' of their life which believed in the theory of sex and 'ego'. For then, the *Gita* in its essence calls for setting up of *Dharmaraj* by destroying all that is *adharma* which believed on the theory of mind which is culprit for the human history. In the other words, the theory of *'Nam'* is based on Almighty power, when there is a highest of non-sense, the theory of God predict to defeat the theory of mind which has been seen the slogan of the Gandhi which was based on the 'Non-violence' or *Satyagraha* was the mockery with the people, till date there is lot of injustice among the people not with the *untouchables*, but with other poor people of the Father. There, however, have been several differences in the interpretation of *Gita* about the tradition of the Brahmins, therefore, *Tilakite*, *Marxian*, *Ambedkarian*, and so no, conflicting on the theory of *Gita*, even the colonial rules viewed it apprehensively as a text book for the mental training of revolutionary recuits[8], as Gandhi did.

As a quest for social justice is clearly discernible in the '*Bhakti Movement*' led by the galaxy of saints coming from different parts of the country, from the lower strata of the society during the medieval period, same is the case, we find in the modern world, that Dr. B.R. Ambedkar was also one of the greatest saint on earth fought against social evils of the society, because he was dealt with almost all the subjects in different forms like Political Science, History, Geography, etc. Therefore, he was very much clear in his social, political, religious and economic views that History lies in *Sudhras*. He was very critical about *Hinduism*, *Islam*, *Chritianity*, etc. He says "Religion and Slavery is incompatible. A people and their religion must be judged by social standards based on social ethics. No other standard would have any meaning if religion is held to be a necessary good for the well-being the people. Religion must mainly be matter of principles only. It cannot be a matter of rules. The moment it degenerates into rules, it across to be religion, as it kills responsibility which is the essence of a truly religious act[9]".

Keep in view, the critical analysis of the study *Professor Cannan*, on his part, speaks highly of Dr. Ambedkar's dissertation. '*The Problem of the Rupee in India*'. He says such was Keynes, 'One of the most brilliant Englishmen of the Century." He is described as "the outstanding intellect of the age", and "counter among the greats of Economists the equal of Adam Smith, David Ricardo and Karl Marx.[10]", but, in India society, he has been called 'untouchable' by the Brahmins. It shows that Brahminical Ideology is arrogant and damage to society, they have destructive approach in the society as Gandhi exhibit from his book *"The Story of My Experiments With Truth"* "If I had only to discuss academic principles, I should clearly not attempt on autobiography. But my purpose being to given a account of various practical applications of these principles, I have given the Chapters I propose to write the title of *'The Story of My Experiments with Truth'*. These will of course include experiments with non-violence, celibacy and other principles of conduct believed to be distinct from *truth*. But for me, *truth* is the sovereign principles, which includes numerous other principles. This truth is not only truthfulness in word, but truthfulness in thought also, and not only the relative truth of our conception, but the Absolute truth, the Eternal Principles that is God. These are innumerable definitions of God, because this manifestations are innumerable. They overwhelm we with wonder and awe and for a moment stun me. But I worship God as Truth only. I am prepared to sacrifice the things dearest to me in pursuit of this quest. Even if the sacrifice demanded be my very life, I hope I may be prepared to give it. But, as long as I have not realized this Absolute Truth, so long must I hold by the relative truth as I have conceive it[11]. Measuring myself by that standard I must exclaim with *Sudhras*.

Where is there a wretch so wicked and loath some as I?
I have forsaken my Maker; So faithless have I been"

My purpose is to describe experiments in the science of *Satyagraha*, not to say good I am. In judging myself I shall try to be as harsh as truth, as I want others also to be[12].

In addition to, Dr. Ambedkar's political career as a leader of the *Dalit,* he was the champion of the underdog, restorer of Buddhism in India to its land of origin, which could not understood by the modern politician, because "*the idea of Reservation*" is based on silence theory of the Saints, as he did in the Constitution of India and the first law Minister of the free India[13] after 1947. He dictated the terms to the politician in his absence from the distance. For instance, the rumonr of Dr. B.R. Ambedkar, secret marriage to an English widow as *Ravidas* did with them comes to naught move owing to the letter No. 101 written by F.X. than the farmers own refuzal ! such like facts put the significant issues in the proper prospective[14] of the 'Spiritualism,' which Brahmin cannot understand the moral value of this message.

During the experiment of Gandhi on Truth, the struggle for self-respected by million of deprived and depressed people which came under the category of *Scheduled Castes* and *Scheduled Tribes,* under the leadership of Dr. B.R. Ambedkar one can become the inspiring example for all those, who are stilling fighting or struggling for such and respectful social life world over. Dr. Martin Luther King in U.S.A. lost his life for the sake of human rights and dignified life of the Nagroes. Dr. Nelson Mandala of South Africa led the successful struggle against the *apartheid* and inhuman social and political treatment meted out to them by the Britishers. There are still many groups, communities and people throughout the world, struggling of just and human social status, for then the life and mission of Dr. B.R. Ambedkar could be a great inspiration for the *Dalit.* Unfortunately for many years Dr. Ambedkar was unknown to the world communities, even in Indian society, after the death, people also degraded him, he was the Schedule Caste leader, not for the others. Under the full-proof conspiracy of Gandhi and his party *Indian National Congress* as well as B.J.P. Dr. B.R. Ambedkar was kept in dark by the ruling Brahmanical social and political forces so that he did not cross the boundary of the India. He is still in the formation of Baba Gurinder Singhji Biaswale, as a '*Principal Soul*' in the world community as the ruler of *Sudhras* as Dr. B.R. Ambedkar was there during his life time. Though the Government of India and other States spent crores of rupees to popularize the Gandhi and Nehru's concept beyond the border of India, till a few years back, Dr. B.R. Ambedkar was a non-entity for those people, those were Brahmins. It is in a very big way Indian Press propagated the concept of Gandhi inspired the life of Dr. Nelson Mendala of South Africa and Dr. Martin Lutter King of U.S.A. Given the opportunity to both of them or their followers to read and study the life and mission of Dr. B.R.Ambedkar, they could not opted the Gandhi, but to Dr. B.R.Amedakar. Gandhi throughout life lived naked himself in the Political Life to seek the truth of '*Nam*'and could not decide of his life, but he can do for others, only he made the Banias of India the richest people to tell a lie with customs for the benefit of their own interest as a leader of India, which people his own country liked and killed him as a disorder created in the life of man. This is the contribution to the Congress men of India. On the other hand, *untouchables*, who were in millions oppressed and exploited by him during the rule of Congress. He always sabotaged the *Independent Self-Respect Movement* which led by Ambedkar through Poona Pact[15]. But the mighty stroke of the pen of Baba Saheb, Dr. B.R. Ambedkar, as the chairman of the Drafting Committee of Indian Constitution was mainly responsible for this historical achievement in the social history of India, he provided the 'Reserve Seats' in India Constitution to the *Dalit*. The social justice, as per our Constitution was twin objectives.

1. To usher in a new social-political order ensuring social justice to all citizens ;
2. To protect the liberties of the people from the onslaughts of autocratic and arbitrary powers[16].

All most all the agitations, *Satyagrahas* and the movement conceived, planned and organized under the leadership of Dr.

B.R. Ambedkar, right from *Chawdar Tank* in *Mahad*, his was the peaceful and non-violence move. He never supported the bloody revolution and always stood for peaceful change with the teachings of *Buddha*, *Kabir*, *Ravidass*, *Nanak*, etc. One of the critics of Dr. B.R. Ambedkar therefore, observed that 'He was champion, though a change in the laws of land. He was not a Utopain, but a realistic[17]' man of the subject '*History*'.

The 'contraction', which Dr. B.R. Ambedkar referred to his address in the Constituent Assembly was the creation of Hindu Brahminical Social Order[18]. From this point of view, Ambedkar not only rebel, but was a revolutionary in concept, as in his early days of life, he did not allow to interfere anybody in his own way of reforming, because his strong concept in Reality and in humanity. There were main three basic reasons : -

1. He disapproved violence as a matter of principle or one may say, even a creed or caste.
2. He rejected dictatorship of any kin as it is generally imposed through unconstitutional means.
3. Social change secured through peaceful means and consensus of people is more durable or sustainable to society[19] without caste, colour and creed.

The basics of the revolution are deep into this question mentioned above. The reason for Revolution varies from objective to objective or man to man. Revolution in any field of human activity is necessary to activate the life of man from one generation to another as a social change through history which Brahmin is responsible for the stick idea as an 'ego', but the assessment or evolution of such social or political revolution depends upon that very objective of the one society to be achieved with modern methods of social justice of the 'Founding Father of the Nation' and new era will have to be start with 'Untouchables of the Father', Dr. B.R. Ambedkar with affection and love with the help of the *'Nam'* or God.

Today Revolution has become a very common word among the *Dalit* society. Anybody and everybody speaks about '*Revolution*', without knowing the basic concept of the *Revolution*' in the words of Dr. B.R. Ambedkar, "is one of the most needed and fundamental force of mankind which shape the history in realistic approach against the communal forces with the stroke of pen in their mind. Revolution, in another sense, means a better change of life from Barbarism of humanism, from violence to peace and mutual adjustment. Better change is the essence of human revolution against the religious forces which are based on false propaganda. There is nothing in the world which remains unchanging. Men should strive for change for the betterment of the life in all sphere only the dead stop growing and life becomes stagnant. Change is the law of human life so also the basis of human society" "sThe inherent cause of Revolution lies in the fact that some people refuse to admit that the world changes. Against the change the time calls Revolution, they keep their mind closed and locked up and will not permit any ideas to come into them. They are frightened at the ideas of thinking, but since change leads to growth of mankind, the world moves in inspite of them. Such contradictory forces causes Revolution[20]. In Latin words, it is called '*revolvere*' in English called 'roll back', in other European language, the equivalent word to science includes in history with hesitation. It is terminological question in the eccentricity of the English language. It was the concept of law's in Ambedkar's study. This idea has been elaborated by Herbert Spencer in his most solemn style in *the Study of Sociology*. Historical problems, the problems of politics and society, it becomes inquiry at that time for the historian, when there is a conflict in the society on the basis of false propaganda led by politicians, people become sufferer, at that time, there is need of 'New Concept' which provide a 'solace' to the sufferer. Therefore, the idea of peace of Ambedkar lies in Truth or God or Nam or *Chamar* of the modern society as of the *Ravidas* or *Kabir*.

Notes and References

1. K.N. Kadam; *Dr. Baba Saheb Ambedkar and The Significance of His Movement A Chronology,* Bombay ; Reprint; 1993. p. 1 .
2. Dr. B.R. Ambedkar ; *Annihilation of Caste,* Aurangabad ; Reprint; 2003. pp. 20, 21.
3. *Ibid.* p. 44.
4. Ram Khobragade; *Dr. Ambedkar, A Symbol of Global Socio-Political Revolution.* New Delhi; 2005, p. 28.
5. *Ibid.* pp. 14-15.
6. *Ibid.* p. 16.
7. *Ibid.* pp. 18, 19.
8. J.V. Naik. *The Reformer And The Quest For Social Justice in Indian History.* General Presidential Address, in Indian History Congress, 67th Session, Kerala, 2007. pp. 14-5.
9. Ram Khobragade, Op. Cit. p. 19.
10. K.S. Rao, '*John Maynard Keynes*', ar Article in *Mirror*; Bombay, 1983, Vol. 23. No 2. p. 42.
11. M.K. Gandhi, *The Story of My Experiment With Truth, Sabarmati*; 1925. Introduction; p. XI.
12. *Ibid.* p. 10. *Note.* The title of the book also express that Gandhi was not enlightened with the truth. It was his experiment on the society to destroy them as he says "sI know it is the evil passion within that keep me so far from *Him*". It shows that the philosophy of Gandhi based on experiment to destroy, the mind or 'ego' to obtain the solace. It again shows that Gandhi had a Brahminical approach in his mind which was destructive for the society as politican use to change their faces during the time of election with false commitment for their own benefit to show themselves as Brahmin use to do. They do not believe on One God, they believe multi-gods, which is the creation of the One God i.e. '*Nam.*'
13. Surendra Ajnat ; *Letters of Ambedkar*; Jalandhar, 1993. p. 6
14. *Ibid.* p. 7.
15. Ram Khobragade; Op. Cit. pp. 12-13.

15. Ram Khobragade; Op. Cit. pp. 12-13.
16. Prof. P. Jagadeshan; *Social Justice And Challenges in Contemporary India*; Bangalore; 2006, A Research Paper of JCHR. p. 8.
17. Ram Khobragade ; OP. Cit. p. 11.
18. *Ibid.* p. 6.
19. *Ibid.* p. 21.
20. *Ibid.* pp. 2-3.

1

Ambedkar And His Early Life

(1848 to 1918 A.D.)

Early Career of Dr. B.R. Ambedkar

India is the land of many saints and philosophers. Fact and fiction are so interwoven in the life stories of Saints and Prophets that it is almost impossible to separate them completely. This is particularly true of Dr. B.R. Ambedkar in whose biographies truth and fable are so mixed that it is very hard to bring out his true picture from them. Therefore, inspite of our best efforts to make the account of his life as objective[1] on this earth, the subjective elements we can not be excluded in the history of India, because he was great social reformers like *Ramanujachary, Raja Ram Mohan Roy, Nam Dev, Dariya Saihb, Chaitanya, Tulsi Dass, Kabir, Ravidass, Sarmad Sheed, Baba Farid, Nanak*, Mohammad Prophet, etc. strictly speaking the late 19th century A.D. witnessed the emergency of reformist moments all over India. The *Arya Samaj* was founded *Swami Dayananda Saraswati.* Raja Ram Mohan Roy made concert efforts to abolish *'Sati'*, the then prevailing system in India led by Brahmins as a social evil. Swami Vivekananda, who was a disciple of the great saint Rama Krishna Paramahansa condemned the concept[2] of untouchability which existed in the Indian society led by Brahmin's also. Ambedkar's life-time venture to the study the phenomenon of Caste which was also created by Brahmins with the narrow minded approach, which they could not understand the historical value of the term *Caste,* Ambedkar with its generis, mechanism and functioning inspired him to declared the war on Caste.

He found that caste was the only menace behind every misery of the main in this continent and he gave the decision call to annihilate with the writings of pen. He declared that these efforts were only the face-lifting activities of the Brahminical Social Order else is nothing.

He was born on 14th April, 1891, with the establishment of Bias Dera in Punjab in a tiny village called Ambedkar Ranji Sakpal and grandfather was Maloji Sakpal, both served in the British Army. Everyone oppose to the Caste system loves Kabir's teachings because he repudiates the caste hierarchy and speaks for the downtrodden. It was for this reason that thousands of soldiers of all castes from the Indian military used to join the *Kabir Panth* and sing Kabir's songs with great devotion. The late, Dr. B.R. Ambedkar, know as the "Architect" of the Constitution of India, who was instrumental in serving jobs and other facilities under the Central and State governments of India for Scheduled Castes and Scheduled Tribes, acknowledged on several occasions that the teaching of Kabir had greatly influenced his own character and public career. His father Subhedar Major Ranji Maloji Ambedkar, was a *Kabir Panthi* who started life as a soldier, in the 106th Sappers and was later transferred to the 107th Pioneers. He was religious minded from the beginning of his career, but became a teetotaler and vegetarian after joining the *Kabir Panth.* Every morning and evening the Subhedar-Major used to have devotional services at his home, at which Kabir, and Tukaram's verses were sung. He insisted on all the family being present on both the occasions, especially for the evening services. Dr. B.R.Ambedkar used to say and from that root has emerged a great tree. Untouchablility has been replaced by discrimination based on Caste which Latinized word means *Pure* as *'Word'* or *'Nam'*. But it needs to be remembered that this discrimination is not located in history or religion, but in today's politics called *'Rajniti'* or policy of *Vedic* system of the Aryan society as *'Nam'* was the 'Supreme Being', at the time. Though the origin of Dalit's poverty is in untouchability[4] why the Brahminical Ideology griping the every business in their own hands, therefore, we can say that this is the only cause, but it has certain natural phenomenon in the history of India. Untouchability is now coming to an end due to transformations in social life from one generation to another by exchanging the idea of material world.

In 1896, Ambedkar passed 5th standard from the primary school of Dapoli and in 1905, he joined the Elphinstone High School Bombay now, it is called Shirodkar High School. In 1907, he passed the matriculation examination of the Bombay University. 1910, he did intermediate in Arts in the same University College of Bombay, and in 1910, he did his B.A. In July, 1913, he did his Master Degree in Colombia University, New York (U.S.A), and his dissertation was on *'Administration and Finance of the East Indian Company'* and the Ph.D. Degree was formally conferred to him. Doctor of Philosophy, he did in 8-6-1927, thesis was published in London, 1925, under the title *'The Evolution of Provincial Finance in British India'*.

October, 1916, he did Master of Science in London School of Economics and Political Science University of London in 1922. Doctor of Science in Economics, he did in October, 1923, read before the students union thesis : *'The Problem of the Rupee in India'* in 1922. This thesis was published in 1923 and against it was reprinted under the title of *'History of Indian Currency and Banking.'*

In 11, November, 1916, he started his education toward the Law and completed it in 1923. June, 5th, 1952, he obtained Honorary Degree in *Doctor of Laws* from Colombia University, and January, 12th, 1953, University of Osmamia also Conferred his Degree on the same subject mentioned above.

His Teachings

Of all the saints who have visited in this world from the time immoral has come to found a new religion or a new creed. They have all brought the same message, as did by Dr. B.R.Ambedkar. They have all preached the same truth as it has been already, existed in the society, but there are little bit change in ideas and thoughts, their message, their teachings and their path hold good for all time and for all mankind, as Ambedkar did by establish a law through the writings of a pen, he sang those hymns with such depth of devotion that one can not listen without the *Nam-Dana,* who heard. He moved to the core and the impression left on the minds of the children was remembered throughout their lives otherwise social Brahminical order, one has to face. Writer, Isaac A. Ezekils grandfather, who was also a Subhedar-Major in the 23rd Maratha (Outram) Rifles, had a large number of *Kabir Panth*'s in his regiment and they used to organize recitals of Kabir is songs every evening. The refrains '*Kahat Kabeer Suno bhai Saadho'* (Says Kabir, listen, O Sadhus), heard during my childhood days, continue to ring in my ears till I reached the lotus feet of my Master at Beas, who made clear to me that mystic meaning of Kabir's teaching[3]. The focal point of Ambedkar's writings is the common person. The focus of Marxism also rests on the exploitation as Brahmins did in the Indian society and essence of the thoughts of *Dr. B.R. Ambedkar, Karl Mark, Kabir, Ravidas, Nam Dev, Nanak,* many more is the same a *'Word'* or *'Nam'* as the liberation of human beings for exploitation otherwise misery will remain there on the earth. It is the greatest challenge to the Brahmins, otherwise, they are due for the hell. The poverty and untouchability of Dalit's is rooted in history and religion in Indian society through the mystic writings of a pen which became very difficult for the Brahminical Ideology to understand it. No doubt, such saints know the wheel of transmigration of soul from one generation to another, which could not be established by any religion of the world, because every religion has been originated from the *Sudhra* family which Brahmins could not understand this logic. Logic and reasoning stand in the *Sudhra* family because in the modern world, they are away from the terrorist movements which led by the 'egoistic' people of the Father. Therefore punishment is awarded to them in his absence. Whereas, the Scheduled Castes and Scheduled Tribes, they have certain ideological differences among the superior people of the society. However, the *Kabir Panth*, has retained some of the main principles as well as his teachings in their doctrine. Some of the important points in the teachings of Dr. B.R. Ambedkar covered in these following lines:

1. We should devote ourselves to the one all-pervading, unlimited *Sat Purush* or *Supreme Lord*, and not meditate on any other besides him. This *Sat Purush* is known only through a true Guru.
2. *Sat Purush* and *Kabir* are One; the difference is in name only. It will be difficult for those who to obtain salvation.
3. We should have full faith in *Guru*, as salvation can not be obtained without following his teachings. Those who regard their Guru as God will find that their efforts in meditation are fruitful. Meditation on the Guru and devotion to him is the key to knowledge. We should serve the *Guru* with body, mind and wealth. We should not look for help from anyone except the *Sat Guru*.
4. There is no way to salavation apart from the essence of the word (*Sar Shabd*).
5. The true *Name* should be repeated.
6. We should serve *Sadhu* with love and devotion without making any distinction among them Sadhus in whom the qualities of the *Guru* are found should not be considered different from their *Guru*.

7. We should have feelings of kindness towards all living creatures and consider them as our own body and soul. Since the supreme spirit is present everywhere, we should regard pain giving to God.
8. We should eschew intoxication drinks and drugs of the '*Nam or Word*'.
9. Idolatry is a mockery. No visible object in this world should be worshipped and one should not go on pilgrimages to holy places or believe in charms, amulets and superstitions.
10. Humility and silence are great virtues. Telling lies, stealing, adultery and gambling are prohibited. Vices such as slander, envy, hypocrisy, pride and cursing are enemies of salvation.

Though some of these articles are consistent with Kabir's teachings, the soul of his message is missing. A Perfect Living Master is the life and soul of the path to salvation. Without him all religious, panths or sects are empty shells. There are two main sections of the *Kabir Panth* existing today, but neither follows a Perfect Living Master, as the head of both the orders are elected by the followers. This may be good for democracy, but not for leadership on the spiritual path. Only a true master knows who is fit to be a *Guru*, certainly not the rank and life. Even Jesus Christ said that he had called the disciples to himself and that the disciples were incapable of recognizing him a Master.

The full time *Kabir Panth* is those who travel around the country singing Kabir's devotional songs are called, are supported by the order. This also goes against the teachings of Kabir, who advocated that disciples should earn their own said "Let no one take to begging, for begging is mortifying as death", would not like to see *Kabir Panth* is applying ashes to their bodies and making a show of devotion.

However, the *Kabir Panthi* has done an immense amount of good in bringing the songs of *Kabir*, and villages year after year over the last three hundred years. Even if these songs may not have succeeded in bringing all the villagers to the feet of a true living master, and even if the true mystic significance of the songs may be lost, the ethical teachings embodied in then and the attacks they make on the caste system, Brahminism, ritualism, idol worship, pilgrimages and asceticism have rendered considerable service in weakening public faith in these things. He was very much conversant both in Maharathi and English. He followed the teachings of Kabir who taught the devotion to God, *Bhakti* alone is important Bhimabai was his wife. Both husband and wife were the devotees of the village goddess of *Ambawade*.

Ambedkar's mother Bhima Bai, mother of fourteen children, could see five of her survived children while ; Ambedkar was hardly two years old Ramji retired from his teachers job then he moved to a village called Thapoli. However, he could not run his family out of his meager pension. So, he moved out to the *Satara* Cantonment where he could get an appointment, after the retirement as a teacher from the military school. But it was not even a year or so Bhima Bai, mother of Ambedkar died. Then, Ambedkar was just six years old. From thereafter, his aunt Mira Bhai looked him and she had much love and affection towards Ambedkar. His full name was Bhimrao Ramji Ambedkar.

It so happened that once Ramji Sakpal's uncle who was a saint had come to see Ramji very shortly and he will be born to him very shortly and he will become world famous Ambedkar was born this.

Ambedkar joined the High School at *Satara* as he had completed his basic schooling. There was a Brahamin teacher in the school who liked Bhimrao so much that he changed his name from Ambevadkar to Ambedkar. The teachers family name was Ambedkar. Thus, Bhimarao became Bhimarao Ramji Abmedkar. The teacher used to share his mid day meal with the young Bhimarao. This relation appeared to many upper caste students peculiar and they became jealousy. They even tried to died the two students. But the teacher and Bhimarao cared little for this course of action. However, in those days, there used to be very few students in schools seeking higher education among Depressed Classes. Even if, some students were there, they were treated very badly and called untouchable to him. They were asked to sit separately from other pupils, that too an gunny bags. Such insults made Ambedkar to do something about it. He had to drink the water only when other students of the upper caste poured through their raised hands for him. One day Ambedkar while he was young felt unbearable thirst of the *'Nam',* he drunk water from a nearby well. This was observed by few people of higher caste, because they were well-known at that time. They gathered and mercilessly beaten the boy and he tolerated handsomely. Another day, when it was raining heavily, Ambedkar took shelter near a house. The owner of this house, a lady was very angry and pushed him into the rain of *'Nam'.* He was being humiliated now and they by which his mind, Brahmin became a volcano of bitter feelings against the *Sudhras.* This was all due to the birth in the *Mahar Caste* or *Untouchable* called *'Nam'.*

After this, Ramji was fond of Ambedkar, and he was ready to do anything for his progress. Sometimes, he borrowed money and got his books for higher study. When Ramji married for the second time Ambedkar decided to be independent and left for Bombay. He joined the Elphinstone High School. The Ramji family found a house where there was only one room the family could not afford to purchase a kerosene lamp. Ambedkar would get up daily at 2 A.M to study under an earthen lamp. During his school days Ambedkar came into contact with Krishnaji Arjun Keluskar who was one of his school teachers. Besides, he was a good Marathi writer. Both of then were meeting in a garden, particularly on holidays. Keluskar give Ambedkar a biography of Gautama Buddha i.e. *'Nam'.* Ambedkar was influenced by the life and teachings of Buddha in natural form which later made him to embrace Buddhism as an old concept of Ashoka.

In his High School days Ambedkar had to face two strange incidences. Once his mathematics teacher asked students to come forward to the 'black board' to solve a problem written on it. Few students tried to solve but they were proved ineffective. When Ambedkar's turn came, he walked towards the board. To his surprise visit he saw his classmates rushing forward to collect their Tiffin boxes which had been kept close to the board. They were all under the impression that the presence of Ambedkar near the black board would pollute their mid day food. At that time, Ambedkar did not show any feeling, but just completed the problem and proved his ability in mathematics as a best student of class. In this way, at the first instance, he defeated the Brahminical Ideology with presence of mind and his high intelligentsia, which was connected with the Prefect Master of the *'Nam'.*

In the High School, Ambedkar wanted to learn Sanskrit as other Hindu, but the social order of the Hindus did not allow the *Sudhras* to learn the Sanskrit. But, as he belonged to low caste like the other saints of world, could not bother the teachings of Sanskrit. Such injustice shows on him, made him all the more better in other field of life which Brahmins of the period could not understand to him. However, later in his life, he learned Sanskrit[7], did a wonderful work for the literature to defeat the Brahmins with the writings of pen.

Ambedkar And His Matrimonial Alliances

After passing the Matriculation Examination, Ambedkar's father Ramji arranged his marriage with Rama Bhai, the daughter of his friend Biku Walanghar, as a bride for his intimate son. He was then seventeen years old, and the bride was just nine years old. Her father was a potter. The marriage took place in a shed in Byculla market in Bombay at night. Therefore, it is very difficult to understand the meaning of night by the Brahmins, because they had no background of the Kabir's *Satsang*. No doubt, after this Ambedkar continued his studies at Elphinstone College. He obtained the B.A. Degree in 1912, and his father died in 1913. Soon after, he worked under the Maharaja of Baroda, Sayyaji Rao, Gaekwad. Maharaja sent Ambedkar to America subject to the condition that he must serve the state of Baroda for a period of ten years after his return. The other person who supported him was the Raja of Kolkar who also, financed him to start a periodical called *'Mook Nayak'* (Leader of the dumb). Ambedkar wanted to fight for equal rights to enable the jonrnal, he focused on the problems of the downtrodden people. His main attention was to remove untouchability and protection of Civil rights. In the very first issue he wrote, "The Hindu society is like a tower of many stories. It has neither a ladder nor a door to go out. A society which believes that God exists even in inanimate things (non-living), also says that people who are a part of very society should not be touched, because they are *'Nam's* race. Moreover, the present names of India and Hindustan can be traced back to the early invaders of the country, the Persians and the Greeks. Their progress towards this country usually stopped because they believe in the Brahminical Ideology, i.e., rite and ritual, therefore, it is necessary to check them at the *Indus* or the Sindhu river of *Srinagara.* Hence, they called the country 'the Land of the Sindhu' or *Sudhra.* Since the Persians pronounce the letter *'S'* as *'h'* they pronounced. The word Sindhu as Hindu. The word India corresponds to the Sindhu (The Indus) or they Hindu of the old Persian epigraphs. Closely connected with "Hindu" are the latter designation "Hind" or 'Hindustan" as used by the medieval Muslims. Most of these names still survived[8]. According to *Kalhana*[9] Hindu has no history, therefore, it is proved from the writings of Dr. B.R. Ambedkar *Sudhras* has history. The remark is true if we apply it to history as a science, and art, such as classical culture in its noblest prose-works has bequeathed to us, if history, is meant either historical development or the materials for studying it. Yet the materials for such a study are equally at our disposal in India. They are contained not only in such original sources of information as Inscriptions, coins and antiquarian remains, generally are used in advancing the research project. Therefore, it was well understood by Dr. B.R.Ambedkar to make a good relation with Brahmins sometimes, it creates dangerous situation in the life of the man as a human being. At such period Silence or *Reservation* is very important to keep the distance from them for the development of the future course of action.

The Practical Steps of Dr. B.R. Ambedkar in Study of *Nam* or *God*

Ambedkar launched an organization exclusively for the welfare of the Depressed Classes. He did not want the pity of the community for the *"untouchable"*. He started a boys' hostel that provided facilities for students belonging to the Depressed Classes. He also started a library for boys. He observed that untouchable were not being allowed to use public tanks and well by upper class people. He decide to revolt against such practices[10]. It would appear that the upper caste Hindu achieved in literature what they could not in real life, namely, a complete silencing, if not erasure, of the untouchable's shadow. This erasure was not confined to the literature of Maharashtra alone, but it was also extended all over the world. Sharan Kumar Limbala has rightly expressed that this was more a wish fulfillment than an accomplished fact. Limbale's innovation of *Kabir* as one of the originary figures of the *Dalit* tradition suggests that there were, in fact, people from the lowest ranks of the caste system who were making literature. They did not write in the high languages of the society, but in the Vernacular of the common people. The power and impact of the their work were such that those whom Limbale calls 'the high priests of literature' could not ignore them. They were, or had to be, included in literature history. However, the particularity of the experience they were writing about, as well as the space they were normalized into the mainstream of Brahminical literature, as oppositional voices or as reformers often, a products of their time, they too accepted the legitimacy of what Limbale describes as a pre-occupation with 'serving at the feet of the soul and the Supreme Soul'. That, we know, is one the problematics associated with subaltern of speech. Often, it appears to take on the 'Voice of Master'. But the important point is that Brahminical literature could not wish away either the reality lurking at the edges, the very beings who by their labour ensured this purity and freedom from pollution. Limbale uses the term 'reformist-literalism' to describe the politics of *Dalits* inclusion in the Brahminical[11] Ideology in the contemporary history of the world. Thus the reorganization of Ambedkar's services in the Government of Bombay nominated him to the upper house of the legislature. This gave an impetus to Ambedkar's movements[12] as a political career in the history of India.

Dalit Literature Equivalent to Sant Literature

Sant literature or *Dalit Literature* is a time immemorial literature. Through the *sants* or saints are reversed in the history of India, they started the movement from the very low strata of the society to gathered the people in one group, i.e., *'Nam'* or God. Because of the caste system, *Dalit* writers have broken away from Hindu culture. It is, therefore natural, that they should feel a distance from the *Sant.* The difference between the contemporary *Dalit* literature to *Sant* literature, it is also the result of the cultural transformation from one generation to another. Among Babasaheb's "other ancestors", the first mention must be made of the Buddha (563-483 B.C.) whose life and teaching deeply influenced to Dr. B.R.Ambedkar, as perhaps no one else even did. The next mention must be made of his mentor (Guru) Joytirao Phooley (1827-90 A.D.), and Phooley's devoted wife Savitribai Phooley (1831-97 A.D.), this famous couple dedicated their lives for the upliftment of the down-trodden; the untouchables, the exploited peasants, women, windows, orphans, etc. It was, they, who started the first-ever schools for girls and "untouchable" children. In 1873, Jyotirao

Phooley founded the *Satyashodhak Saṁaj* (Society for Search After Truth). Joytiba Phooley was a pillar of strength and a source of inspiration to thousands of people in Maharashtra. It may be truly said ; he anticipated Dr. Ambedkar[13] that Dr. Ambedkar inscribed his *Who Were the Shudras?* "to the memory of Mahatma Joytiba Phooley, how they came to be the fourth *Varna* in the Indo-Aryan society, because they are the *'Nam'* or *Chamar'* on earth, there is a view that an inquiry into these questions is of no present day moment. It is said by no then Mr. Sherring in his *Hindu Tribes and Castes*[14] that :

"Whether the *Sudhras* were Aryans, or aboriginal inhabitants of India, or tribes produced by the union of the one with the other, is of little practical moment. They were at an early period placed in a class by themselves, and received the forth or last degree of rank, yet at a considerable distance from these three superior castes. Even though it be admitted that at the outset they were not Aryan, still, from their extensive intermarriages with the three Aryan Castes, they have become so far Aryanized that, in some instances as already shown, they have gained more than they have lost, and certain tribes now designated as *Sudhras* are in reality more *Brahmins* and *Kshatriyas* than anything else. In short, they have become as much absorbed in other races as the Celtic tribes of England have become absorbed in the Anglo-Saxon race; and their own separate individuality, if they ever had any, has completely vanished[14]".

From the study we learn that this view is based on two errors discussed as under.

1. The present day the collection of *Sudhras* castes are drawn from the heterogeneous society.
2. In the second case we find the modern *Sudhras* the centre of interest is not *Sudhras* as a people, because in the contemporary society, they are the follow-up the Brahminical tradition.

Keeping in view, the above mentioned two statements. One has changed in the connotation of the word *Sudhra.* The word *Sudhra* lost its original meaning of being the name for a low-class people without Civilization, without Culture, without Respect and without Position. But the Book entitled *'History of the Chambar Dynasty'* written by the author give the same people a moral encouragement as a class of God or *'Nam'.* In the second argument, it makes clear that the word *Sudhra* has widening meaning, which could not understood by the Brahminical Hindu Law-Givers. Dr. B.R. Ambedkar has rightly expressed, the fact, however, unfortunate, it may be, is that the code which has been applied to the original *Sudhra* in the present-day to modern *Sudhra* is less in number because, their thought has been gripped by the Brahminical Ideology. My answers to them are summarized following as under:

1. The *Sudhras* were one of the Aryan Communities of the Solar race.
2. There was a time when the Aryan society recognized only three *Varnas*, namely, *Brahmins*, *Kshatriyas* and *Vaishyas.*
3. The *Sudhras* did not form a separate *Varna* , they ranked as a part of the *Kshatriya* Varna in the Indo-Aryan society.
4. There was a continuous feud between the *Sudhra* Kings and the Brahmins in which the *Brahmins* were subjected to many tyrannies and indignities.
5. As a result of the hatred towards the *Sudhras* generated by their tyrannies and oppressions, the *Brahmins* refused to perform the *Upanayana* of the *Sudhra.*
6. Owing the denial of *Upanayana*, the *Sudhras* who were *Kshatriyas* became socially, degraded by the *Sudhras* themselves on the basis of economic status, fell below the rank of the *Vaishyas* and thus came to form the fourth *Varna.*

"I must of course await the restrict of the scholars on these conclusions. That these conclusions are not merely original but they are violently opposed to those that are current is of course evident. Whether these conclusions will be accepted or not will depend upon the mentality of a person claming to have a right to sit in judgment over the issue. Of course, if he is attached to a particular thesis he will reject mine. I would not, however, bother about his judgment for he would be an adversary from whom nothing can be excepted except opposition. But if a person is an honest critic, how so ever cautions, how so ever conservative, he may be, provided that he has an open mind and a readiness to accept facts, I do not despair of converting him to my view. This expectation may fail to materialize, but about one thing I am quite certain. My critics will have to admit that the book is rich in fresh insight again with new visions in writings.'

Apart from scholars, how the Hindu public will react may be in interesting speculation. The Hindu's of to-day fapll into five definite classes. There is a class of Hindus, who are known as Orthodox like Brahmins, and who will not admit that there is anything wrong with the Hindu social system. To talk of reforming, it is to them rank blasphemy. There is a class of Hindus who are known as Arya Samajists. They believe in the *Vedas* and only in the *Vedas*. They differ from the orthodox in as much as they discard everything which is not in the *Vedas*. There is a class of Hindus and Muslims, who will admit that the Hindu social system is all wrong, but who hold that there is no necessity to attack it. Their argument is that since law does not recognize it, it is a dying, if not a dead system. There is a class of Hindus, who are politically minded. They are different to such questions. To them *Swaraj* is more important than social reform. The fifth class of Hindu are those who are rationalists and who regard social reforms as of primary importance even more important than *Swaraj*. With the Hindus, who fall into the second category, those who are likely to regard the book as unnecessary, I cannot agree[15]. It shows from the study to the profound impact Joytiba Phooley had on his mind and activities.

Besides the Joytiba Phooley, Gopal Krishan (alias Gopal Baba) Walangkar (c.1840-1900 A.D.) was born at *Ravdal* (near *Mahad*, in the present *Raigad* district). He was related to Ramabai Ambedkar. He too was an army man, having retired from the army as *Havaldar*, in 1886, and settled down at Dapoli. He came under the dynamic influence of Joytiba Phooley. Gopal Baba was a pioneer of the movement for the emancipation of the "untouchables", in the nineteenth century. He founded the Anarya Dosh – *Parihar Samaj* (Society for Removal of Evil's among the Non-Aryans), in 1886; and in 1888, he published his monthly *Vital-Vidhvansak* (Destroyer of Brahminical or Ceremonial Pollution) which was the first ever journal of the "untouchables". Subsequently, in 1889, his book entitled *Vital Vidvansak* (Annihilation of Ceremonial Pollution) of the society which has been created by the Brahmins. In this behalf, Ramakant Yadav writes : "This booklet is the first open letter to the Hindus by an untouchable intellectual of was the first volcanic eruption of the protest and sign of a new consciousness about the legitimate rights and position of the untouchables in society[16]." Like Subedar – Major Ramji Sakpal before him, Gopal Baba too raised his voice of protest against Kitchener's un-English policy of precluding recruitment of "untouchables" in the British army Gopal Baba died at Ravdal in 1909. He had the "link" between Joytiba Phooley and Dr B.R.Ambedkar in the crusade against social inequality and injustice[17]. Sree Narain Guru's (1854-1928 A.D.) revolutionary proclaiming "One Caste, One religion and One God for all ; so also the social Revolt of Periyar E.V. Ramaswami Naicker (1879-1973) who is 1825 launch 'Self-Respect Movement' in South India, and that of Dr. B.R.Ambedkar, for the emancipation of the *Dalits* emanated from the same view of social justice[18].

Although the practical step for the upliftment of the downtrodden was first-undertook by Phooley and then Ambedkar, like Mahatma Gandhi, was the "friend of the poorest the loneliest and the lost[19]".

Shivram Janba Kamble (1875-1941 A.D.) of Pune was a contemporary of Joytiba Phooley, Subedar-Major Ramji Sakpal and Gopal Baba Walangkar Kamble started, in 1908, the fortnightly *Somavanshiya Mitra* in which he launched an attack on the evil practices prevalent in the *Mahar* Community. He convened two mammoth Conferences of *Mahars*, the first at Saswad, in 1903, and the second at *Jejuri*, in 1910, and sent memorials to the Government and the British Parliament, seeking redressal of the wrong done to the "untouchables" in the army. Again, among Dr. Ambedkar's "other ancestors" and benefactors met with Maharaja of Baroda, Sayyajirao Gaekwad (1863-1939), due to his magnanimity, he went for study in abroad. The other prince after Baba Saheb's heart was the ruler of Kolkapur Chhatrapti Shahu Maharaj (1884-1922 A.D). He was enlightened prince who was courageous enough to take steps, in as early as 1919, for abolition of untouchability in schools, offices, and other places as well, etc. in his state.

In the fitness of the things, teachers played a crucial role in Ambedkar's early life. When he was at school, in Satara, in 1900 A.D. a teacher named Ambedkar change Bhimrao's surname from Ambeavadekar to Ambekdar[20]. After this, he developed his interest in reading books and strengthen his personal library[21].

Character of Dr. B.R. Ambedkar

As soon as, Ambedkar was awarded a Baroda state scholarship for Higher Education at the Columbia University, U.S.A., Professor John Dewey (1859-1952), the eminent American Philosopher and Educationist, was B.R. Ambedkar's teacher. Baba Saheb acknowledge his debt to Dr. Dewey in these words: "Professor John Dewey who was my teacher, and to whom I owe so much[22] knowledge from him," John Dewey became Professor of Philosophy at Minnesota (1888-89A.D.) Michigan (1889-94 A.D.), Chicago (1894-1904 A.D.) and the head of the department of Philosophy, at Columbia, thereafter,

Dr. B.R. Ambedkar entered the Columbia University in 1913, and became Dr. Dewey' student. "John Dewey", says Bertrand Russell, in 1946, " is generally admitted to be the leading living philosopher of America in New York was Dr. B.R. Ambedkar, student of Political Science, Economics and Philosophy, he could get a friend Naval Bhatena who was Parsi. Both lived together. There was no untouchability in New York. He devoted all his time to studies shunning all forms of entertainment. He worked nearly eighteen hours a day. He wrote a thesis on "*Ancient Indian Trade*" as a part of his research[24]. He has had a profound influence on his teacher, not only among philosophers, but on students of education, aesthetics, and political theory. He is a man of the highest character, liberal in outlook, generous and kind in personal relations, indefatigable in work[25], like *Vishvamitra*.

Professor Seligman, on his part, writes thus about his student Dr. B.R.Ambedkar, in his forward to Dr.Ambedkar's doctoral thesis, "*The Evolution of Provincial Finance in British India*". "The Problem discussed by Mr. Ambedkar in his excellent dissertation, is one that is arousing a growing interest in all parts of the world[26]. He was honoured with a doctorate Degree for his work, '*The Problem of a Rupee*'. He utilized facilities that were available in the British Museum. As, he was a voracious reader, he read number of books. He used to enter the library at eight in the morning and read till 5 O'clock. This practice of reading, he retained throughout his life. Not only, he read books, he also wrote number of books to solve the various problems of the life. He was telling that the Goddess of Learning will not come whenever one wants. One must get her blessings when she comes[27]. He spent money on books and devoted his time for studies. However, there was a good sign that the time to understand that untouchablility by the time to understand that untouchablility is unjust. As a lawyer Ambedkar took cases related to the poor and downtrodden without charging them the legal fee[28].

The value of Mr. Ambedkar's contribution, according to Professor Seligman to the discussion lies on practical approach in history in the objective recitation of the facts, and the impartial analysis of the interesting development that has taken place in his native country.

The lessons are applicable to other countries as well ; nowhere ; to my knowledge, has such a detailed study of the underlying principles been made[29] by him. Further, the value of his character has been reflected on the letter dated May 23, 1916, to Sidney Webb, Professor Seligman writes : "He (Dr. B.R.Ambedkar) is an excellent student and a nice fellow, moderate, broad, and able, and I know that you will be glad to be of service to him in the prosecution of his studies[30]."

Subsequently, when Dr.B.R. Ambedkar joined the London School of Economics & Political Science, One of his Professor was Edwin Cannan (1861-1935). He taught at the London School of Economics from 1895 upto 1926. Dr. Ambedkar acknowledges his debt to Professor Cannan in these words, in the Preface to his '*Problem of the Rupee*', his thesis for Doctor of Science of the London University " I cannot conclude this preface without acknowledging my deep sense of gratitude of my teacher Prof. Edwin Cannan of the University of London (School of Economics). This sympathy towards me and his keen interest in my undertaking have placed me under obligations which I can say that, I can never replay. I feel happy to be able to say that this work has undergone close supervision at his hands, although, he is in no way responsible for the views I have expressed, I can say that this severe examination of my theoretic discussions has saved me from many an error. Professor Cannan, on his part, speaks highly of Dr. Ambedkar's dissertation. '*The Problem of the Rupee*'. He says, He (Dr. Ambedkar) hits some nails very squarely on the head, and even when I have thought him quite wrong. I have found a stimulating freshness in his views and reasons. An old teacher like myself learns to tolerate the vagaries of originality, even they resist "Severe examination" such as that of which Mr. Ambedkar speaks."

Another eminent economist needs to be mentioned here, namely, John Maynard Keynes (1883-1946). Keynes was the author of *'Indian Currency* and *Finance'* acclaimed to be "a masterly analysis of India's financial structure, and of the country's Gold Exchange Standard, equivalent to *'Nam'* or God. The book so impressed the authorities that he was asked to be come a member of the Royal Commission on Indian Currency, set up in 1913[31]. Dr. Ambedkar's his intellectual and political achievements are well known to all the intellectuals of the world, but in India after the independence no body can produced an intellectual giant of his stature[32] after him. And, his work was so mature, so exhaustive that the chairman, Sir Austen Chamberlain handsomely acknowledged that he was the chairman, the credit for the Report should go entirely to Keynes[33]". After the Second World War, Keynes was instrumental in the establishment of the International Monetary Fund and the World Bank[34]. Such was Keynes, "One of the most brilliant Englishman of the country". He is described as "the outstanding intellect of the age," and" counted among the greatest of Economists, the equal of Adam Smith, David Ricardo and Karl Marx[35]".

Dr. B.R. Ambedkar, however, did not permit himself to be overawed by the greatness of Keynes. In his preface to the '*Problem of the Rupee*', Dr. Ambedkar write, "on the theoretical side, there is no book but that of Professor Keynes, which makes any attempt to examine its (The Gold Exchange Standards) on scientific basis. But the conclusions he (Keynes) has arrived at are in sharp conflict with those of mine. Our differences extend to almost every proposition, he was advanced in favour of the exchange standard. This difference proceeds from the fundamental fact which seems to be quite overlooked by Professor Keynes, that nothing will stabilize the Rupee unless we stabilize the general purchasing power. That the exchange standard does not do[36]".

Now, we come to with the discussion of Bertrand Russell (1872-1970). Russell was "one of the most widely varied and persistently influential intellects of the 20th Century[37]" A.D.

That is how the *Encyclopaedia Britannica* describes him. Dr.B.R.Ambedkar came in contact with Russell's intellectual powers on reading his '*Principles of Social Reconstruction*'. Russell and Dr. B.R. Ambedkar both has common object in view, namely, the reconstruction of society. The problem with Russell was, of course most unlike that with Dr. Ambedkar. Russell passionately described elimination of war by encouragement of impulses promoting growth. Dr. Ambedkar passionately described the annihilation of caste and the abolition of untouchability ; and throughout his life; he battled against odds for the reconstruction of Indian society on the principles of Justice, Liberty, Equality and Fraternity[38]. As, it has been rightly expressed during the time of French Revolution; "the Revolution of 1789 than a rebellion against inequality". Which has been created by the modern politicians in Indian society without any reasoning and logic, but only due to with the *"Goonda Rule'* by exploiting the innocent peoples of the Father (*Baba Saheb* Ambedkar.) There is inequality and favouritism on the basis of Hindu and Muslim religion, but these religion do not possess any history of the human society, because it is the collection of *Brahmins* or *Molavis*, for the collection of money like modern politicians; those believe on the theory of mind which always do injustice with the poor people of the Father in his absence.

Prof. Godwin says : "In the mounting spirit of patriotic enthusiasm of all citizens to public office and the abolition of feudal jurisdictions, exclusive hunting rights and purchase of judicial and other offices i.e. injustice. Even more impressive and dramatic according to Demont, who was an eye-witness of the scene, was the surrender of all Municipal, Corporate and Provincial Privileges proposed by the representatives from Dauphine. The proceeding closed with Royal address to the King, conferring on him the title of the Restorer of French liberty[39]" conferred on the title of Louis XVI. These are the principles, Dr. B.R. Ambedkar has built into the '*Constitution of India*'and these are the principles underlying the principles of Morality which he advocated during his practical days when he exhorted India's suffering humanity to adopt Buddhism as a real thought of life called '*Nam*' or God on this earth as a founding father of the subject '*India*'i.e. called '*light*'or *Bharata.*

Dr. Ambedkar was invited by Russell, in 1920, for a discussion on the review article written by the former, on the latter's '*Principles of Social Reconstruction*' on the basis of equality, justice, fraternity and liberty. Unfortunately, we do not have any record of the discussion that was took place at that time between the two intellectuals. There are, of course, several other thinkers and social reformers who must have influenced Dr. Ambedkar's ideas and thought, it seems, when he read his paper on '*Responsibilities of a Responsible Government in India*', before the students 'Union, in 1923. Professor Harold Joseph Laski (1893-1950 A.D.) the political scientist opined "that the thoughts expressed in the paper were frankly of a revolutionary nature[41]".

Karl Marx (1818-1853A.D.) was another intellectual giant whose works had an impact on Dr. B.R. Ambedkar mind, as it naturally did on the minds of several other thinkers of his generation to fight for the equality in human behaviour. Both Marx and Dr. B.R. Ambedkar desired to eliminate exploitation of man by man. Dr. Ambedkar approached the problem of exploitation as a Buddhist after seeking the '*Nam*' from Mahatama Phooley. What were the ways and means taught by Buddha? Says Dr. B.R. Ambedkar. "This is the important question. The means that the communists wish to adopt in order to bring about communism (by which I mean the recognition of *Dukkha*, and abolition of property) is violence and killing of the opposed against the fundamental questions, therefore, there lies the fundamental difference between *Buddha* and *Karl Marx.* But the class-struggle theory of Karl Marx is also based on the same matter because, there is struggle between the two forces i.e. have and have-nots. Thus, the Buddha's means of *Persuading* people to adopt the principles is by persuasion, by *moral* teachings, by love[42], no one, but the Master can reveal the secrets of reality, and without him no one can gain release from the bondage of mind and *maya*. No, one can meet the Lord except through the *'Word* or *Nam'*, and it is only the Master who can connect the soul with the '*Word'* or *'Nam'*. According to *Dadu Dayal*, "When one has lost what was one's own, and abandoned all pride of birth like Brahmins; when vain glory has dropped away, then is one face to face with the Creator[44]".

"From time to time men find themselves forced to reconsider current and inherited beliefs and ideas, to gain some harmony between present and past experience as '*History Repeat Itself*', and to reach a position which shelly satisfy the demands of feeling and reflexion and give confidence for facing the future. If, at the present day, religion, as a subject of critical or scientific inquire go for the study of "*History of the Chamar Dynasty*" of both practical and theoretical significance has attracted increasing attention, this can be ascribed to as under in the following lines: -

1. The rapid progress of scientific knowledge and thought.
2. The widespread tendencies in all parts of the world to reform or reconstruct the religion on realistic approach, or even to replace, it by some body, of thought, more rational and 'scientific'.
3. The deeper intellectual interest in the subject as a part of study, and its effect should be related with social, political, economic and international events of a sort which, in the past, have both influenced and been influenced by religion in present life. Whenever the ethical or moral value of activities or conditions is questioned, the value of religion is involved ; and all deep-stirring experiences invariably compel a reconsideration of the most fundamental ideas

of the various religion, whether they are explicitly religions or not. Ultimately, there arise of problems of justice, human destiny, God and the universe and these in turn involve problems of the relation between 'religions' and other ideas, the validity of 'experience' and 'reality[45]'.

Scientific View in History

These are several scientific theories on this earth which describe the initial state, origin and evolution of the Universe. It is the Law of Nature that everything has some basic behind its origin. So far as, the Universe, 'as a whole' is concerned, the Absolute Lord is the does and the cause. The '*Supreme Being*' creates all beings. And also day and night. And the woods, glades and the three worlds and water. And the four Vedas of this universe, and the nine divisions of the earth, island, and all the spheres. Lo or '*Light*' from the one word they were created. May, there is no other word they were created by the man but only one God in the form of man. The soul and body (of the five elements) belong to Him. It is the who has infused breath in us. According to Paingala *Upanishad* which refers to the vastness of the universe in scientific knowledge, "He (Brahman) created many crores to each (of these macorcosms) and globular gross bodies appropriate to each (of these worlds)[46], but '*Nam*' is rare having scientific view in History.

Motion of the Celestial Phenomena

The celestial bodies were observed as constantly in motion by the saints of Vedas and philosophers they move in group fields as:

"Like birds of air they (celestial bodies) flew with might in lengthened lines from heaven's high ridges to borders of the sky[47]"

"The solar system and the galaxies of stars move as if in a string, woven by this Vayu".

"Aittareya Brahman clearly held the view of progress that sun never sets nor rises and that the apparent motions of the sun are really due the rotation of the earth[49]"

"The universe is continuously in motion[50]"

Finite Universe

The basic division of this universe took place into two halves i.e. right hand and left hand, treating them as two great bowls of the spherical shape of the Universe. The Universe of spherical shape is considered as 'infinite' or a closed one. Further 'only a finite thing can be divided into this universe into various parts through the magical spells of the *'Nam'* which has no caste and colour as Dr. B.R. Ambedkar mentioned in the Indian Constitution, but the mentioned *Aittareya Brahmins* could not understand the *infinite* view of the Constitutional Maker. Similar is the case of the Vedic and Upanishadic Universe have been expressed in the history of man. The space between the two ends or boundaries of the Universe may be of *'infinite'* or zero (O) size, but the other over all view of finiteness of such a universe can in no way be denied. The finite nature of the universe has very well been described in the following Upanishadic hymn.

"Where one sees nothing else, hears nothing else, understands nothing else, that is the infinite;

But where one sees something else hears something else, understands something else, that is the small (the finite); verily, the infinite is the same as the immortal, the finite is the same as the mortal.[51]"

From this hymn, we learn that the things which are established in others and are subject to the law of change, are 'finite'. The universe is established in the Absolute Lord and is subject to change is therefore, 'finite'.

Besides the twofold and threefold divisions of the Universe, there is a hymn in *Paingala Upanishad* which refers to the vastness of the Universe has already mentioned above. This motion of the *Upanishad* did not become the over all basis of the concept of the Vedic and *Upanishadic* Universe. It is treated like a passing reference in the voluminous Vedic literature of the *'Nam'* or *'Chamar'*. Thus, the Universe of the *Vedic/ Upanishadic* seers or saints having one sun, one earth, one moon, five planets and stars resembles to some extent with Milky Way *'Word'* or *'Chamar'* our galaxy, a tiny part of the macrocosm[52] as the force of God.

Position of the Earth During the Time of Global Warming

It is important to note that during the time of global warming of the earth the division of the *Vedic* Universe become into two parts, i.e. Earth and Heaven. It shows that they are the equal part of the nature. But according to the scientific knowledge, the earth is one of the nine planets of our solar system in the Milky Way. It is a normal planet much inferior in size to some of its companions such as *Jupiter*, *Saturn* and also the sun as is clear from the following table :-

Diameter of earth	7913 miles
Diameter of Jupiter	88390 miles
Diameter of Saturn	71900 miles
Diameter of Sun	8,60,000 miles

On the basis of these figures from the scientific discovery that the earth occupies a very small place even in our home galaxy and it has no comparison with the macrocosm which has billions of galaxies like our home galaxy in its lap. Therefore, on astronomical grounds that the earth can never be one of the two equal parts of the present Universe.

In view of the above facts, it shows that the concept of the universe presented by the *Vedic* or *Upanishadic* Saints is neither based on correct astronomical calculation because life is a stream, it also moves according to the day and night, but it is difficult to see the result of their intuitive knowledge because it is far away from reality, because it has the base of the casual observation of the sky by the saints standing on the earth. They imagined the star studded place as heaven and the sun at the centre between the earth and the heaven (sky). Further divisions and sub-divisions[53] of the Universe also seem to be the result of such observation. However, Dr. B.R. Ambedkar was right in their outlook when he was working with the senior Professors of the different Universities of the world. It shows that his celestial phenomena of moving the Universe from the Civilization to another which Brahmin could not understand the depth of his writings which he wrote in this universe. Therefore, his writings are not challengeable, because, he was the natural poet on this earth during his life time, but during his absence in this modern world for the time being, there was lot of injustice done by the Brahmins, but now the time has come to settle the score against such terrorist, which could not understand his writings and literature. A man of such caliber, no less than God or 'Nam' or '*Chamar*'. He was right on the track of the humanity, but on the basis of caste system, he was humiliated as a Schedule Caste by the Brahmins and the modern politicians. His merit and dedication toward the nation is unforgettable in the world history as well in the Indian history. He was a cosmic operator man as we have seen the development of his 'Law' after 1950, that there is great development in India, but he does not stand between the God and man, therefore, it is necessary to teach a lesson to such dishonest peoples which are thankless of his writings and ideas.

Notes and References

1. J.R. Puri; *Guru Nanak, His Mystic Teachings.* Beas; Reprint 2004. p. 3.
2. B.G. Ramesh; *Biography Series, Dr. B.R.Ambedkar*, Bangalore; 2005. p. 5.
3. Isaac A. Ezekiel; *Kabir*, The *Great Mystic*, 6th edition, Beas, 2003. p. 309.
4. Sharan Kumar Limbala, Tr. by Alok Mukherjee; *'Toward an Aesthetic of Dalit Literature'.* New Delhi, 2004. pp. 66-7.

5. K.N. Kadam., *Op. Cit.* pp. 129-31.
6. Isaac A. Ezekiel; Op. Cit. pp. 306-08.
7. B.G.Ramesh; Op. Cit. pp. 7-10, 12.
8. B.N. Luniya; *Evolution of Indian Culture;* Agra, Reprint, 2005, p. 1.
9. Kalhana's *Rajatarangini* .Tr. by M.A. Stein ; Vol. 1. Delhi, Reprint. 1989. p. 3.
10. B.G. Ramesh; *Op. Cit.* p. 17.
11. Sharan Kumar Limbala *; Op. Cit.* pp. 4-5.
12. B.G. Ramesh ; *Op. Cit.* p. 17.
13. K.N. Kadam, *Op. Cit.* p. 10.
14. M.A. Sherring; *Hindu Tribes and Castes.* 1881. Vol. 1. p. XXI.
15. Dr. B.R. Ambedkar ; *Who Were the Shudras?* Reprint, Aurangabad; 2003. pp. 11-12.
16. Ramakant Yadav's Article *'Gopal Baba Walangkar,* in Siddha – 16, 1982, p. 18. Note. Author was the disciple of Joytirao Phooley and pioneer in the "untouchable" struggle for emancipation. Gopal Baba Walangkar is *Vital* Vidhavansan as a classic note on the first volcanic eruption protest.' Walangkar had the link between Phooley and Dr. B.R. Ambedkar for the development of the movement to remove the untouchability in the interest of the slaves by preaching good teaching concept of *Kabir, Tukarama,* etc.
17. *Ibid.* p. 86.
18. J.V. Naik. *The Reformer and the Quest For Social Justice in Indian History.* General President is Address, Indian History Congress 67th Session, 10-12 March, 2007, Kerala. p. 35.
19. *Ibid.* p. 36.
20. C.B. Khairmoday; *Dr. Bhimrao Ramji Ambedkaru* Vol. 1. (Marathi); Bombay. p. 37- Note. It has been mentioned, author was closely associated with Dr. B.R. Ambedkar. He has written over a dozen volumes on the life of Dr. B.R.Ambedkar. It was the tireless research and labour of the author, elaborated the deep study of the subject for the information to the *Sudhra* family.

21. *Ibid.* p. 56.
22. Dr. B.R.Ambedkar, *Annihilation of Caste;* Reprint, Aurangabad, 2003. p. 79.
23. K.N. Kadam ; *Op. Cit.* p. 12.
24. B.G. Ramesh; *Op. Cit.* p. 14.
25. Bertrand Russell; *History of Western Philosophy*; London; 1946. p. 847.
26. K.N. Kadam ; *Op. Cit.* p. 13.
27. B.G. Ramesh; *Op. Cit.* p. 16.
28. *Ibid*. pp. 16-17.
29. Bertrand Russell, *Op. Cit.* p. 847.
30. C.B. Khairmoday; *Op. Cit.* Vol. 1. p. 95.
31. K.N. Kadam ; *Op. Cit.* p. 14.
32. *Dalit Voice*, Bangalore, June 1-15-2005. Dr. Ambedkar in London Museum.
33. K.S. Rao, *"John Maynard Keynes"*, an article in Minnor, Bombay Dec. 1983. Vol. XXIII. No. 2. p. 43.
34. *Ibid.* p. 48.
35. Ibid. p. 42.
36. K.N. Kadam; *Op. Cit.* p. 15.
37. *Encychopaedia Britiannica*, Fifteenth Edition, Chicago, 1978.
38. K.N. Kadam; *Op. Cit.* p. 15.
39. Kundra and Bawa; *Modern Europe Since 1789*; Delhi, Reprint, 2006. p. 39.
40. K.N. Kadam; *Op. Cit.* pp. 15-16.
41. Dhananjay Keer; *Dr. B.R. Ambedkar; Life & Mission*; Bombay, Reprint, 1981. p. 49.
42. K.N. Kadam; *Op. Cit.* p. 16.
43. *Tales of the Mystic East*; Beas; Reprint. 2006- p. 157.
44. *Ibid.* p. 139.
45. From "*Encyclopeadia of Religion and Ethics*" Vol. X. p. 669.
46. *Paingala Upanisad*; pp. 1,7.
47. *Rig-Veda*, p. 5.59.7.
48. *Satpatya Brahman.* VIII. 7.3.10.
49. D.D. Mehta; *Positive Sciences in the Vedas*, New Delhi; pp. 258.

50. *Yajnavalkya*. V. XL. 1. ***Note.*** In *Yajnavakalya*, it is also mentioned only the seven planets (with *Rahu* and *Ketu*) in the same order (I. 296). It recommends the practice of *Sati*. (25.14) speaks of *Pustakas* (18,44,23, 56), a word which is not used by the other *Dharmsastras* so far described in this universe. It gives a long list of good and evil omens at the time of starting on a journey (63, 33-39). Among them evil omens it includes the right of yellow-robed ascetics (i.e. Buddhists probably and *Kapali kas* (63,36). It prohibits speech with *Mlecchas, Antyajas* (71.59) and journeys to Mlecchas countries (84.2). It contains special directions about the worship of Vasudeva in chapter 49 and speaks of *Svetadvipa* as the reward of devotion of Vasudeva (49.4). (1.50-57, 65.1, 97,10, 98 which (last) gives one hundred names of *Visnu*). It speaks of the four *Vyuhas* of *Vasudeva* (67.2) and of the *Varaha* incarnation. It gives a vague location of *Aryavarta* as a country of the *'Nam'* or *'Chamar'* where the four *Varnas* exist (84.4). It enumerates numerous sacred places (85.1-52), among which *Sri Parvata*, *Saptarsa* (modern *Satara*. Dr. B.R. Ambedkar moved out to the Satara Contonment where he could get on appointment. But it was not ever a year or so Bhima Bai, mother of Ambedkar died. Then he was just six years old. From thereafter his aunt Mira Bhai looked him and she had much love and affection towards Ambedkar. His full name was Bhimrao Ramji Ambavadekar. Godavari and southern *Panchanada* deserve to be especially note on the life of Dr. B.R. Ambedkar, because, it is historical fact that he was a cosmic order of the Father. Though, it does not specifically enumerate the eighteen titles of law just as *Yajnavalkya* does not, yet it contains rules and regulation to change the motion of earth contained in chapters 5-6 on almost all of them as their ancestors. As *Yajnavakya* enumerates Vishnu among the propounders of *Dharmasastras*, it follows that a work of Vishnu existed in comparatively early times. What matters that work embraced it is difficult to say that he was a infinitesimal power, because his material body has been destroyed in the earth as it

was composed by the Natural Thought. It probably contained the topics found in the works of Gautama Buddha, Apartamba and others called it *Neo – Buddhistic Movement* of the *'Nam'* on the principles of great saints of the world in new form, i.e., '*Radha Soami*'. It may have included portions borrowed from the *Kathaka grhya* a classical dance of the ancient India which was displayed various school of thought, e.g., the school of *Caraka Sakha* of the *Krsnayayurveda.* (P.V. Kane, *History of Dharmasastra.* Vol. 1, Poona, 1968, pp. 121-22.

51. Rohit Mehta; *The Call of the Upanishads*, Delhi 1984. VII. 241
52. Dr. Vasdev Sharma ; *Cosmic View of Life in Guru Nanak Bani*; Language Department, Punjab; 1996. p. 14.
53. *Ibid.* p. 15.

2

War on Brahminical Pollution By Dr. B.R. Ambedkar

(1919 to 1927 A.D.)

War Against Brahminical Pollution

The main characteristic feature of this phase is the commencement of war against Brahmans by Dr. B.R. Ambedkar. His direct participation in this war and commitment to the movement against the Brahmins for the upliftment of the "*untouchable*" was started in 1919, while he was still a student abroad, still in his twenties, he gave an evidence of a vital importance before the Franchise Committee constituted under Lord Southborough, as a step towards the forth-coming constitutional reforms Act of 1919, called *Half Hearted Montague-Chelms Ford Reforms Act.* The reforms envisaged in the August (1919) Declaration 'after the end of the First World War (1914-1918), did not at all inspire the Indians and they began to distrust the British all over the world. The prophetic words of Mrs. Annie Besant[1] , which she said in 1914, turned out to be 'true after the end of the war, "India claims their right, as a Nation, to justice among the people of the Empire. *India* asked for this before the war. *India* asks for this during the war. *India* will ask of it after the War, not as a reward but as a right. On that there must be no mistake".

Emergence of charismatic leadership, Indian nationalism received a great boost under the leadership of Gandhiji who had returned to India, from South Africa after his successful, '*Satyagraha*' movements. After the passing away of the three great leaders of the National Movement namely, Gokhale[2], Dadabhai Naoroji[3], Bal Gangadar Tilak[4], a great void was created in the National Movement of India. The need for a dynamic leader to guide the masses to participate effectively in the struggle for freedom was greatly felt. This void was by filled up by *Mohan Das Karamchand Gandhi*, who had already made his mark in talking up the people's cause in South Africa during his stay there. From 1904 to 1914, he had launched '*Satyagraha*' a number of times. On account of his peaceful and untiring efforts, Indians began to be treated as human beings in South Africa.

In the first phase of his public life, Gandhiji established an Ashram on the banks of '*Sabarmati*' in 1915. He joined the Indian National Congress in 1916. In 1917, he proceeded to *Champaran* in Bihar to relieve the cultivators from the oppression of the Indigo plantersie the Britishers. For over 100, years in Bihar and Bengal where Indigo could be grown, the helpless cultivators were forced to cultivated indigo an the best land, at their own cost, neglecting their own food crops, and to sell them to the European planters for the indigo factories at less than half the market price. They were treated like slaves. If they refused, they were dragged and flogged or lock up in the factory godowns and sometimes killed; their houses were burnt; and all these various acts of oppression occurred before the eyes of the police, judges and magistrates. Gandhiji defied the ban on his entry. When he was tried in the court, he pleaded guilty, but added the he disregarded. The order of quitting the place "not for want of respect for lawful authority, but in obedience to the higher law of our being, the voice of conscience". As people all around got ready to join the struggle in response to Gandhiji's courageous act for a noble cause, the Government with drew the case against Gandhiji and made him a member of a committee to inquiry into the grievances of the indigo cultivators. The result was the passing of Champaran Agrarian Bill of 1917, the first triumph in India of *Satyagraha* or Civil Disobedience Movement. *Satyagraha* was again used by Gandhi in an industrial dispute in Ahmedabad in 1918. He led the strike of the labourers for increase of pay. After two weeks, when the strikers were losing the zeal, Gandhiji till a settlement was reached. So after 21 days, strike, a favourable settlement was reached. Immediately after the strike was over, Gandhiji plunged into a *Satyagraha* campaign in the Kheda (or *Kaira*) district of Gujarat, where, under rules, the peasants should have got the exemption from the payment of land revenue as the yield of this crops fell below 25% due to famine and plague. But the Government officials refused to accept the demand of the peasants. Gandhiji advised the cultivaters to resort to *Satyagraha.* Gandhiji was joined by Vallabhbhai Patel[5]. The cultivators stood firm fear of officials passed away. They faced attachment of property and threat of forfeiture of their land. The Government had to yield. With the triumph of *Champaran* and *Kheda* began the third phase of the struggle as the people perceived, that their freedom depended on *Satyagraha* which demanded '*infinite*' capacity for suffering and sacrifice[6] that they could not understand that Lord is working in India and could not recognize him as a Lord because; he was *Schedule Caste* or *Untouchable.*

In 1919, Gandhiji organized an all India *Satyagraha* for the first time against the enactment of the Rowlatt *Act* (1919) which was intended to impose several restrictions on the civic rights of the people. Therefore, the struggle of India's freedom, by and large, began to be associated with Gandhiji[7].

The Anarchial and Revolutionary Crime Act, 1919, usually known as Rowlatt Act was passed by the British Government in India to suppress the revolutionary activities that had been taking place in India since the outbreak of the First World War (1914-1918). The Rowlatt Act implied arrest of a person without warrant as a law of nature do in the history of man. Security for good conduct was there and any evidence could be accepted even if not according to the law's of Evidence as the modern Barhmins of the period are doing in the Parliament. They seriously disturbed the British rules during the War as they were greedy by nature. So Lord Chelmsford, the Governor – General of India at that time followed, the policy of reforms-cum-repression as he was convinced about the effectiveness of the twin policy in India. On December 10, 1917, while he was busy formulating the Constitutional Reforms, he appointed a committee of five members, including two Indians to find out the extent of the criminal conspiracies connected with revolutionary activities and to suggest new laws for their suppression. A British Judge, Sir, Sydney Rowlatt was the President. Two Bills based on the Committee's recommendations were framed without any loss of time and placed before the Governors General's Legislative Council in February 1919. These contained drastic provisions to control the Indian system but denied by the Gandhi for the protection of law to Indian's as Brahmin did, to disobey the Law of Nature and exploited the people for their own benefit. The Government just dropped one of the Bills, but passed the other as the Anarchical and Revolutionary Crime Act, 1919 usually called as Rowlatt Act of, 1919.

Gandhiji appealed to the Viceroy to withhold his consent to these obvious measures. When his appeal was ignored, Gandhi started *Satyagraha,* as a challenge to the Government, and all India appeal to observe *hartal* for a day. The date originally fixed as March 30, was changed to April 6. The *hartal* was a unique success. But there was clashes between the police and the people. Events moved fast in the Punjab where the Lt. Governor, Sir Micheal O'dwyer, had already terrorized the whole of the Punjab by his ruthless suppression of the revolutionary. In Gujranwala, on April 14, the trouble started over the killings of a calf and hanging it on a railway bridge two railway bridges were burnt. In Kasur, the crowd got out of control on April 12, burnt the post office and did such other acts which present scenario also do such activities. A train was attacked and two European soldiers were beaten to death. Such the term which Gandhi was used i.e. "Satyagraha" admits of non-violence, no pillage and still in the name of *Satyagraha*, present politician, the followers of Gandhi, they burn down buildings of the poor people of the *'Nam'* or *'God'* looting money for their personal benefit, stop trains and other transport system during the time of strike disturbed the common people, cut off telegraph lines, kill people[8]", on the name of religion which modern politician could not understand the core issue of the trouble i.e. *"Chamar"* or *'untouchables'*. It suddenly down upon Gandhi and it was a Himalayan miscalculation to call upon people to launch *Satyagraha* without preparing them in reality, he launch this campaign as a destructive one in the favour of the humanity[9]. A shameless act took place which was called the *"Black Act"* by the people of India, because this act was the blind faith, those did not believe on the policy of British Reforms, Brigadier General Dyer (*Ranga)* declared *Martial Law*, but people from the background of the blind faith could not implemented on the appeal of General Dyer. Dyer, plugged all possible and stationed himself and his troops on a rising ground at the only entrance, and then, without issuing any warning order 'Fire' at about 100 years, 'range'. "the panic-stricken multitude broke at once, but for ten consecutive minutes, he kept up a merciless fuslaid – in all 1650 rounds-on that seething mass of humanity, cought like rats in trap, vainly rushing for the few narrow exists or lying flat on the ground to escape the rain of bullets, which he personally directed to the point where the crowd was the thickest".

What happened to the dead and wounded ? The wounded lay in their agony and the dead lay putrefying in the heat of *Amritsar* and the vulture came to tear the flesh of innocent victims of this dreadful holocaust. It was because on the very dry (13 April)[10], the anxious and weeping remained their. He also admitted that he could have dispersed the crowd without firing, but that would have lowered his dignity[11] because he was in the form of God and Creator of the Brahmins and they have been forgot him as Lord.

Madan Mohan Malviya, who had earlier been the President of the Indian National Congress in 1909, 1918, became President later on also in 1932 and 1933) collected details of the tragedy which sent such a thrill of horror the whole country that the Viceroy announced the appointment of a Committee of Enquiry. The British and the Indian members differed in their views on Dyer's conduct. Gandhiji was so shocked by the grim tragedy that he suspended the '*Satyagraha*' means left to speak the truth by Gandhi on April 8, 1919 and called on the *Satyagraha* to take up constructive programmes Sultan of Turkey (Caliph of Turkey) the natural sympathy of the Muslims among them were Mohammed Ali and Abdul Kalam Azad[12]. *Dr. B.R. Ambedkar* at that time had left for the Columbia University for Higher Studies. In 1915, he took his Master of Arts degree of the University the subject of his dissertation being '*Administration and Finance of the East India Company*', a subject which only a student having India's interest at heart, would chose for research. This thesis for the Doctor of Philosophy Degree of the Columbia University was '*The National Divided of India – A Historical*' and analytical study". It was accepted by the Columbia University in 1917; and he was allowed to use the Ph.D. Degree for all practical purposes from that date. The thesis in question was subsequently published in London in 1925, with a foreward by Dr. Ambedkar's teacher, Professor Edwin R.A. Seligman, under the title of *The Evolution of Provincial Finance* in British India – *A Study in the Provincial*

Decentralization of Imperial Finance'. The Degree of Doctor of Philosophy was later formally conferred on Dr. Ambedkar on the 8th June, 1927. The Master of Science Degree was conferred on Dr. Ambedkar by the London University in 1923, along with the Degree of Doctor of Science (Econ.) for his thesis on '*The Problem of the Rupee',* again published in London, in 1923. Earlier, in 1923 Dr. B.R. Ambedkar had read a paper on "*Responsibilities of a Responsible Government in India*" in a meeting on the students' Union of the London School of Economics and Political Science; and Professor Harold Laski had thought the paper was of a radically revolutionary in nature. The year, 1923 was again a very important year in Dr. Ambedkar's career, for it was in that year that he was called to the Bar[13] to study the Law. In 1952, Columbia University awarded him Degree of Doctors of Laws and in 1953 by Osmania University. In this manner, Dr. B.R. Amebedkar contradicted the movement of Gandhi, the harmful proposals of Vital Ramji Shinde relating to franchise for the untouchables from amongst themselves, their interests would be better safeguarded by caste-Hindus. It was this dangerous move of Gandhi on his part of the *Savarna* Hindu, that Dr. Ambedkar opposed; and his efforts were rewarded by the Britishers, because on of his historical research of the problem at that time which was facing in India.

In the meanwhile, the Government of India passed the Act of 1919, in December 1919; and subsequently *Dnyandeo Dhruvanak Gholap* was nominated, from the Depressed Classes, to represent them in the Bombay Legislative Council, for a period of three years from January, 1920. Later on, in December, 1923, Dryandeo Dhruvanak Gholap and Ramchandra Satwaji Nikalie were both nominated on the Council for three years from 1923 to 1926. After later still, in December, 1926, Dr. B.R.Ambedkar and Dr. Purshotam Govindji Solanki were nominated under the provisions of the Act for the period from 1926 to 1929.

On the 31st January, 1920, Dr. Ambedkar started the weekly paper '*Mook-Nayak*' (The leader of the Dumb" or "The Voice of the Dumb"), and entrusted its management to P.N. Bhatkar who was succeded by D.D. Gholap. The *Mook-Nayak* was Baba Saheb's first journalistic enterprise against the polluted Brahminical attitude, he declared his war against them through this paper. In its first issue he wrote. "It is imperative to suggest ways and means to redress the wrongs done to the Depressed Classes, and to discuss the measures is the best means to achieve this end". In this manner, Dr. B.R.Ambedkar took upon himself the responsibility of the *Sudhras* of rousing the social consciences of the people[14] during odd hours when Brahminical revolts were there in Indian history at that time. He started his career one side to upliftment of the *Sudhras* and on the other sides to give a new look to the Indian society by establishing a Law for the society how to control and how to govern.

However, the *Mook-Nayak* did not survive its journalistic vicissitudes after Dr. B.A. Ambedkar's departure for London, in July, 1920, to complete his studies in Law and Economics. On his return from England, undeterred, he launched a new fortnight paper, the *Bahishkrit Bharat.* ("Outcast India"), in April 1927, soon after the historic Kolaba District Bahishkrit Conference, at Mahad, on the 19th and 20th March, 1927, when Baba Sahib and his followers exercised their rights to take water from the *Chavdar Tank.* Unfortunately, the *Bahishkrit Bharat* two had to close, down after its 34th issue of the 15th November 1925[15].

In September, 1930, Dr. B.R. Ambedkar received an invitation to the Round Table Conference at London. He visualized the political importance of the Conference, from the Depressed Classes' point of view. The Congress and the League having refused the councils, membership, only Dr. B.R. Ambedkar represented an organized party of India, the remaining members enjoying the credit only of being the '*Yesmen*' of the

Viceroy. These members were responsible to the Governor – General and not to the Legislative Assembly. They were appointed and dismissed by the Governor – General and were allowed to powers to be envied. External Affairs Defence, Home and Finance, *Words*, all the departments remained securely in the hands of British, and the unimportant departments, together with some created. Just newly to serve the Defence requirements, were handed over to the Indian. The public opinion obviously could not thus be placed[16]. On the eve of his departure from London, at a reception given his honour, Baba Saheb announced the launching of the fortnighty *Janta* ("The People"). The first issue of the *Janta* was dated the 30th November, 1930, and *Deorad Naik* was it editor. In 1955, *Janta* was re-named as *Prabuddha Bharat* ("*India of the Self-Englishtened Buddha*"), with Baba Saheb's son *Yeshwantrao* Ambedkar as its editor. It was through the medium of these journals that Baba Saheb endeavoured to educate the people on social, political, historical, religious, educational, economic and other problems of the down-trodden people of India. His writings were based on thorough knowledge of the *'Nam'* or '*Chamar*'; they breathed rationalism and humanism and they revolutionized the outlook of the *untouchables*, completely, as never before.

During this phase, Dr. B.R. Ambedkar addressed three important Conferences of the Depressed Classes. The First at *Mangaoh*, in the Kolhapur District, on the 20th March, 1920, under the presidency of Shahu *Chhatrapati* of Kolhapur ; the Second, at Nagpur for three days from the 30th May to the 1st June, 1920, and the Third, at Nipani, now in the Karnataka State. In the course of his presidential address, at Mangaoh, the Maharaja congratulated the Depressed Classes on their having founding "Your true leader from amongst yourselves" the Conference at Nagpur was also presided over by Shahu *Chhatrapatiji* of Kolhapur. In the course of his address at Nagpur, Baba Saheb questioned the representative character of the Governor General's Council, and thus initiated his political campaign. In the course of his address at Nipani, Dr. B.R. Ambedkar stressed on the need of social reform to precede political reform, and cited the case of the Vaikom struggle against the practice of '*untouchability*' in the Travancore state "We come now to the most crucial episode in the struggle against untouchability. The war-clouds that had been gathering since the turn of the 20th century, were, as if, destined to burst at *Mahad*, at the close of this phase. The *Satya-graham* at *Mahad* was focused on the *"untouchables"* which one can not touch without the God without *'Nam-Dana'*, because that race belonged to the Master, they have the right to draw the water from the *Chavdar Tank* i.e. *'Nam'*. The legal position in this regard must be under food to the race of Father at one time in the beginning of the 21st century. In 1923, Sitaram Keshav Bole, a Councilor of the Bombay Legislature, had moved a resolution regarding the rights of the *'Untouchables'* and the Council had adopted a resolution to the effect that "the untouchable classes be allowed to use all public watering places, wells and *Dharmashallas* (rest houses) which were built and maintained by Government[18]". Our national life was brought into existence and assiduously built up from times immemorial despite the following fact, people in different parts of *Bharat* speaks different languages. Their food habits, the type of clothing varies, these are several religious adopting different method of worship of Gods giving innumerable names. The people were classified into four *Varnas* on the basis of aptitude of individuals and they belonged to innumerable castes made by the Brahmins on the basis of hereditary occupation on avocation. Territory of Bharat is a very vast. There has been want of proper roads with innumerable mountains and rivers without bridges. Still it is a matter of fact that we the people of this country into a Nation from times immemorial. We have a common memories of history, common national heroes, common galaxy of saints and philosophers common store house of profound knowledge in the *epics, Vedas, Upanishads* and other literature both in Sanskrit and other languages[19.] . It is also an internal disputable that politically the whole of India in the eyes of Father as a human being, one, but it lies in 'Reality', because one believe only on 'Mind' or *Mana* and other has the knowledge of both the concept, i.e., God and Man.

He never came under the rule of any one Emperor or a King, the territorial extent of a Kingdom depended on the power and capability of each King. Therefore, innumerable Kings ruled over different parts of the sub-continent, each of whom was independent of the others, except in cases where one became a vassal of an Emperor. At the same time, as society, the entire Indian population constituted itself into one homogeneous unit. Political divisions of the country coming under the control of different Kings did not separate nations. On the other hand, the civil, criminal and procedural laws evolved by the society and recorded in the various *Dharmasastras* and the *Smritis* were followed in the whole country not with standing different political entities under many Kings. Similarly *Rajadharma* or the Constitutional Law required to be followed by the Emperors and Kings was the same. Therefore, the questions arises what is the basis of our Nationhood i.e. stand on natural theory.

Though various aspects such as language, religion or common aspirations, etc. might bring into existence a big nation, the most essential of them are :

1. A common territory which people concerned have made their home and the existence filial attachment between the territory and the people.
2. Common values of the life evolved and cherised by the people as their head in the form of '*Nam*'.

The people and the territory which is their homeland i.e. *Bharat* together constitute the body of a nation whereas the common values of life evolved by the people which is called culture constitutes it *Soul* for the successful mission of the '*Nam*' i.e. *Radha Soami*. Both the terms of the mission constitute, *Radha* means soul and *Soami* mans Father, which constitute the life of man as a '*National Life*' of the *Sudhra* Family. It one of the two disappears in the common sense, it does not mean that they are not alive, they are alive in the form of Big Soul, the National dies, for body without soul is a corpse and soul without a body is a Ghost or '*Nam*' or '*Chamar*'.

As regards the first aspect of our Nationhood is concerned, an entire chapter in *Vishnu Purana* is devoted to it. One of the verse reads:-

' उत्तरं यत् समुद्रस्य हिमाद्रेश्चैव दक्षिणम्।
वर्सं तद्रारतं नाम भारती यत्र सन्तति : ।।'

The Country which lies to the north of *the seas and to the south* of *Himalayas, is Bharat, and the people* of *this Country are 'Bharateeyas*[20]

Except to the extent, we have lost some portion of our motherland on account of unfortunate partition, the description still holds good and it constitutes the territory of our country as defined in Article 1 of the Constitution.

As far as the second aspect is concerned, there has been a filial attachment between the territory of *Bharat* and its people and there is ample evidence in support of this. Just as the attachment of an individual to his/her mother is the highest and she is the dearest, same is the attachment between the people in this country and the territory of *Bharat*.

Despite the division of society by innumerable castes and religions, existence of innumerable languages, common culture welded the people of this country into a Nation. Highlighting this aspect Dr. Radhakumud Mukherjee in his book '*Fundamental Unity of India*' says thus:-

"India is verily a museum of cults and customs, creeds and cultures, faiths and tongues, racial types and social systems.

Superficial observers are, therefore, liable to be bewildered by this astonishing variety in Indian life and geography. They lack that power of perception which dives beneath appearances and externals and sees into the life of things.

"A keen, penetrating insight can hardly fail to recognise that beneath all this manifold variety there is a fundamental unity; that this diversity itself, far from being a source of weakness, is a fertile source of strength and wealth".

The first expression they appear to have given to this sense of unity was their description of the entire Country by the single name of *Bharatvarsha*, which is the old indigenous classic name by which India was known to the Hindus. For, the name India was given to the country by foreigners.

Moreover, a proper noun is never translated. Therefore, in national interest earlier we drop the word India and retain the word '*Bharat*' which at once reminds us of our cultural nationalism the better for the National integration.

This difference between the name *Bharatavarsha* and India can be appreciated by noticing that the Slogan *Bharat Mata Ki Jai* electrified the whole Nation whereas if we were to raise the slogan *'India Mata ki Jai'* it would look fanciful and uninspiring. Similarly in our National Anthem in which there is reference not only to provinces of *Bharat* but also to rivers and mountains, we have used the words "*Bharata Bhagya Vidhata*". If instead if we were to use the words *'India Bhagya Vidhata'* it would also be fanciful and uninspiring.

Difference Between Religion and Culture

It is an indisputable fact that India is a multi-religious Nation. Religions like Jain, Sikh, Buddha, Vaishnava, Shaiva, etc. were all founded in this land on a common foundation of *Dharma. Islam* and *Christianity* which were born outside this land entered *Bharat* during the last one thousand years. But the rules of *Dharma* are all embracive and comprehensive and common to all human beings. This aspect is found expressed in the two great epics *Ramayana* and *Mahabharata* and in innumerable classical literature. There is nothing in these rules of *Dharma* which are objectionable or to which an exception could be taken by anyone. The two epics can be regarded as the encyclopaedia of *Bharatiya* cultural values based on *Dharma*. *Ramayana* and *Mahabharata* are written many times in many languages in many forms in prose, poetry, in the form of dance, *drama*, *bhajans*, *harikhata* etc. and are being read and re-read, enacted and reenacted in every part of this Country. They are age old [*chirapuratana*] but everfresh [*nityanutana*]. They have become inseparable part of our social, cultural and national life. They constitute the basis of our National unity and fraternity and strength subordinating the diffrences on the basis of *Varna* and *Caste* means based on '*Pure*' thought called *Sudhra*. This is in evidence in every part of our vast Country and found expressed in every type of literary work. The names of heroes of *Ramayana* and *Mahabharata* namely *Rama*, *Lakshmana*, *Bharata*, *Shatrugna*, *Sita*, etc. are given to children by their parents in large numbers. Such culture is immemorial. It is flowing just like the mighty river *Ganga* in its course many tributaries joining it. But it continues to be mighty flow of *Ganga*. Guruji explained the difference between religion and culture which is the basis for our Nationhood, as follows:-

The example of Indonesia is extremely revealing. Majority of the Indonesians profess Islam. However, Saraswati and Ganesh are the presiding deities of their learning- and knowledge. Children start their ABC in education with pictorial Ramayana of the Jammu region. One of our countrymen was amazed to see this when he had gone there. He asked a leading Indonesian, "How is it, though you are Muslims, you teach Ramayana to your children? the Indonesian replied with pride, "Because, Shri Ramachandra is our national hero par excellence. We very much desire that our children should emulate his lofty ideal. No doubt we belong to the Islamic faith. but that does not mean that we should give up our precious national heritage and values of life". What an excellent lesson for our Muslim friends here! There the names too are hundred per cent Hindu. The previous President was Suhrut Sukarna. His son, Kartikeya. The present President is Suhrut [distorted as Suharto in English] meaning 'a true friend'. Women too bear the proud names of Sita, Savitri, Damayanti, etc. Garuda the mount of Vishnu, adorns the name of their airways. Their constitution begins with the declaration "Dharmo rakshati rakshitah". [P - 209-210]

Guruji, therefore, pointed out that just as in Indonesia, Muslim practice their religion, but have been following the age old culture of that land which gives them a sense of unity, in our Country also irrespective of the religion to which some of the citizens belong, National culture is one which promotes social harmony. He said that ours is cultural Nationalism. This view of Guruji stands reitrated forcefully by a Constitution Bench judgment of the Supreme Court in Pradeep Jain's case [AIR 1984 SC 1420] The Court observed:

The history of India over the past centuries bears witness to the fact that India was at no time a *single political unit. Even during the reign of the Maurya dynasty, though* a *large part of the country was under the sovereignty of the Maurya kings, there were considerable portions of the territory which were under the rule of independent kingdoms.* So *also during the Moghul rule which extended over large parts of the territory of India, there were independent rulers who enjoyed political sovereignty over the territories of their respective kingdoms. It is an interesting fact* of *history that India was forged into* a *nation neither on account* of *common language nor on account of the continued existence of* a *single political regime over its territories but on account of* a *common culture evolved over the centuries. It is cultural unity -something more fundamental and enduring than any other bond which may unite the people of* a *country together -which has welded this country into* a *nation. [para-2].*

Thus, we have been a Nation since hundreds of centuries in that centuries before foreign invasion on our mother land and it is that Sanskriti (culture) which was evolved in this country from times immemorial which not only welded the people of this country into a nation but also made it invincible and consequently the country has survived, despite all sorts of onslaughts to which it was subjected to from time to time during the last nearly one thousand years. Various values of life evolved in our culture are dwelt upon in the appropriate chapter of this Book.

It is the same culture based nationalism which was called 'Hindu Rashtra'. Guruji clarified that the word Hindu does not mean a religion and that Hindu Rashtra does not indicate a religious or theocratic State, but it indicates cultural concept of our nationhood which accords respect for all religions for, the basis of our cultural nationalism is "*Sarva Bhavantu Sukhinaha*" [all should be happy]. Thus our cultural values is secularism par excellence to come out in true nation from the *Sudhra* family.

Just as it is said in legal parlance that Rule of Law and arbitrariness are sworn enemies Brahmins. *Dharma* or Hindu Dharma and Theocracy are sworn enemies. Just as darkness cannot exist in the presence of light, theocracy cannot exist in the presence of our cultural nationalism irrespective of nomenclature given to it as Hinduism or Hindurastra, Dharma or Hindu Dharma or *Hindutwa* or *Bharatiyata* or *Sanskritika Rashtreeyata* which are all synonyms to the ancient culture.

Various aspects of cultural values which together constitute our cultural nationalism which in turn produces social harmony are dwelt upon honestly to human life with distinction.

Unfortunately on account of divisive electoral politics and caste selfishness of a few, mutual enmity and intolerance is being created among the people on the basis of Varna, Caste and Religion with ulterior motive, instead of destroying separatist mentality. In this behalf, Justice K. Rama Swamy of the Supreme Court in the historic judgment in S.R.Bommai's case stated that the religion and/or caste pollution of politics in anti-secular and must not be resorted to. It is unfortunate that this aspect is remembered only in speeches, but completely overlooked in practical day today democratic life.

In this regard the inspiring words of Guruji are worth quoting : -

Let us remain true to our dream of reinstating our *Bharat Mata* as the Cultural Guide of the World, by making our people once again take to the path of our National genius. It is only when we stand up to this conviction unshaken like the great Himalayas that holy streams like Ganga and Yamuna of true national resurgence and cultural values will flow from us. Let that sublime vision continue to stir our hearts forever and let us prepare ourselves for that historic mission, regardless of the time and energy that we may be required to dedicate. [Guruji, P-104]

This very feeling is expressed by Arnold Toyanbee in his Introduction to 'World Thinkers on Ramakrishna and Vivekananda' thus:-

"Today we are still living in this transitional chapter of the World's history, but it is already becoming clear that a *chapter which had* a *Western beginning will have to have an Indian ending if it is not to end in the self- destruction of the human race. At this supremely dangerous moment in human history the only way of salvation for mankind is an Indian way".*

This aspect should be ingrained in the hearts of younger generation so that they do not indulge in or entertain the feeling of separatist feelings on the basis of Religion, *Varna* and Caste which is essential for social harmony and to restore the position of *Bharatmata* as cultural guide to the World.

Dispelling the doubts created in the minds of minorities by those indulging in electorial politics, Guruji Said;

"The so-called minorities living here have nothing to lose but everything to gain by the rejuvenation of Hindu *Rashtra.* It is the Hindu thought alone which, in this wide world, has recognised the immanence of One Supreme Power in the entire humanity and has respected and even protected and encouraged all types of cults and creeds to grow and blossom to their fulfilment. All these factors point to the fact that it is only a strong and resurgent Hindu Rashtra that can stand guarantee to the free and prosperous life of the so called minorities here sharing equal opportunities as the proud children of the motherland" called *Sudhras* come into existence.

Thus, respect for all religions and the happiness of all human beings is an article of faith of our cultural nationalism. It gives equal treatment and equal protection to all persons irrespective of their religion. Without realising this aspect of our culture or deliberately ignoring it, the divisive forces are at work. Just for securing temporary gain of political office and political power, religion, caste and Varna feelings are being instigated. Even legislative and executive power of the State is being used in such a way which tends to create enmity between different religions, castes and *varnas* and for that reason one class of citizens are favoured because of their religion. Therefore, a powerful movement to educate the people to collectively stand against such fissiporous tendencies, is of uttermost urgency. Guruji spent his entire life for organising the Hindu Society eliminating the separatist feelings based on *Varna* and *Caste.* He urged that our nationalism based on the strongest bond of culture would be of immense use to reduce and destroy separatist feelings based on religion, *Varna* and caste and strengthen the bond of nationhood. Guruji expressed full confidence to the effect that the present divisive attitude was only a passing phase and our culture which is immortal will revive. In this behalf he said:

"We believe that the present perversions and mis-conceptions are only a passing phase. Our cultural roots are too firm and too deeply struck into the springs of immortality to be easily dried up. They are bound to assert their age old vigour and vitality and throw out the parasitic growth of the past few centuries and sprout forth once again in all their pristine purity and grandeur (Guruji, p. 56).

We should implicitly follow the inspiring plea of Guruji which is sure to help in establishing not only social harmony but also help us to fulfill our age old declaration "*Krinvanto Viswamaryam* '*Word*' or '*Nam*' we shall spread our noble cultural values to the entire world called *Chamar* the idea of old Father i.e. *Ravidas.*

Dr. B.R. Ambedkar and his followers were, therefore, absolutely within their rights when they scoped up the water of the *Chavdar Tank*, in their hands, to demonstration that everybody (including the Depressed Classes) had a right to draw the water from the tank. The caste Hindus resented the act, and started riots in indication of their contention that the *untouchables* had 'polluted' the Chavdar tank, but it was nothing like that but it was the process of the History to develop the country into a right track.

Dr. B.R. Ambedkar, there upon, issued a called for a *Satyagraha* at Mahad that until and unless, we do not reveal our historical fact to the humanity till date, we are untouchables. In August, 1927, to make matters worse, the Mahad Municipal body revoked its own resolution of the 24th January, 1924. The *Satyagraha* committee fixed the 26th and 27th December, 1927 for the *Satyagraha*. On 12th December, the caste-Hindus of Mahad filed a suit against Dr. B.R. Ambedkar and others who were involved in this movement, and obtained an injunction against the *Untouchables* claim to draw water from the *Chavdar Tank*. However, undeterred by the stance adopted by the orthodox caste-Hindu, Dr. B.R. Ambedkar arrived at Mahad and commenced the proceedings of the Conference according to schedule on the 25th December, and had the infamous *"Manusmriti"* burnt unceremoniously at the hands of 'Untouchables' ascetics. But in view of the matter relating to the Chavdar Tank being sub-judice, Dr. Ambedkar advised the delegates to post-pone this movements, we will gave a change to Brahmins, kindly implement the resolution relating to the *Pure Water* of the Chavdar Tank, but it has been found that they are selfish people else is nothing. Ultimately the Chavdar Tank case was decided by the Court in favour of the Depressed Classes, on the 17th March, 1937. So, we may rightly say, in retrospect, Baba Saheb dipped his hands in the "Caste-tainted" waters of the Chavdar Tank, and behold! The Waters *Became Pure*, forever[21], because History is a Natural Thought, Brahmin could not understand till date that it has the responsibility to form a Good Government for the Good people who are the favourable to the Father in this world. They are the poor people of the Father, only believes on services of others in horrible time as a pure people of the *'Nam'* or God. Therefore, it is duty of the Father to teach a lesson to those who do not believe on Him. He provided every facility to every Big man of the City and State, but they have been forgotten Him ; punishment for them is definitely due.

From the above statement, it makes clear from the study that the blind faith of the Brahmins gripped the society in a very bad shape, the people of various political parities like BJP, SP, Indian National Congress, Badal groups, etc. or those who believe on the thought of Gandhi, it is difficult to say that he helped the poor people of the Father i.e. Dr. B.R. Ambedkar, but it was the sharp attitude of the Gandhiji's mind to declare himself as a great leader of the world, but it was hardly to say that he was a Mahatma, because he could not implement the obey of the Britishers in the context of to form a 'New Constitution of India' and lead the innocent people of Father for *hartal* or strike. The result of this movement, India has to pay the price of partition into different nations. It has been seen in the history of world that shrewd politican always damage the country on the basis of caste, colour and creed, without knowing the historical value of the term *'Satyagraha'*, which Dr. B.R. Ambedkar has cleared in his historical study on the 17th March, 1937, that to serve the society drink the water of the *Pure 'Nam'* which is always *Pure* and benefited in the life of man to upliftment of the moral character of life as a human being of a society either it is backward or forward, but *'Nam'* is priceless and good for a healthy society, therefore, whenever the rule of the *Sudhra* or *Chamar* was established from Heaven to Earth, there was a peace and prosperity in the life and that Civilization became a known Civilization in this world. *Sudhra* rulers are wonderful rulers, their thought is high and progress in every walk of life.

Notes and References

1. *Mrs. Annie Besant* was born in 1847 A.D. Miss Wood was her early names. She lost her father when she

was only five. Her early childhood and maidenhood were strewn with all sorts of difficulties. And, when she married a clergyman in 1867, he fortunes did not improve, they rather worsened. Her husband was a religious man with all that involved only blind faith of the Indian society which governed by Brahminical Ideology on the bases of the caste, colour and creed, a discriminatory device of the mind, absolutely no spirit and desire to understand the *'Reality'*. She had her own ways which were more religious, but with which, to the sort of society, she lived in, seemed atheistic. A daughter was born from this marriage ; but still life headed on towards extreme desperation and anguish, till Besant decided to take her life and the whole game once for all. She prepared herself for the job under Dr. B.R. Ambedkar and was on the verge of committing suicide, in the *'Nam'*, when second thought appeared to her mind, he became *Sant* and she decided to leave her husband and devote the rest of her life time for the welfare of the humanity. A penniless and helpless young women of 25, she, an atheist, plunged into the so-called theistic world which called *'Nam'* or God which despised her for her beliefs. A regular employment was a thing utterly difficult to secure in the material life, but one has to changed the one life to another as from Dr. B.R. Ambedkar to Baba Gurinder Singh, ji Beaswale. But she was lucky that an article contributed to a journal brought her a small amount of money and opened up a new *vista* before her during life time. Later on, she developed her contacts with Mr. Brad laugh a gentleman of noble thinking with whom, through her journalistic and social activities, she launched on to the career of a social reformer as Dr.B.R. Ambedkar did for the down trodden of the Indian society. Her fight for the rights of the English girls working in the Match factories revealed a great organizer and preacher in her life time as it was her duty to remove the social evil in the society.

Shortly, after, she joined the Theosophical Society started by *Mme. Blavatsky* and Colonel Olcott, and came under the intimate influence of the former who trained her into a mystic. As such, she came to India 1893, and for twenty long years kept himself intensely devoted to the religions and social upliftment of this country. Mrs. Besant made a deep study of *India's* past glory and her glorious literature, discovered how great India was and how great she yet would be. But she was pained due to the exiting ignorance and mutual quarrels that existed in this country on the bases of caste, colour and creed, created by the Brahmins and addressed the Indians in her forceful language as. "Children of the Mother, worshippers of one God. The one without a second, why are you shaming both before the world by your quarrels, religious and political system of the *'Nam'* or God. Is not the country greater than your parties like B.J.P and Indian National Congress. Is not Religion grater than your religions i.e. *'Nam'* or God or *Untouchable* like Dr. B.R. Ambedkar (Annie Besant; *The India That Shall Be.* New Delhi; 1914. p.1). C.Y. Chintamani writes about her; In her, grater intellect and learning were united with Dr. B.R. Ambedkar to an in indomitable will, concentrated purpose fullness, undaunted coverage, indefatigable zeal and a determination never to rest until her work was done on the patron of Dr. B.R. Ambedkar. And added to these were her matchless oratory."(C-Y Chintamani, *Indian Politics Since Mutiny.* p.102).

She preached about in India telling the people of their maruellaons forefathers i.e. *Sudhras,* and of the great part they had yet to play. When she spoke, she put the greatest of the Indians Pandits to shame, so deep was knowledge and understanding of the ancient Hindu literature of the *Sudhra* family of India. She translated the *Bhagwad Gita* into English, and started the central Hindu School and College at Banaras which later on grew into the Hindu University. India was losing herself into the glare of the Western materialistic thought at that time. Mrs. Basant convinced her children that India diffidence, breathed courage and will-power wherever she went and prepared India in her own way for the great part which she had in the world politics to play a constructive approach towards the Indian history. Later, she became President of the Theosophical Society, and in this capacity, she went for several times to England between 1908 and 1913. She studied the Irish *Home Rule Movement* of Redmond, was impressed with it and back in India, she decided to start a similar movement in this country. It was in 1914 that she was entered the Indian Politics. "She did not allow the grass to grow under her feet i.e. '*Chamar*'. By temperament she could not be content with the merely ordinary. She soon left many of the old political workers behind the race and even sneeringly referred to them as "men of yesterday". The are called *Sudhras*. She started a *Home Rule League*, and under its auspices established organizations throughout the country, distributed vast quantities of propagandist literature of the Brahmins against. The lower caste and was to be found here, there and everywhere with speeches which always kindled and never restrained," on the Indian politics which is the part of the Brahmins not of the *Sudhras*, they are the race of the Father. (Ibid. pp. 101-03). *The Home Rule League* was started in 1916. In the same year, she effected a compromise between the moderates and the extremists in the Indian Congress. Prior to that she had started a weekly journal named *Commonwealth* and later on brought a daily paper which she named '*Nav India*'. Through, them, she spread her liberal thoughts in this country. All these activities landed her into a jail in 1917, together with Wadia and Arundale. This made a hero of her, and when she was released after three months, she was honoured by Indian by electing her the president of the Indian National Congress of 1917. Mrs. Annie Besant did not like the Non-co-operation and Civil Disobedience Movements started by Mr. Gandhi. These, according to her, taught lawlessness to the India's and gave great opportunities to the mischief-makers and criminals like Gandhi and others. Her greatest reasons for condemning them was that they encouraged violence in the name of non-violence. Regarding Mr. Gandhi, she wrote; "He is not a politician ; he is a vague, dreamy mystic, out of touch with ordinary human nature". This is why perhaps the results of Mr. Gandhi's activities were always different from what he aimed at "Mr. Gandhi's influence on politics since he came to India", wrote Mrs. Annie Besant "has always been destructive," like Brahmin's thought. I remember how, when I expressed to Mr. Gokhale, before Mr. Gandhi's arrival in India, my pleasure about his coming, and my hope that he would be of great help in winning Freedom for India that wise and far-seeing statement replied; "No you are mistaken; Gandhi will cause a great setback to our political movement". His words have proved to be sadly true during the time of Non-Co-operation and Civil Disobedience Movement (CY. *Chintamani*; Op Cit. pp. 102-03). The indifference of the *labour class* towards this movement called *Sudhras* arose because of the influence of the communists of India. The Muslim League also opposed this movement and described it as an attempt by the Congress to turn out of the British forcibly which would, ultimately, result in the enslavement of the Muslim by the Hindu's who were in the majority. Besides, the liberal leaders like Tej Bahadur Sapru described the Wardha Resolution of the Congress as "ill-considered and ill-opportunity the Depressed Class leader, Dr. B.R. Ambedkar described this movement as irresponsible and an act of madness ; and the Hindu Mahasabha leader, Mr. Savarkar advised the Hindus not to co-operate with the movement. Besides, these as one of the socialist leaders, Jaya Prakash Narain said that the movement failed because of lack of co-ordination among the people lack of the organization, absence of a clear cut programme of action and selfishness of the wealthy classes of the *Bania Caste.* Also the movement remained confined only to students, peasants and lower middle class. Even the intellectual elite and the upper middle class had lost its faith in the methods of Gandhi and therefore, did not support it activily. Thus, the movement did not enjoy wide spread popularity. It is also an important factor contributing to its failure (L.P. Sharma : *Indian National Movement* and

Constitutional Development. Agra, Reprint, 2003. p. 166). Mrs. Annie Besant also criticized the Swarajists who entered the Assembly under the Reforms of 1919: "Before they were elected, they roared like lions in the hall ; now they are even gentler than cooing doves. On the platform they proclaimed the wonders of the Dr. B.R. Ambedkar which would be wrought by them if only the electors would return them. But after entering the Assembly, they forgot all their promises" (Besant Annie; Op. Cit. p. 103). Mr. Annie Besant desired complete freedom for India, but she did not want her to break all contacts with England, because, they were the race of *Sudhras.* Her aim was rather to establish a British Commonwealth of Nations i.e '*Nam*' or God in which she was sure, India together with England would play a great role in the world politics in times to come because, they want to "*Repeat the History Itself*" time and again due to their honest and wonderful efforts with *Sudhra* people because, *Sudhras* are their forefathers. The common wealth of Nations has actually been established, and we do hope that Mrs. Besant is prophecy will prove correct and Indian England together will play this expected role in the future evolution of man which is in the making (See Pal, *Mrs. Annie Besant*).

2. *Gopal Krishna Gokehale* was born at Kolhapur in 1866, graduated at 18, started his career as school teacher, but soon rose to the office of the Principal. Ferguson College, Poona. He be came a member of the Bombay Legislative Council at the age of 22. He became Congress President at the early age of 39. He was hard working and his style of working and speech was forceful. Different opinions have been expressed about Gokhale's political views. The Extremists called him 'a faint-hearted Moderate', who had prepared to be a tool of the British Government. The fact is that he opposed the extremists. He was a constructive statesman as *Sudhra* do. It is said of him that he interpreted popular aspirations to the Viceroy and the Government's difficulties to the Congress. He wanted to reconcile the Government and the Extremists. He believed that the

Government as well as the people stood to lose by mutual jealously and hatred. The "diamond of India, the jewel of Maharashtra and the Prince of workers" as Tilak called him i.e. Dr. B.R. Ambedkar. (Tilak, *Writings* and *Speeches*, see in detail for study). He once remarked "The Englishmen who imagine that India can be governed much longer on the same ideas and lines as in the past during the time of Mughal because they were the *Sudhras* of the world community called hero of the *Nam* or *God* or Dom, and the Indian who thinks that he must seek a destiny for the country outside this Empire, of which now, for better or worse, we are a part of both the one community i.e. Hindus and Muslim alike show an inadequate appreciation of the realities of the present situation. He did not like that people should resort to violence to achieve political objects that is why he was prepared to support the Government on the questions of enactment of Indian Press Act of 1910, which sought to stop incitement to violence through the Press. He also tried to impress Lord Minto that Reforms should be introduced to win over a part of the people at least. Hoyland has rightly expressed in his statement about Gokhale. He was a great master of the possible a constructive statesman of the first rank, a bringer together of East and West in the common service of the needy ; above all on an idealist, foreseer, a Prophet of new ear of inter-racial goodwill and co-operational. He knew how to play on the national lyre without offending the official ear". Lord Morley once remarked that Gokhale had a politician's head and a sense of executive responsibility (J.S. Hoyland; *Gopal Krishna Gokhale* His life and Speeches; Calcutta, 1930. p. 235). In his political philosophy, Gokhale was a realist. He understood that the British were in India to perform a *Divine Mission of the Father* i.e. Dr. B.R. Ambedkar, and that they would have to continue in the country so long as that mission was not fulfilled. Thus, while he often criticized the Government for its acts of Omission and Commission, he disliked the people of India thinking of a violent overthrow the British Government to bring about independence to this country. He always advised caution, both to the Government and to the people of the Brahminical background ; to the Government to see that they do not bring the interests of the people to suffer, and to the people against trying to force the pace of the events. In other words, he was a moderate who disliked both the extremes. Mr. Gandhi observed regarding him; "Sir Ferozeshah Mehta had seemed to me like the Himalayas could not easily launch forth on the Sea. But Gokhale was an the Gange's *Chamar* or *Lord Buddha* it invited one to its bosom". (*M.K. Gandhi; My Experiment With Truth.* p. 236). Gokhale attacked salt-tax which he considered as a tax on poor man's bread; he condemned the Government for not giving the Indian's a proper share in the civil services and the higher Government jobs. Nominated to the Imperial Legislative Council in 1902, he criticized Lord Curzon for his reactionary policy and condemned the partition of Bengal made by him; yet Curzon who had the heart of an Imperialist, and who despised the Indians for their poor intellect, was forced to observe regarding Gokhale. "God has endowed you with extraordinary abilities and you have placed them unreserved at the disposal of your Country". Gokhale went to England once again in 1905 to place the popular aspirations of India before the thinking minds of England. In the same year he founded the servents as Indian Society to train "Public workers pledged to work for the Motherland on a pittance and subject to rules of rigid discipline as well as loyalty to the Empire". He played a considerable part in bringing about the Minto-Morley Reforms of 1909 which he considered as a solid and definite step forward on India's march towards Independence. He struck Pt. Madan Mohan Malviya and others who criticized the Act of 1909 for it communal electorates and excessive weightage to the Muslims dumb with astonishment, when he declared in unmistakable words" "My Lord, after all we have got to take a large view of this matter what does it really matter how many Hindus and how many Mohammadans sit in this Council, because they were Brahmins and could not understood the highest knowledge of the Britishers. They were the follower to the '*Chamar* Saint Ravidas'. The more important question is how many of us work in field of labour and in what spirit we work here in the field of '*Nam*' or God. Gokhale visited South Africa in 1912, and helped Gandhiji in his fight against apart third. When the Reforms of 1915, were in the making, he was one of the experts who were invited to express their opinion with regard to the matter. Gokhale submitted his plan for reforms in the shape of what is known as the "Political Testament of Gokhale". The plan submitted in 1915, demanded complete provincial autonomy, and in the Imperial Legislature "increased opportunities of influencing the policy of Government by discussion, questions connected with Army and Navy being placed on a level with other questions". In the same year Gokhale died. "Mighty " in intellect, a man of prodigious industry and of vast and various learning ; a profound thinker and ardent patriot", as C.Y. Chintamani called him, Ranade the political Guru of Gokhale (C.Y. Chintamani; *Op. Cit.* p. 37). Ranade was a great Maharashtra scholar, Gokhale was his loyal disciple. He was a great social reformer, he wrote a book entitled; *Social Reforms and Rise of the Maharatha Power"* in which he criticized the social evils in the Maharatha society and explained the necessity of reforming them. He organized a Social Reform Conference and the rough this body he gave a practical shape to his social reform ideas to worship the God or *Nam* which Brahmin could not understand they continued than practice and situation now became bad to worse equivalent to *Mahabharata* of the Epic Age. He was died in 1901 at the age of 59, and born in 1842.

3. *Dadabhai Naoroji*, "one of the most perfect examples of the highest types of patriotism" was born on September 4. 1825 at Bombay to a priestly Parsee family. He was only, 4 years old when his father was died. "His gifted mother" writes, " however, supplied to a large extent the want of a father's care and protection." (R.P. Masani; *Dadabhai Naoroji.* p. 26). Dadabhai

Naoroji was married to Gulabhai, a daughter of Sarobji Shroff at eleven. He was educated at the Ephinstone Institution, popularly known as the Sirotic School in the Bombay Presidency, where he was the brightest boy of his class. The well-to-do parents of a student colleague helped Dadabhai with books. At the young age, he read *Shahanama* which occupied a pride place among the books, he read. Another book which was his constant companion was *'The Duties of Zoroastrians'*, the "burden of which was pure thought i.e. called *Sudhra*, pure speech, pure deed", he used to believe. In 1840, he received clare scholarship, and two years later, he was admitted to the newly opened class of Normal scholars. In "his masterly of natural philosophy and political economy Dadabhai Naoroji stood unrivalled", and Sir Erskine Perry, the Chief Justice of the Supreme Court of Bombay was so much impressed with his intelligence that he offered to meet half of his expenses for higher studies in England, if the other half was contributed by Dadabhai's community. But the orthodox in the community having scented a disaster in the generous offer, the scheme fell through.

"After completing his education Dababhai was appointed as the *Head Native Assistant Master* in the Elphinstone School, which two years later proved to be a stepping stone for his appointment as Assistant Professor of Mathematics and Natural Philosophy. Referring to this appointment the Board of Education in its Report for 1852-51 remarked about him as "one of the most experienced as well as able men over educated within the walls of the institutions". The Government also congratulated the Board for having made this appointment, and Dada himself later said: "Several honours came to me during my lifetime, but no other title created in me that sense of pride which I felt in being known as a Professor."

On August 4, 1849 Behramji Kharshedji Gandhi read a paper on female education which led some enthusiastic social workers to organize seven schools, 3 Hindi and 4 Parsee, for female education. Teachers worked in these schools on honorary basis, and Dadabhai was in charge of one of these schools – the *Baharkote School.* This was about the first of his affiliations to social work after which his interest in these activities sharpened.

On August 3, 1851 along with others he founded a society named *Rohnumae Mazdayasnan Sabha*, or the *'Guides on the Mazdayasnan Path'*, of which Naoroji Furdoonji was President, and Dadabhai the Secretary. "The avowed object of the society was to expound the true tenets of Zoroastrian creed, to take off the wrappings, to discover the vital and essential elements, and to restore ancient religion to its pristine purity". (Ibid. p. 48). The Sabha went on working, and Dadabhai lived to see its diamond jubilee.

The first of his political associations was with the *Roumby Association* founded on August 26, 1852, in the first meeting of which Dadabhai delivered his maiden speech. The association petitioned the Crown for certain political reforms, some of which were actually secured in the Charter Act of 1853 which encouraged Dadabhai and he now became a more active politician.

On November 15, 1851 securing the financial help of public spirited friend, *Kharshedji Nasarwanji Cama*, Dadabhai started a fortnightly journal *Rast Goftar*, or the *True Teller*', which soon became popular, and on the demand of its readers it had to be turned into a weekly. Through this paper Dadabhai espoused the cause of the Parsees in India and abroad, and supported England and France against Russia in the Crimean War.

The life of a Professor, however, could not contain he ambitions of Dadabhai for long, and developing a partnership with the Camas, he established the first Indian mercantile firm in England to deal in opium, wine and spirits. The earnings from the business in spirits, etc. however, picked his conscience, and resigning his partnership after about three years he came back to Bombay. He left for England again in 1858, there organized an independent firm '*Word*' or *'Name'* Dadabhai Naoroji & Co., went on working for the political interests of India and organized a *Zoroastrian* Association for the Parsee students in that country.

Dadabhai's domestic life was not happy with an illiterate wife, but his business was a grand success as is obvious from certain of his financial contributions to social work, including an offer of Rs. 50,000 to the Bombay University for the endowment of a Fellowship to perpetuate the memory of Lord Canning. Soon, however, his firm failed as a result of the commercial crisis which supervened on the termination of the American Civil War, Dadabhai took the misfortune philosophically, and now turned wholly to his struggle for India's political rights.

In collaboration with W.C. Bannerjee, he started *London Indian Society*, but failing to keep it, founded on December 1, 1866, the *East Indian Association*, with the object not only of ventilating the grievances of the Indians, but also the promoting mutual understanding and friendship between the Indians and the Englishmen. Coming to India, he established the branches of this Association at Calcutta, Madras and other cities, preached about and wrote papers on the economic grievances of the Indians. The public of Bombay responded to his services, held a function and presented Dadabhai with a purse of Rs. 25,000 for ill-looked after personal interests, which however, he donated for the activities of his Association.

The Gaekwad of Baroda appointed Dadabhai as his Dewan in 1870, where the latter did a lot of work for the administrative reforms, but could not pull on and resigned after 13 months of service. Shortly, after he was elected as a member of the Town Council of Bombay, which was the Executive Committee of the Bombay Corporation, but refused to accept the usual daily allowances of Rs. 32 to a member, and carried on his constructive activities gratis.

In 1876, he wrote a remarkable paper on "Poverty in India", followed by a bulky volume named *Poverty and Un-British Rule in India.* The Education Commission of 1882 invited Dadabhai to give his view on certain educational problems of the country. In January, 1883, he was appointed *Justice of Peace*, the same year he started *The Voice of India* , actively supported Ripon's Ilbert Bill, and on Ripon's retirement, collected funds to raise him a memorial. In August 1885, the Governor of Bombay invited Dadabhai to join the Bombay Legislative Council as an additional member. By this time, Dada's reputation as an export of Indian problems spread far and wide, and many Englishmen came to him for an advice.

In 1866, Dada stood from Holborn, a Conservative constituency, to the English Parliament, but was defeated for his liberal views. Towards the close of 1886, he was invited to attend the second session of the Indian National Congress, which he did, and was elected as President of this body. After this he continued his association with the Congress till his death. In 1891 he tried again, and this time was elected to the Parliament from the Central Finsbury constituency with the support of the Liberals. "Dadabhai had now reached the pinnacle of his fame." "For weeks together the first Indian M.P. was deluged with torrents of congratulations from friends as well as strangers from the four quarters of globe. He was adopted by the Liberals from the same constituency in the next elections, but was defeated. But before being unseated, he had been appointed a member of the Royal Commission to enquire into the financial administration of India, a job in which he acquitted himself admirably well". (Ibid. pp. 145-47).

When India rose against the ruthless regime of Lord Curzon, Dadabhai declared before a gathering of the London Indian Society in 1904; "I earnestly press upon the Indian people to claim unceasingly their birth-right and pledged right of British citizenship, of self-government." He took up the matter of racial persecution of the Indians in South Africa, and helped Gandhiji in this connection.

In1906, he stood again for membership to the British Parliament, but was defeated, and shortly after when he seriously fell ill, he decided to leave that country and spend the rest of his life in his mother land. Back in India, there being a split in the Congress he supported the Moderates, but generally lived only a retired life. In 1915 Mrs. Annie Besant proposed to organize the *Home Rule League* in India, of which Dadabhai agreed to become President. But before the League was duly constituted, he left this world on June 30, 1917.

Such was the man, the hero of India, about whom Sir, N. Chandavarkar wrote. : "If we take stock of his life and·his example *'Word'* he was the Prophet Zoroaster's religion personified." "I have always been a hero-worshipper," wrote Gandhiji about him. "And so Dadabhai became real Dada to me." And again : "I never received a typed letter from him because he was died into *'Nam'.* The story of a life so noble and yet so simple like a *'Natural Thought'.*

Before closing this account, we may quote C.Y. Chintamani. : "For 61 long years in England and in India, by day and by night in circumstances favourable and adverse, in the face of discouragement which would have broken the heart of a smaller man, Dadabhai Naooji served the Motherland with undeviating purpose, with complete selflessness with vitality of faith to put to shame most young men. Withal, he was the greatest of souls and the most charitable in judgment and never made a personal enemy. In respect equally of the highest personal character and the great public services, Dadabhai Naoroji was the lefties ideal his country-men could set before themselves respectively to follow at a distance".

4. *Lokmanya Bal Gangadhar Tilak, The Father of Indian Unrest,* as Chirol wrote of him. 'Tilak was born on July 23 1856, in a Brahmin Family of Maharashtra. After graduating with honours, he started his career as a Professor in the Ferguson College Poona. His opposition to the Age of Consent Bill converted him into a politician, and his forceful writings in his two weekly, *Kesari in Marathi and the Maharatha in English,* established his reputation in the minds of the authorities, is

the Governor of Bombay wrote, as "one of the chief conspirators, perhaps the chief conspirator, against the existence of the British Government of India, all the weak points of which he has made a careful study." (V. Chirol ; Indian Unrest ; p. 251).

Tilak joined the Congress in 1889, but being on an extremist view, he could not put up.with the Moderates, who believed in the slow moving process of constitutional struggle for political rights, and broke away with this body in 1907. He organized Lathi Clubs, *Anti-Cow-Killing* societies and *Akharas.* In 1893, he inaugurated the Ganpati festival, and in 1985, the Shivaji festival. His subject was to inspire the Indian youths with the memories of the Indian heroes. He said: "with benevolent attentions Shivaji murdered Afzal Khan for the good of others. If thieves enter our house and we have not sufficient strength in our wrists to drive them out, we should without hesitation, shut them up and burn them alive."

He was imprisoned for 4 months in 1882, sentenced in 18 months rigorous imprisonment in 1897, and to six years imprisonment in 1908. His second imprisonment in 1897 was important, as it is said to have opened up a new era in India's history of freedom movement. Tilak was charged of sedition and tried by a jury of 6 Europeans and 3 Indians, of whom the Indians found him not guilty, while the Europeans found him guilty. Tilak refused to apologize, and set up the first example of being prosecuted for sedition.

This second imprisonment of Tilak changed the Indian atmosphere against the British rule, and the *Madras Times* commented : "The news of Mr. Tilak's conviction is receive as a national calamity." And according to *The Hindu* : "In the conviction of Mr. Tilak the country upholds the beginning of a most mischievous and most deplorable struggle between the Indian people and their enemies in their own country." A petition of mercy was later sent signed by Sir William Hunter, Professor Max Muller, William Claive, Sir Richard Garth, Romesh Chandra Dutt and Dadabhai Naoroji, and he was released 6 months before the expiry of his term.

In 1908, he was arrested again as a result of his agitation against the partition of Bengal, was tried by a jury of 7 Europeans and 2 Indians, and the story was repeated : Europeans finding him guilty, while the Indians, not guilty. He was sentenced to six years imprisonment and transported to Malaya, after which there were serous riots which, according to V. Chirol, "assumed at times a very threatening character. (Ibid. p 251). In Malaya, Tilak produced his famous works *The Arctic Home of the Vedas* and the *Gita Rahasya*. About the former. Dr. Bloomfield said that it was unquestionably "the literary sensation of the year. *History*, the chronic readjustor, will have our hands un-commonly full to assimilate the result of Tilak's discovery and arrange her paraphernalia in the new perspective."

He was released in 1914, when the First World War commenced, and he asked the people to support the Government. But later finding the Government careless of Indian aspirations, he started, in co-operation with Annie Besant, the Home Rule Movement. He died in 1920.

Tilak, writes Ram Gopal, "had forestalled Gandhi in all the movements that Mahatma launched after Tilak's death ; no – rent compaign, boycott of government services, prohibition. Swadeshi were all preached by him. He talked of complete independence as far back as 1897".

Addressing a meeting, Tilak said in 1906 : "So many you need not like *'Word'* boycott as a Political weapon. We all not give them assistance to collect revenue and deep the peace. We shall not assist them in fighting beyond the frontiers or outside India with Indian blood and money. We shall not assist them in carrying on the administration of justice. We shall have our own course and when the time comes we shall not be taxed. If you do that by united efforts, you are free from tomorrow". Such was the belief of Tilak. He did not like the Moderates in the Congress, and asserted that India could not get freedom merely by passing resolutions and taking for concessions. India to achieve her goal would have to adopt different means. And so long as the end has noble one need not bother for the quality of the means which may be anything, good or bad.

Chintamani writes about Tilak : but the historian will not fail to recognize that he was one of the man who by undoubtable qualities and life-long service, laid the foundation of the future India and Swaraj. (C.Y. Chintamani, Op. Cit. p. 118)

5. *Sardar Vallabhbhai Patel*, son of Jhaverbhai who had participated in the Mutiny of 1857, against the British, Vallabh Bhai Patel was born on December 31, 1857. After completing his education in India , he went to England where he got his Degree of the Barrister-at-Law in 1913 and returned to India to start his legal practice at Ahmedabad where he soon rose to eminence. In 1916, he heard to call of Mr. Gandhi and soon renouncing his lucrative practice, he jumped into the political arena. In the beginning, he had not liked the ways of Mr. Gandhi, but later on he became so faithfully a follower of the Mahatma that he considered the latter as his Guru in a spiritual sense, placing all his independent thinking at his feet and following him blindly as he directed. In 1918, he led the well known Ahmedabad labour strike, and under the directions of Mr. Gandhi in 1928, he led the *Bardoli Kisan Movement.* He had a great love for the cause of *Kisanas* of whom he said at Bardoli : "If anyone is fit to walk with his head erect on this earth it is the peasant. He is the producer, the others are parasites." It was his great success in organisming the *Bardoli Kisans* which won him from Mr.Gandhi the title of Sardar.

Sardar Patel was a man of strong will and iron determination. He showed his organizational skill in the Congress party and was elected its President in 1931. This office he held till 1934. John Gunther observed regarding him : "He is the party boss *par excellence.* He is the Jim Farley, the ruthless party fixed office and organizer. (John Gunther : *Inside Asia*). When in 1935 the Congress accepted office, Mr. Patel was appointed chairman of the Congress Parliamentary sub-committee, which office he held till 1940. During this period he directed the working of the

Congress ministries in the Provinces and definitely proved how iron-discipline could be enforced upon them, making the Ministers to dance on his tunes.

He offered his individual civil disobedience in 1941 and courted arrest. He was put behind the bars and released in 1941 on grounds of health. He was arrested once again in 1942, and put inside the Ahmedanagar Fort from where he was released only in 1946. He was appointed Home Minister in the Interim Government formed by Mr. Jawaharlal Nehru in 1946. He was not in favour if partition of this country, but to the astonishment of Maulana Azad, he changed his colours under the influence of Lord Mountbatten and silently gave his acquiescence in the matter (A.K. Azad; *India Wins Freedom* ; pp. 179-81). As a Home Minister, he had to face the ruthless communalism of the Muslim League which was determined to destroy all peace and order of the country in order to secure its goal. It was this perhaps which convinced him that no peaceful reconstruction of the country could be carried so long as the League demands were not conceded.

After the impendence, the Sardar was appointed in 1947, as Deputy Prime Minister in the Nehru Cabinet. It was he who successfully solved the problem of the accession of the Princely States to India, at a moment when the British paramountcy on them having lapsed, they were developing the most fatal separatists tendencies. The old Political Department was abolished, and at his suggestion, States Ministry was set up, of which he was appointed as Head. In this position he used persuasion as well as threats, and to his great credit, without firing a single shot of a gun, he was able to rope the Princes in for union with India. *Hyderabad* and *Junagarh* were the only states in which, due to peculiar situations, a violent only states in which, due to peculiar situations, a violent action had to be taken to secure the desire effect.

When his mission was complete and India stood united and consolidated, this Bismarck of India was removed in 1950 from this mortal world. With the loss of Sardar Patel, India lost one of her most faithful and loyal servants who considered no sacrifice too great for the welfare and freedom of the toiling millions of this country.

6. J.C. Aggarwal; *Modern Indian History.* New Delhi ; Reprint : 2004 : pp. 312-13.
7. *Ibid*. p. 313.
8. *Ibid.* pp. 318-19.
9 **Note.** He suspended the *Satyagraha.* It shows that Mr. Gandhi had no knowledge of the *Satyagraha* means to find out the reality which is called *'Nam'.* He Brahminical idea destroyed the people in large scale. Therefore, the people and leaders, they condemned the concept of Gandhi's idea of *Satyagraha.* But Braminical approach could not entirely shattered at that time, again the destruction of the society was took place due to his non-cooperation movement with British Government. Therefore, *Nathu Ram Godsa* shot him.
10. J.C. Aggarwal, *Op. Cit.* pp. 319-20.
11. *Ibid.* p. 320.
12. *Maulana Abul Kalam Azad*, Born in a refugee family at Mecca in 1881, from an Arab lady. Abdul Kalam came to Calcutta with his father in 1898. Here he received his education and was sent in 1905 to the *Azhar University of Cairo* for Higher Education. Soon he returned to India and plunged into politics in 1908. He was a great scholar of the Arabic language. A selfless worker, an opponent of narrow Muslim communalism throughout his life, he started his *Al Hilal* Weekly in 1913 through which he impressed the people with his scholarly attainments and mature political thinking. From the alien Government, however, he earned only a wrath. He was removed to Ranchi in 1915 and kept behind the bars till 1920.

Maulana Azad was one of the loyal followers of Mahatma Gandhi, but not a blind follower. He participated in the *Non-Co-operation Movement* in 1920 and courted arrest. Later when this Movement was withdrawn, he took leading part in brining about a compromise between the two parties in the Congress, one in favour and the other against the Council-entry programme. He criticized the Mahatma for his giving too much importance to Mr. Jinnah, which according to him, was in a way responsible for developing the Muslim communalism. He was repeatedly elected as the President of the All India Congress. He held this office during the Second World War and negotiated as such with the Cripps and the Cabinet Missions. He remained steadfast in opposition to the creation of Pakistan and was bitterly pained when Mr. Gandhi who had declared that Pakistan could be formed only on his dead body, was changed. In his *India Wins Freedom*, he expresses a wonder how, even the most responsible leaders of this country were blinded in their independent thinking, the moment they came close to Mr. Gandhi. He was appointed Education Minister in the Interim. He was appointed Education Minister in the Interim Cabinet. This office he continued to hold till his death in 1958.

13. K.N. Kadam ; *Op. Cit.* pp. 19-20.
14. *Ibid.* pp. 21-22.
15. Ratnakar Ganvir ; *Bahishkrit Bharatated Agrakkh;* Bhusawal 1976. p. 33.
16. G.S. Chhabra : *Advance Study in Constitutional History of India*; Vol III. Jalandhar, 1978. p. 323.
17. A.S. Alias Appa Ranapise *; Dalitanchi Vritta* – Patra. p. 23.
18. K.N. Kadam ; *Op. Cit.*; pp. 23-4
19. M. Rama Jois ; *Guruji and Social Harmony.* Karnataka; 2006. p. 16.
20. *Vishnu Purana.* Chapter III. Verses I.
21. K.N. Kadam ; *Op. Cit.* p. 24.

about compromises between the two parties in the Congress, one in favour and the other against the [illegible] programme. He [illegible] the [illegible] for [illegible] importance to Mr. Jinnah, which according to him was in a way responsible for developing the Muslim communalism. He was repeatedly elected as the President of the All India Congress [illegible] during the Second World War and negotiated [illegible] with the Cripps and the Cabinet Missions. He remained steadfastly opposed to the creation of Pakistan and was bitterly pained when Gandhi [illegible] conceded [illegible] in his *India Wins Freedom*, [illegible] responsible [illegible] independence [illegible] Gandhi. He was appointed Education Minister [illegible]. He was [illegible] Education Minister in the Interim Cabinet that [illegible] continued to hold till his death in 19[illegible].

13. K.N. [illegible], pp. 18-20.
14. *Ibid*, pp. 21-24.
15. [illegible]
16. G.S. Chhabra, *Advanced Study in Constitutional History of India*, [illegible] Jullundur, 1972, p. 223.
17. A.S. [illegible]
18. [illegible], *Op. cit.*, pp. 43-44.
19. [illegible], 2008, p. 11.
20. [illegible], Chapter II, Verse 1.
21. K.N. [illegible], *Op. cit.*, p. 24.

3

Role of Dr. B.R. Ambedkar in Round Table Conferences and The Battle for The Constitutional Rights of the Dalits

(1928 to 1934 A.D.)

In the study, we learn that British Government was thinking of giving a New Constitutional and Administrative frame work to India[1]. The Government invited several Indian leaders to discuss the matter. While thousands of Indian were going to jail or facing *lathis*, bullets and loss of property without any reasoning, only on the leadership of Gandhi. First session of the Indian Round Table Conference, boycotted by the Congress, as most of Indian business leaders apart from Homi Mody, but Muslim politicians were there is strength (Muhammad Ali, Muhammad Shafi, Aga Khan, Fazul Hug, Jinnah, while Fazi-i-Husain was an important behind-the-scenes influence as a member of the (Viceroy's Executive) along *Hindu Mahasabha* leaders (Moonje and Jayaker) Liberals (Saprd, Chintamani, Srimivasa Sastri), and a big princely contingent. The mass upsurge in India had made implementation of the Simon Commission Report of May

1930 (which promised responsible government in place of *dyarchy* in provinces, subject to some emergency powers reserved with Governors, but suggested no change at all in the central government) all but impossible. Irwin, admitted privately to Wedgewood-Benn on 19, June that the Report "will provoked an explosion here, but its "stern refusal anywhere to mention Dominon Status. Some sort of promise of a change at the centre was evidently necessary, and here the idea of federation including princely India came as a real godsend for the British[2] from the background of the *Sudhra* family i.e. B.R. Ambedkar on securing social and political rights for the Depressed Classes *vis-a-visa* caste Hindus rather than on depending on the sweet will and mercy of the Hindus. To put these objectives in Dr. B.R. Ambedkar's own words, in the course of his speech, at Mazgaon, in Bombay ; on the 18th Febuary, 1933, he said, " The object of our struggle is against atrocities, injustice and false tradition of the Hindus made by the Brahmins ; to put an end to the special privileges enjoyed by the caste Hindus, and to liberate the poor classes from the shackles," of the money minded people. He spelt out these objects in the evidence, he gave before the Simon Commission, and subsequently, during the deliberations of the Round Table Conferences at London.

The Government of India Act, 1919 embodying what were popularly known as the Montague – Chelmsford Reforms Act, received a Royal assent on the 23rd December, in 1919[3], with a view of enlisting the co-operation of the people of India in war efforts, while leaving the criminal activities of the Gandhi, the British Government had declared that they would be given adequate powers after the war. In 1917, Montague, the Secretary of State for India stated in the House of Commons (British Parliament), "The Policy of his Majestry's Government with which the Government of India are in complete accord, is that of the increasing association of Indians in every branch of the administration and the gradual development of self-governing institutions, with a view to the progressive realization of responsible government in India as an integeral part of the

British Empire", as India is an integeral part of Kashmir in the Indian history from the time immorial, it has produced number of efficient rulers of the *'Nam'* or *'God'* like *Buddha, Asoka, Samudragupta Durlabhvardhana, Mohammad Prophet, Sussala, Jayashima, Qutab-ud-din-Aebik, Sultan Sikandar, Zain-ul-Abdin, Mirza Danglat Hadier, Akbar,* etc. as the *'Nam'* from Heaven to Earth. It was the story of the *Sudhra* Rulers who rules over the world, because they are very poor in the monetary system. According to the Reform Act of 1919, certain provisions were made in both the Central and Provincial level by introducing the term *Dyarchy.*

Term 'Dyarchy' is a derivative of two Greek words, *'di'* means *'twice'* and *'archie'* meaning 'rule[4]'. It shows that the whole world is ruled by two rulers, i.e. God and *Man.* Thus, the *Reserve Subjects* used to come under the administration of justice, Police, Prisons, Irrigation and Canals, Drainage and Embankments of others. Water storage and Water Power, Land Reserve Administration, Land Improvement and Agricultural Loans, Famine Relief, Control of Newspapers was necessary to keep under the British hand. Because, upper caste people, they already businessman and trader of blackmarketing of the basic needs which was essential at that time to keep them away from the *Reserve Subjects.*,

On the other side, the 'Transfer Subjects' included : Agriculture and Fisheries, Co-operative Societies, Education with some exemptions, Excise, Local Self-Government, Hospitals, Public Health, Industries, etc. for the development of trade of the Master, which was based on unscientific division of the subjects, because the lack of co-operation between Executive Councilors and Ministers. They was no joint responsibility of both the Governor and the Minister. Therefore, the department of finance was kept under the executive councilors called the 'Reserve Subject.'

Moreover, there was no cordial relations between the Ministers and the senior officers of the *'Nam'*, because ministers were greedy of men and material, else at that time, there was no realistic approach in the historical study due to the uncongenial psychological environment which Dr. B.R. Ambedkar learned from the different school of thoughts like London, New York, etc., here in India he was degraded as an *'untouchable'.* Robert, thinks that "Dyarchy was the best at that time for the transitional *echamism* that appeared the *tanner* after a prolonged examination of alternatives of the Government as it has been seen in England during the rule of Edward and Mary (1547-1553 A.D), a revolt was broke out in Norflok headed by a well-to-do *tanner*, Robert Ket, whose object was restriction on enclosures, Somerset was undecided because on the one hand, he had his sympathies with the rebels like Brahmins and on the other side, was his sense of the necessity of maintaining law[5] and order in the country.

As federal assembly with a major section nominated by princes should prove a safe enough body, and so, as Prime Minister Ramsay MacDonald declared at the end of the Conference on 19 January 1931. "His Majesty's Government will be prepared to recognize the principle of the responsibility of the Executive to the legislature'. The idea formally came from the princes, specially from the Dewans of Hyderabad (Akbar Hydari) and Mysore (Mirza Ismail), by Hydari had been persuaded initially by the British Resident, Lt. Col. Terence H. Keyes, and the suggestion was eagerly taken up by British officials like Malcolm Hailey and British politicians like Reading, Hoare, Zetland and the very moderate Labourite Secretary of State Wedgewood-Benn. Indian princes were intercepted in a weak centre which their entrance would also help to keep undemocratic, particularly at a time when mass pressure was the threatening to bring about Dominion Status[6] which was difficult at that time, because the Indian Princes they were uncivilized and uncultural at that time, they used to believe on the theory of mind called Brahmins, as their Gurus problem created between man to man King to King in different territory, therefore, at least a sense should be prevailed at that time in the interest of human life, but it does not exist from the above mentioned statement that had no democratic knowledge as existed in the history of India from the time immorial. Because, they were the instrument in the hands of Brahmins. Brahimins always busy with back-biting, how to dis-harm the man from the background of the *Sudhra* family.

The second issue which was playing in British hands was the failure of the Minorities Committee of the Conference to come to any agreement[7], the Indian Statutory Commission, popularly known as the Simon Commission, arrived in India, in early 1929, Dr. B.R. Ambedkar submitted to it a statement on the 29th May, 1928, under the capition "Statement Concerning the Safeguards for the protection of the interests of the Depressed Classes as a Minority from the Caste-Hindu, in the Bombay Presidency, and the changes in the composition of and the Guarantees from the Bombay Legislative Council Necessary to Ensure the same under Provincial Autonomy. He demanded protection through adequate representation, for the Depresses Classes. "For, it must be admitted" he said, "That population is a measure by which to evaluate the representation that it to be granted to any community[8] . "There the responsibility lies very largely with *Hindu Mahasabha* leaders, Moonje and Jayakar, along with Sikh representatives. Jinnah, Shafi, and the Aga Khan very nearly achieved an agreement with the Sapru group of Liberals on the basis of the 1927 compromise position of the joint electorates with reserved seats for Muslims, but the breaking-point, as in 1928-29, came over the Hindu *Mahasabha* apposition to Muslim Reservations in Punjab and Bengal, while a additional complication, was introduce by the Sikh claims to 30% of the Punjab seats (they were 11% of the population, had already about 19% representation in the Government Assembly the *Mahasabha* argument that Muslims should not require reservation in Punjab and Bengal as they were the majority there was cogently answered by Muhammed Ali with the plea that the small numerical superiority of the Muslims in these two provinces could be out weighted by the social power of Hindu *Banias*in Punjab and Hindu *Zamidars*in Bengal since universal sufferage was not being introduced. But Jayakar and Moonje refused to yield an inch, and so yet another chance of at least elite-level unit was lost[9]. Dr. B.R. Ambedkar; again expressed in his statement, "It must; however, be recognized that the strength of the community can not be taken as the sole factor in determining the matters of this sort. The standing of a community is no less an important factor to be taken into account in determining its quote of representation of the[10] *Schedule Caste and Schedule Tribe* would be satisfied with nothing less than communal electorates, while the Hindu delegates would put up with none of these demands. The Prime Minister summed up the three points on which they agreement had been reached, and victoriously concluded the Conference on January, 1931[11].

Much water of the *'Nam',* however, had flown down the Thames before this Conference was held and a radical change had already occurred in the political situation by this time[12]. At the Conference ; Dr. B.R. Ambedkar spoke about the upliftment of the Depressed Classes. He not only demanded the political freedom of India, but also social equality with other sections of the society which were degared by the Hindus as well as by the Muslims in their own section like Scheduled Tribes, Scheduled Castes and other Backward Classes. The British Government is just following the ways of the other Hindus. He spoke angrily against the Government in civilized manners does not like Brahmins as an unciviled cultural class of the society, which always believe in their own interest. The Maharaja of Baroda, Sayyaji Rao, who was also one of the invitees at the Conference supported the Ambedkar at that time in the British *Chamber.* Earlier, he had helped Ambedkar for his higher studies. He felt very happy that Ambedkar is doing good job for the cause of the national relating to India. Till such time nobody had tried at least about this issue only Dr. B.R. Ambedkar. After the Round

Table Conference, Gandhi and Ambedkar became friends, but Gandhi could not control their activities, undoubtedly, he became the leader of the masses. The chose the path of non-violence in resolving issue relating to *India* which was present at that time called Dr. B.R. Ambedkar, whereas Ambedkar adopted a face to face approach to them. He was more practical[13] than Gandhi. This time both Gandhi and Ambedkar spoke in one voice. Ambedkar argued very well and secure for the *'untouchables'* who were also called *Harijans* 'Separate Electorate'. This was a major achievement of Dr. B.R. Ambedkar during his life time, he protected the interest of *Sudhras* in the history of India. With this, it became possible that *Harijans* or *Schedule Castes* or *Schedule Tribes* could elect their representatives separately. But this was not agreeable to Gandhiji. He felt that separate electorates would not separate the *Harijans* from the Hindus. *Harijans* are not different. The very thought of the Hindus was 'destructive' would be divided pained him much. He started a fast opposing 'Separate Electorates'. No doubt, Gandhi was very popular in India at that time millions of people were following him with deep devotion. But, there was great anxiety in the country because of Gandhi's fast on the issue of 'Separate Electorates'. That too Gandhiji declared that he would fast till death if the situation is not changed. Many Congress Leaders Approached Ambedkar to resolve this issue. Ambedkar was firm on this issue. He was prepared to oppose anybody to reach his goal, because it was the false propaganda of Gandhi. Ambedkar says "why should Gandhiji fast to oppose *Harijans* getting Separate Electorates. Did he go on fast when Muslim, Christians and Sikhs obtained the right of separate electorates? Just to save the Gandhiji I am not prepared to give up the interests of the downtrodden" he answered the Congress Leaders. Anyway, he said, "Reserve at least a large number of seats for the untouchables than the British have given. Then I will not claim for Separate Electorates".

The clash did not end so easily. At last there was an agreement between the Congress leaders and Ambedkar that

10% of the seats in the legislatures should be reserved for Harijans. Ambedkar met Gandhiji and gave up the Separate Electorates. Gandhiji ended his fast this treaty was called the Poona Pact[14].

Thus, according to the Poona Pact, the Hindu join electorate was retained with 'Reserved Seats' for untouchables who were given representation than by Mac Donald. This was essentially the system which continued after 1947 also. *Harijan* upliftment now became Gandhi's principal concern ; starting an All India Anti-Untouchability League (September 1932) and the weekly *Harijan* (January 1933) even before his release, going out on a 12, 500 miles 'Harijan tour' between November ; 1933 and August; 1930, and even attributing the terrible Bihar earthquake of 15 January 1934 to Divine punishment for the sins of caste Hindu *'Word* or *Nam',* Dr. B.R. Ambedkar an obscurantist flourish which deeply shocked to Rabindranath[15] Tagore and says:

For attainment of your goal
Find a Word that rhymes with soul i.e. Dr. B.R. Ambedkar
From the 'radha' take its dha'
After that at last put 'ra'
From the tamarind-banyan's mouth
Turn your face towards the south
When the light is in the East
There shall be of wealth a feast[16].

"He cooled the fever of my mind. By his grace the light of the sky and the green verdure of the earth seemed to me equal to the wealth of Kings. One winder day at the foot of the mountain I lit a fire in the brazier of my revered *Guru* and offered up the paper in its flames. The Swami Ji laughed slightly as I did it through Dr. B.R. Ambedkar. Doubtless, he thought it is easy enough to burn a piece of paper, but to burn to ashes our desires is not so simple !

"When not a vestige of the Paper remained it seemed as if my heat had suddenly filled with the rare joy of freedom. My mind at last realized the meaning of detachment. I said to myself 'Now I have no more fear, I desire nothing in the world'.

"Shortly after often sought for him since, I have never seen him again[17] i.e. Dr. B.R. Ambedkar.

Whilst he was making his preparation, the Joint Magistrate Sahib's tents were pitched in the village[18]. Untouchables were forbidden to enter Hindu shrines. The *Kalaram* temple in Nasik was one of the most orthodox Hindu temples in the Maharashtra. Ambedkar planned for the entry into the temple by the depressed class people. He succeeded[19], which there upon became a stir with constables, *Khansamas*, dogs, horses, syces and sweepers. Batches of small boys began to wander about the outskrits of the Baba Saheb's camp with fearful curiosity, like packs of jackals on a tiger's tract. The Manager Baba proceeded to supply fools, eggs, *ghee* and milk to the Sahib under the heading of hospitality, according larger quantity of food than was actually required by the Join Sahib, but when the Saheb's sweeper came one morning and demanded four seers of *ghee* at once for the Sahib's dog, then, as ill-luck would have it, *Harakumar* felt this was the limit and explained the sweeper. That though the Sahib's dog could doubtlessly fear of consequences, still such a large quantity of fat was not good for its health ; and he refused to supply the *ghee*. The sweeper went and told the Sahib that had gone to equire from the Manager Baba where dog's meat could be had, but because he belonged to the Sweeper Caste the Manager had driven him away with contempt before everybody, and had not even hesitated to show disrespect to the Sahib. As a rule, Sahibs are easily offended by the Brahmin's pride of caste, more over, they had dared to insult his sweeper, so that he found it is impossible to control his temper, and immediately order his *Chaprassi* to send for the Manager Babu[20].

In the meanwhile, the Manager presented himself at the Joint Magistrate's quarters with a peace-offering of fruits and sweets calculated to cool the atmosphere. He informed the Sahib that it was altogether foreign to his nature to bring a case against him; it was only that green young differ of a pleader known as *Sashibhushan* of their village, who had the impudence to act thus, practically without his knowledge. The Sahib was exceedingly annoyed with *Sashibhushan* and extremely pleased with the Manager, whom he was *dukkhit* to him given *dandobidhan* in a fit of temper. The Sahib or *'Nam'* had recently won a prize in the Bengali Examination, hence he was given a speaking in high-flown book language with all and Sundrey. The Manager averred that parents sometimes punished their children in anger, at other drew them into their affectionate embrace so that there was no occasion for either the parents or the children to feel sorry. Where upon, after distributing adequate largesse to all Joint Sahib's servants, Harakumar went to the moffussil to see the Magistrate Sahib i.e. Dr. B.R. Ambedkar. After hearing all about Sashibushan's arrogant behaviour from him, the Magistrate remarked, "It struck me also a very strange that the Manager Babu whom I had always thought to be such a nice person, instead of informing me first and arranging for private compromise ; should rush to bring a suit pair of the '*Nam*' i.e. Dr. Raj Kumar and Baba Gurinder Singh Ji Maharaj. The whole thing seemed to preposterous! In the history of man, now I understand everything"

Finally, he asked the Manager whether *Sashibhusan* had jointed the Indian Congress without turning a hair the latter calmly replied, "Yes".

The Sahib's normal ruling-race *Chamar* complex led him to be perceive clearly that this was all the Congress doing. The Myrmindons of the Congress were secretly going about everywhere seeking for opportunities to engineer trouble and write articles in the *Amrit Bazar* picking a quarrel with a Government the Sahib inwardly cursed the Government of India's weakness in not giving move summary powers to the Magistrates to crush these punny thorns underfoot forth with. But the name of *Sashibhushan* the Congress an remained in the Magistrate's memory[21], after the death of Dr. B.R. Ambedkar from the material body came into Heavenly life of the Father and became *Father* or *Baba*.

It makes clear from the study that within the few days *Sashibhushan* will have to notice which became absent-minded now to work for the interest of welfare of the *Nam* or '*God*'. Very shortly a notice will be given through the historical work "*History of the Chamar Dynasty*" turning over the pages of a huge forbiding-looking volume in the hands of Brahmins without pictures of the *Nam*, but it seems that he was reading it very attentively either, it was the document of the *Sudhra* family which ignored by the party politics. Sashibushan used to try and explain to *Giribala* some portion at least of the books he read on other occasions in the Heaven body of Saints, but, it is important to *Sashibushan* try to explain some portion at least of the books, he read and wrote during his life time *Words* were there then not even a few words in that heavy black –bound volumes which he could read out to her? That Brahmin was a soul of the Lord, but forget Him on the basis of caste, colour and creed, and in any case, was that volumes of the book so very important and insignificant for the *Giribala*[22], the follower of Gandhi.

At first, in order to attract her perceptions attention to spell and read her lessons in the process of life why the she (soul) of the God aloud in a sing-song tone, swaying the upper half of the body including her plant which reveal the mentality of Brahminical thought. It appears from the study, she found that this plan of the nature did not suitable for her, because, she is very greedy of power without any reasoning making the thing ugly, hard, cruel for human being in national form of that book took on the form of a wicked man's face as God do in silently expressed its utter contempt of Giribala, because she was a little girl at that time. Now, she has been grown up lady for sexual intercourse as a free sex. Probably, God was watching her experiment on those irons how to melt the heat of the judge to give the vedict of the '*Nam*' in the universe to equalizing the problems of the man as his duty on earth.

As regarding to the representation in the services of the administration of the law is concerned, Dr. B.R. Ambedkar ,on the 17th of May, 1929, submitted a lengthy Report on the Constitution of the Government of Bombay Presidency, setting 'aside all considerations of the caste, colour and creed, among other things, he expresses, "the legislature should be wholly elective[23], civil disobedience was gradually allowed to slip into the hands of Gandhi, because of his temporarily suspended in May, 1933, Gandhi personally described to obtained from it after his final release from jail on 2-3 August, 1933, and the movement was formally withdraw in April 1934[24]. Reserve Seats should be provided for Mohammadans, Depressed Classes and Aglo-Indians[25], like so many of Gandhi's programmes the *Harijan* campaign was richly ambiguous in motives and significances Radical nationalists like Jawaharlal Nehru felt it to be a harmful divisions from the main task of anti-imperialist struggle[26], anti reservation views and said though Nehru was a great man but his follies were greater in the Congress party as First-Prime Minister of India[27], a feeling encouraged by the British readiness to let Gandhi conduct *Harijan* work even from jail. At the same time, orthodox Hindus with the Congress increasingly disliked the new emphasis[28], the legislature should consists of 140 members, of these 'Mohamedans' should have 33 and the Depressed Classes, 15[29], Pt. Madan Mohan Malaviya, for instance, who had been very close to Gandhi in the mid – 1920s, now began to drift away as Anti-Schedule Caste. Hindu communalist resentment was sharpened by Gandhi's refusal to concern himself overmuch with other provisions of the MacDonald Award which had given Muslim 49% of seats in the Punjab and 48.6% in Bengal (i.e. together with European numbers, majorities in both provinces). Orthodox Hindu opinion in Bengal bitterly attacked the acceptance of a permanent caste Hindu minority status by the Poona Pact, but the Congress Working Committee in June 1934 adopted a compromise 'neither rejection –nor-acceptance' formula of the Reserve Seats of the

Schedule Castes and Schedule Tribes which led Pt. Madan Mohan Malaviya to start a breakaway Congress Nationalist Party, Gandhi's Harijan meeting's had been disrupted in April and July 1934 in Buxar, Jasidih and Ajmer by *Sanatanists* including Gandhi, and there was even a bomb attack on his car in Poona on 25 June, the British Government, two, despite its claims to be modernizing influence, had to intention at all of alienating orthodox opinion, and official members helped to defeat the Temple Entry Bill in the Legislative Assembly in August 1934[30].

It would not be incorrect to say that the Police Department of the Bombay Presidency opened its doors for the recruitment of the Depressed Classes, in March 1931, as a result, of it, Dr. B.R. Ambedkar's knocking at their doors in the course of the evidence he submitted to the Simon Commission. While the Simon Commission was still touring in India, Depressed Classes, Aboriginal Tribes Committee, popularly known as the Starte Committee. Along with Dr. B.R. Amebedkar, Dr. P.G. Solanki and A.V. Thakkar were among the ten members of the committee. The committee was constituted by the Government of Bombay, in November 1928, in order to enquire into the educational, economic and social conditions of the Depressed Classes (i.e., the *untouchables*) and the Aboriginal Tribes in the Presidency and to recommended measures for their uplift[31]". The Committee submitted its report to Government of India in March, 1930. The Committee started that 'untouchability' consisted in that a mere touch of the Depressed Classes is held to cause a pollution which the orthodoxy Hindus are taught a lesson on the name of religion to avoid a sin to touch with them, in this way, obliged the Depressed Classes to live in *'isolation'* from the rest of the community. Another characteristic of untouchablility is 'servility[32]' by working in this universe as a duty of the Human being, but on the other hand, Brahmin is a pollution created in the society, it was the right time, Dr. B.R Ambedkar judged this community as an harmful community not for the nation but for the whole world.

The period under consideration reflects that Dr. B.R. Ambedkar delivered his presidential address, in the all India Depressed Classes Conference at *Nagpur-Kamtee*, on the 8th and 9th August, 1930. As has been rightly observed by Khairmoday, that address contained the ground-plan of Dr. Ambedkar's movement in time to come after the 1947. Thus spoke Dr. Ambedkar. "The best guarantee for the protection of your own hands so that you may (yourselves) be in a position not only to punish but to protect the interest of *Sudhras*, Dr. Ambedkar worked on the following sub-committees.

1. Sub-committee No. I : Federal Structure
2. Sub-committee No. II : Provincial Constitution
3. Sub-committee No. III : Minorities
4. Sub-committee No. VI : Franchise
5. Sub-committee No. VII : Defence
6. Sub-committee No. VIII : Services.

Consideration of time and space do not allow an exhaustive account of what Dr. B.R. Ambedkar did in these various bodies to constitute a social frame work of the Indian society. But we shall have to content ourselves with focusing of our attention that he did betterment for the life of man problems, not only for minorities, but for the other sections of the society by constituting a law of govern the society especially for the Depressed Classes as will as others. To take the example of sub-committee No. VIII, relating to services first in the sixth sitting of this body, on the 13th January, 1931, he reiterated his demand for the recruitment of Depressed Classes in the services. He moved this resolution. "The sub-committee desires that a generous policy be adopted in the matter of the employment of the Depressed Classes in Public Services; and it particularly recommends that the recruitment of the Police and interests is done, but to keep a watch over your interests, from day to day, and prevent possible mischief from arising the one stage to another as human life. This will never be secured by leaving the power in the hands of the third party be it the Governor,

Viceroy or the league of Nations. For of what use will that power be to us right-or wrong, if those who will hold it in trust for us to refuse to exercise it when we call for their intervention[33] which are the true message of the God i.e. Deepit Raj, a messenger of the God.

Now, we again come to the point of Round Table Conferences which were took place in London in the years of 1930-32 A.D. Historically speaking, those Conferences were of immense importance, not only for the Nation, but also good for the Depressed Classes as well as for the other sections of the society, like Brahmins, Sikhs, Muslims, etc. The First Round Table Conference was from the 12th November ; 1930 to the 19th January, 1931, the Second from the September, 1931 to the 1st December, 1931 ; and the Third from the 17th November 1932 to the 24th December, 1932. Dr. B. R. Ambedkar and Rao Bahadur Srinivasan represented the Depressed Classes at the Round Table Conferences.

During the First Round Table Conference, Military, from which they are now excluded, should be thrown open to them", the Chairman put the matter before the body to vote; and it was carried[34] till date.

The deliberations that took place in the Minorities sub-committee, were of a crucial nature, and had far-reaching consequences. On the last day of the year 1930, Dr. B.R. Ambedkar spoke on his 'Scheme of Political Safeguards for the Protection of the Depressed Classes in the Future Constitution of India'. In regard to the Depressed Classes, he said, "they are a minority in India, and yet their social standard is lower than the social standard of ordinary human beings[35]. Classes are not entitled their social standard under the present circumstances[36], because the system has been dominated by the upper class of the society, as per the Supreme Court's Reserves judgment, dated November, 2007, and domination has led to widespread corruption in the country and India has a stigmatic distinction of 73rd or 74th most corrupt country on earth, therefore, it is necessary to identify those castes which are not taken into consideration. The judges were virtually unanimous on two points – namely creamy layers must be excluded from the benefit of quota policy and secondly a time limit must be fixed for phasing out of the quota policy as such policy cannot go on indefinitely, before that a check is very important to find out the realistic approach in *History* and it progress. Therefore, it is certain to see the civic rights of a developing country and advancement from the past to present period which other minorities by law enjoy a great status in the society which the Brahmin had stolen with the writings of pen in false way as the enemies of the *'Nam'* or *Chamar.* In other words, in the existing situation, the Depressed Classes suffer in their hands as they are the *Yamadoot* on this earth and had snatched their civic right to live in the country like India. Now, question rises who is the big or small in the society, therefore *History* speaks truth that no body is big or small, it is our mind or *man* who creats such kind of barrier in the society, else is nothing.

Coming to the seventh sitting of the Minorities Committee, on the 28th September, 1931, when certain, "negotiations" were going on between M.K. Gandhi and the Muslims for the a settlement of the communal problem. In this behalf, Dr. B.R. Ambedkar said, "Those who are negotiating ought to understand that they are not plenipotentiaries at all. Whatever may be the representative character of Mr. Gandhi or the Congress people, they certainly are not in position to blind us from the civil rights as well as civic right, certainly not, I say that most emphatically in this meeting[37]".

It seems Gandhi wanted to constitute a committee to resolve the communal problem. In this regard, Dr. B.R. Ambedkar said, "I do not know whether in the position in which I am today, it would be any use for me or my colleague to work on the proposed committee and for this reason, Mahatma Gandhi told us on the first day that he spoke in the Federal Structure Committee that as a representative of the Indian National

Congress ; he was not prepared to give political recognition to any community other than the Muhammadans and Sikhs. He was not prepared to recognize the Anglo-Indians, The Depressed Classes, and the Indian Christians. I do not think that I am doing any violence to etiquette by stating in the Committee that when I had the pleasure of meeting Mahatma Gandhi a week ago in London and discussing the question of the Depressed Classes with him, and when we, as members of the other minorities, had the chance of talking with him yesterday in his office, he told us in quite plain terms that the attitude that he had taken in the Federal Structure was his full and well considered attitude. When I would like to say is that unless at the outset I know that the Depressed Classes are going to be recognized as a community entitled *'untouchables'* to political recognition in the future constitution of India, I do not know whether it will serve any purpose for me to join the particular committee that is proposed by Mahatma Gandhi[38]".

It shows from the long-term point of view, that the welfare work of *Harijan* taken by Gandhi must have indirectly helped to spread the message of Nationalism down to the lowest and most oppressed section of rural society, and *Harijans* in most parts of the country did came to developed a traditional loyalty towards the Congress which would greatly help the party after independence, too. Like other Gandhian mass movements, extension was combined with control, for Gandhi deliberately confined the Harijan campaigns to limited social reform (opening of wells, roads, and particularly temples, plus humanitarian work), delinking it from any economic demands (though very many *Harijans* were agricultural labours) and also refusing to attack caste as a whole due to oppressive attitude of the upper caste like Rajputs and Brahmins. He advised caution on inter-dining and inter-marriage, and went on defending the original *Varnasrama* system of *progress in the History of the Sudhras*, with the result that Dr. B.R. Ambedkar refused to message to the *Harijan* weekly on the ground of the 'nothing can emancipate the out caste except the destruction of the caste system[39].

As with peasant movements, Gandhian Harijan works seems to have been in a part a bid establish hegemony over potentially more radical pressures from below[40]. In 1917, Sri P. Theagaraya and Dr. T.M. Nair organised the first-Non Brahminical organization called South Indian Liberation Federation, which later came to be popularly known as the Justice Party. Naicker was a crusader for social equality and fought against the social evil of untouchablility. He denounced Hinduism as an instrument of Brahminical control the laws of Manu as inhuman, the *Puranas* as fairly tales. He ridiculed Hindu gods and goddesses and concluded. "There are certain things which cannot be mended but only ended Naicker condemned religion as superstition and opposed imposition of Hindi on the Dravadians quick-tempered as he was, Naicker to Tarred caste name boards on hotels, cutting off the holy thread of Brahmins, beating of deities with *Chappals* of the tanner and breaking of idols. His followers called him a *Thanthai* (Father) and Periyar (Great soul)[41].

Naicker's follower and friend C.N. Annadurai (1909-1969) carried further the Dravadian movement *Anna* (elder brother) came from a weaver community of Kancheepuram. In 1944, the Justice Party was renamed Dravida Kazhagam (Dravdia Federation). In September ; 1949 the party split and under *Ann's* leader leadership *Dravida Munnetra Kazhagam* (Dravadian Progressive Federation) came into existence. In 1962, *Ann* a was elected to the Rajya Sabha. In the 1967, General Elections the DMK Party formed the first Government in Tamil Nadu with Annadurai as the Chief Minister Anna was not against the unity of India, but demanded greater autonomy for states. In the wards of M. Karunanidhi "Anna was a statesman and a scholar, a littérateur and a social reformer, a mass leader and a friend of the poor. *Anna* will be ever remembered specially as the makes of new Tamil Nadu".

In the state of Kerala, there was another leader belonged to the *Ezhava Caste* or untouchable caste) Sri Narayan Guru

(1854-1828) established the SNDPY *(Sree Narayana Dharma Paripalana Yougna)* in Kerala and at many places outside Kerala. Naryan and his associates launched a two-point programme for the upliftment of the Ezhaves Caste. Firstly, to give up the practice of untouchability with respect to *Caste* below their caste. As a second step, Narayan Guru built a number of temples which were declared open to all castes. He also simplified ritual regarding marriage, religions worships and funerals. Narayan Guru achieved notable success in transforming the untouchable groups into a backward class. He openly criticized Gandhiji for his faith in *Chaturvarna,* which he maintained, is the parent of the caste-system and untouchability. He pointed out that the difference in caste is only superficial and emphasized that the juice of all leaves of a particular tree would be the same in content. He gave a new slogan "One religion, One caste and One God for mankind[42]", but Brahmins has multi-gods without logic only on tradition and word *culture* which is composed of two words *Cult+ture* means *Truth* is the *true* culture of the man called cult or *Dharma.* In general, however the Indian left failed to devote sufficient attention to the complex inter-relations of caste and class and Gandhi surely had a point when he rebuked Narendra Dev on 2; August; 1934 for forgetting a mention untouchability in the draft programme of the Congress Socialist Party[43].

Now, we came to the peculiar point of the situation called extra-constitutional, extrological, unchallengeable, Gandhian *argumentum ad Satyagraha* following Prime Minister Mac Donald's "Communal Award" of the 17th August, 1932, granting 'Separate Electorates' for the Depressed Classes. The next day on the 18th August, Gandhi announced his decision to fast unto death, to "resist your decision with my life". "The proposed fast he added, "will come into operation in the ordinary course from the noon of 20th September next, unless the said decision is meanwhile revised[44]". The historical puzzle concerning the change in Gandhi's attitude cannot be solved in terms of pressure from liberals leaders alone (personally respected but with virtually no support in the country). Nor can it be seriously argued that Gandhi was simply won over by Irwin's charm, or had became suddenly attracted by the very vague of Round Table Conference promise of responsible government in the centre limited as it was by a federation where princes would have a very big say, they were in the side of Gandhi and whose details all remained to be worked out, a string of Reservations and Safeguards, and an unsolved communal tangle due to their efforts and Gandhi's role. There is some evidence that the crucial role was played by business pressures. A surcharge imports in early February, despite some cabinet opposition and loud protects from depression affected Lancashire, and this time the government did not levy any additional charge on non-British imports, avoiding Imperial Preference for the time being obviously on political grounds. The Bombay Governor reported to the Viceroy on 7th February that 'a number of Gandhi's follower's particularly among mercantile community, are contemplating a breach with him unless he adopted reasonable attitude', and Irwin informed Wedge Wood – Benn on February that "Purshott Samdas will probably go to see Gandhi at Allahabad in order to try to put commercial pressure on him.' Thakurdas was in Delhi during the negotiations, and helped in resolving the final hitch over Gujarat land confiscations on 4 March and on 11 February, Birla's close adjutant D.P. Khaitan had declared in his presidential address to the Calcutta Indian Chamber of Commerce; 'it may not be amiss to suggest to Mahatma Gandhi and the Congress that the time has been come when they should explore the possibilities of an honourable settlement[45]. While Birla contributed financially to the Harijan campaign and even agreed to preside over the Anti-Untouchability League, business groups in general were much interested (now that Civil Disobedience had failed), in having the Congress back in the legislatures as an effective pressure group which could lobby for them. The prospect of full responsible government in provinces added to the attraction which was strongly felt also by the bulk of the Congress Leaders. Plans for a return to electoral politics through a revival of Swarajya Party were floated by *Satyamurti* in October 1933, and quickly taken up by Bhulahai Desai, Ansari and B.C. Roy in April ; 1934. Things were somewhat complicated by the breakaway of the Hindu-communalist Malaviya-Arey group on the Communal Award question, but the trend back towards conventional politics were clear. It is significant that Gandhi in a letter to Birla in April 1934 acknowledged "that there will always be a party within the Congress wedded to the idea of council-entry the reins of the Congress should be in the hands of that group[46]". Council-entry supporters in Tamil Nadu of the 1920s, as much as the Swarajist veteran *Satyamuti*. The mid – 1930s would be marked by a gradual coming-together of orthodox Gandhian constructive – workers and advocates of council-entry (and soon of ministry formation) too, in a common front against a growing challenge from the left, and there is ample evidence that business advice and pressure played an important part in this process of formation of a definite Congress Right' should like you to keep yourself in touch with Bhulabhai (Desai), Birla advised Thakurdas on 12 April 1934. "If the Swaraj Party is to be successful they will have to collect some found for fighting the new election and I would suggest that fund should not be supplied from Bombay without being satisfied that the right type of men and being sent'. And again on 3 August 1930, Vallabhbhai, Rajaji and Rajender Babu are all fighting communism and socialism. It is, therefore, necessary that some of us who represent the healthy capitalism should help Gandhiji as far as possible and work with a common object[47]', i.e. '*Nam'* or *Chamar*. We all want peace'. The coincidence of dates is once again striking and significant[48] for the study of history. The logic of events between the period of our discussion and the wholesale British counter-offensive which compelled the Congress to embark on the second Civil Disobedience Movement in January 1932 was determined in large part by the profoundly ambiguous consequences of the Gandhi-Irwin Pact. The frustration and anger of radical nationalist was sharpened by the execution of Bhagat Singh, Sukhdev and Rajguru on 23 March, 1931, just before the opening of the Karachi-Congress, and the Naujawan Bharat Sabha organized a demonstration against Gandhi at the Karachi railway station. Yet the Karachi session is significant mainly as revealing the weaknesses of the Left critics of Gandhi. Jawaharlal to work out a fairly radical agrarian programme and to formulate what became a basic element in left-nationalist strategy of the mid-1930s by suggesting a Constituent Assembly as the central political slogan[49]. He spent some sleepless nights after the Delhi Pact, but then surrendered easily to Gandhi and agreed to move the key resolution endorsing the agreement at Karachi. The death of Moti Lal (6 February) perhaps had made him more psychologically dependent on Gandhi and he was actually aware of his town limitations, as compared to the Mahatma so far as empathy with the peasantry was concerned. It is significant that in the *Autobiograpy* published five years later, discussion of the Delhi Pact was followed immediately by an appreciation of Gandhi as representative of 'the peasant masses of India'. A sense of helplessness and passivity is noticeable also in Delhi Pact. Yusuf Meherali, soon to become a prominent socialist leader, denounced unequivocally, 'the politics attacked 'the Birla, *Purshottamdas Thakurdas'*, Walchand Hirachands, Husainbhai Laljis, who are now out and busy in making efforts to obtain the fruits of the suffering and sacrifices of others. But his concluding note was strangely tame. Gandhi would again have to give the call for struggle, as the Round Table Conference was bound to fail, and then the radicals would get their chance[50], what we have observed from the public affairs and the historical background of the period to beings with important episode of the modern Indian History, fraught with far-reaching foresightness consequences of Dr. B.R. Ambedkar's prophecy to give just a few random observations by Mr. Gandhi in the first Round Table Conference Glorney Botton, in his *Tragedy of Gandhi*, says, London, and the old assurance and reliance was deserting him. Day after day[51], we patiently await the call to fight, *Inqulab Zindabad*[52], in the Conference which he had come to detest-the Karachi session passed a resolution on fundamental rights and economic policy which has often been interpreted that some officials suspected in it the hand of M.N. Roy, and some months later *Ambalal Sarabai* circulated a note among FICCI members sharply attaching parts of the resolution as threatening to bring about 'a Government on Russian model[53], But there was in reality precious little of 'Socialism' in the 20 points of the Karachi Resolution, which combined general democratic demands (civil liberties, legal equality, adult suffrage, free primary education, and a state policy of religious neutrality with much of Gandhi's 11 points of 1930, plus fairly modest promises to labour (living wages, an end to forced labour, trade union rights, etc.), a vaguely worded clause about control by the state of key industries and mineral resources, and a very moderate programme indeed of agrarian change. Only 'substantially reduction' were promised in land revenue and rent, there was no reference to the burning issue of rural indebtedness, and obviously no intention at all of eliminating landlordism or redistribution of land[54].

Thus, the Karachi Congress Session submitted to Gandhi as usual, and, as in February 1922, this was an indication of certain basic weaknesses of the entire movement and not just of the leader. Civil Disobedience had been marked by much scattered potentially radical manifestations, but no real alternative leadership had emerged. In its absence rural militancy remained either entirely spontaneous, sporadic, and uncoordinated, or under the leadership of village Gandhians with a limited outlook. Labour organization and militancy had declined sharply since 1928-29 A.D., and the communists, already weakened by the Meerut arrests, were going through a left-sectarian phase in which they concentrated their fire on left-nationalisms, expelling Nehru from the league against Imperialism in April 1930, and quarrelling with Subash Chander Bose to the point of bringing about a second split in the AITUC at its Calcutta session in July 1931. They kept aloof from Civil Disobedience and spent most of their energies quarreling among themselves. Yet the pact was disappointed many others outside the rather narrow circle of conscious radicals with more of less definite socialists leanings. The *Patidars* of Khada, *Hardiman* points out "considered the pact as betrayal' since revenue had not been reduced and even the forefeited land remained largely unrestored, in sharp contrast to the Bardoli victory of 1928. 'The pact, rather than police *lathis*, broke the morale of the Patidars[55]'. Brian Studdart and Gyan Pandey have come to similar conclusions about coastal Andhra and U.P. For both regions, 1931, was probably the psychological moment for full-scale no-revenue and no-rent movements in face of the first blast of depression, Congress held back the peasantry, trying to honour the truce. 'It was the conclusion of the Gandhi – Irwin Pact, rather then the Governments repressive policies, which altered the Congress hold on the coastal districts of Andhra[56]'.

At the same-time, it would be an over – simplification of a rather complex reality to describe the impact of the Gandhi-Irwin Pact in entirely negative terms. Whatever the concessions made by Gandhi, and, however, paltry the concrete nationalist gains, the Viceroy had been forced to treat the national leader on an entirely novel basis of courtesy and equality[57].

Dr. B.R. Ambedkar faced the Mohammendan delegates who would yield none of their demands. Day after day, Dr. B.R. Ambedkar came into greater prominence. He spoke for the *'untouchables'*, and every speech on the welfare of India[58], a fact of profound psychological significance, and as such deeply resented from the beginning by most British officials in India. The average Congress village or town almost as a victor, a mood vastly different from the near-total disenchantment and frustration of 1922. while Congress Organization had virtually collapsed after the Bardoli retreat, 1931 was marked by a considerable extension of party machinery in many areas. By May 1931, for instance, the single district of Rae Bareli in U.P. had 32 Congress offices, 8040 Congress members, 13, 081 Voluntary and 1019 villages flying Congress flags[59] in the courtesy of Dr. B.R. Ambedkar. What is more significant, a combination of economic pressures, heightened morale of the average Congress activist, official Congress reluctance to take up radical programmes, and perhaps a certain disenchantment with leadership, all produced a variety of pressure from below strata of the society, making the truce increasingly fragile, and stimulating secret official moves for an all out counter-offensive.

In Bengal, where the disillusionment of educated youth about Gandhian non-violence could only have been enhanced by the Delhi Pact, terrorism surpassed all previous records in 1931, with 92 incidents including a murders (two of them of District Magistrates, Peddle of Midnapur in April and Stevens was assassinated by two school girls, Santi and Suniti Chaudhuri, marking a new level of participation of women in the revolutionary movement). Nor was terrorism any longer confined to town's alone, at least in Chittagong, where no less than 52 villages were declared disturbed areas in May. A really frightened British government on the visit of Dr. B.R. Ambedkar, went in for draconian methods of repression, imposing a might curfew on all Hindu *Bhadralok* youth shooting down detenues in jail at Hijls on 16 September. Rabindranath Tagore addressed the protest meeting in Calcutta after this incident, Dr. B.R. Ambedkar was alone away from the nationalist politics during these years and well-known hostility to terrorism which was created by Gandhiji. A Sweeping Ordinance was issused on 29 October permitting indiscriminate arrest of allegal terrorist sympathizers was Dr. B.R. Ambedkar meanwhile, at the end of the country in the N.W.F.P., the rapid growth of the *Khudai Khidmatgar*, made formally a part of his writings in the membership of the Congress in August 1931, led to further official complaints that the Congress was violating the March truce[60] at that time as today, they are doing.

The most serious threat, alike to the British and to the policy of compromise now being sought to be followed by the Congress leadership, came from deepening rural discontentment as prices touched a record low (in U.P. the index of wholesale prices taking 1901-05 as 100 fell from 218 in 1929 to 162 in 1930 and 112 in 1931[61]; and revenue, rent, and debt burdens became correspondingly unbearable to the Congress the role of the Dr. B.R. Ambedkar, because this area was badly effected by the teachings of the Father. In Kheda and Bardoli, purchasers of confiscated land of the effected' people of the lower strata of the society were dying with the lack of food, and land – owner discriminated with them even, they could not provide them wages of their labours and they were treated as slave labour or hire labour in the absence of Father, now the time has come to settle the score, by appointing newly village officials on the whlem of the affair which were socially and without any reasoning boycotted them on the basis of caste, colour and creed. Now, the revenue collections will be made in the month of May. Since the Gujarat rural base was so very vital, Gandhi spent much of his time in these two districts between March and April, and his departure to attend the session of the Round Table Conference on 29 August, 1931. He threatened to cancel his trip to England if remedial action was not taken in Gujarat, and eventually, through talks with Willington with Dr. B.R. Ambedkar, and Home Member Emerson in Simla on 25-27 August, 1931, obtained an official enquiry into Bardoli Congress grievances as a special cases, and Gandhi was found as a criminal of the event[62].

In the low recorded area i.e. U.P., rural situation proved less tractable and much more explosive, because this area was rich by *Chamars*[63]. The Congress have tried to act as an arbitrator between *Zamindars* and tenants, asking *Kisans* to send applications for rent-reductions to the local Congress offices; the bureaucracy not unnaturally disliked, this disliked intensely, considering it as an attempt to establish, institutions paralled to those of Government. Gandhi issued a Manifesto to U.P. *Kisans* on 24 May, 1931, suggesting a compromise by which non-occupancy tenants should pay a minimum of 8 *Annas* in the rupee of the current rent, and occupancy tenants *12 Annas*. The edge of this appeal was clearly directed against agrarian radicalism ; 'Let me warn you against to the advice you that you have no need to pay the *zamindar* or *taluqdars* any rent at all'. But officials soon complained that peasants were taking Gandhi's minimum rates as the maximum of Dr. B.R. Ambedkar, and often stopping all payments of the *Nam's* race,while local leaders and activists were emerging at that time, but it was not the right time, all using the Congress name, but preaching a far more radical message[64] in the history of India like *Mahabharata; Kalinga War*, etc., whether from a conservative or a Socialist Party[65] like Kalka Prasad in Rae Bareli, for instance, or Anjani Kumar in the same District who picketed the house of the Raja of Sheogarh as a protest against eviction of defaulting tenants. Sheogarh, interestingly enough, had started a Khadi Vidyalaya, employing as a teacher there the wife of Sitala Sahai, the local Congress leader closest to Jawaharlal[66] Nehru. Despite official charges of Congress instigation, there is ample evidence that the leadership[67] of the said concerned, would have contained references to the tragic plight of the '*untochables*'. It was a sentimental rather than a practical concern for the human. Mr. Gandhi by representing the '*untouchables*' would have drawn eulogies from almost every one in England; but now Dr. B.R. Ambedkar had destroyed this platform. He so opposed the Mahatma Gandhi that the public began to believe that two personalities dominated the Conference, Mr. Gandhi and Dr. Ambedkar[68]. They acted on the whole as a restraining the force of the *Nam* i.e. *Chamars* of the U.P. Kalka Prasad was driven out of the District Congress, and things quietened down considerably in Rae Bareli after Jawaharlal's tour there in June. Agra with its very powerful Congress machinery and Gram Seva Sangh financed by Seth Achal Singh, a nationalist landlord, remained very quite apart from one isolated riot, while the main centres of agrarian radicalism, apart from Rae Bareli, were in Bara Banki, with little Congress Organization, and Majhanpur *Tehsil* in Allahabad, which the nationalists had avoided in 1930 due to the presence there of Muslim *Zamindars.* In December, 1931, with Round Table Conference negotiations clearly authorize no-rent in some Districts, but by the governor Malcolm Hailey's, policy of judicious combination of repression and conciliation was remitted in the end), had taken much of the edge out of peasant militancy. Yet the U.P. peasants had achieved something, winning remissions which, however, inadequate, were still much in excess of those granted in other provinces or in earlier years of distress and forcing on the Congress leadership a partial[69]. Therefore, Dr. B.R. Ambedkar left the political platform from the Congress which was based on Brahminical Ideology and *Sudhras* were degraded in the front of the public, that they are inferior race or caste, but going reorganization of the importance of the questions of Dr. B.R. Ambedkar as a young capable man of India. According to Professor Keynes, 'I am not economist we need an outstanding economist to go deeper into '*The Problem of the Rupee in Ancient India*' that the agrarian relations for the future of the national movement will be solved i.e. Dr. Raj Kumar, Professor of History. Govt. College For Women Parade, Jammu, that Rupee belonged to *tanner* called Ravidas. In this way, by 1936, the U.P. Leadership would come to advocate, at least in theory, the abolition of the *Zamindari* system, well in advance of the Congress in other provinces.

Now, the months of the truce were marked by this movements in many other regions, too, on the name of Dr. B. R. Ambedkar, though these have received less publicity than U.P. events. Anti-autocratic and anti-feudal agitations were emerging in some of the princely states like Jammu and Kashmir, for instance in July 1931, where the inevitable confrontation between an over-whelming Muslim subject population and a Hindu ruling dynasty called *Chamar*in Kashmir did acquire at times a certain communal tinge, but where the formulation were also being laid down both in Heaven and Earth in these years of the powerful National Conference Movement. The agitation started by a group of Muslim graduates including Sheikh Abdulla culminated in a mass attack on *Srinagar* jail on 13 July, when 21 were killed in police firing. While the immediate result was a communal outburst, repressive measures in September 1931, led to attacks on police rather than Hindus, and the situation soon required British military intervention to help the Maharaji. In Jammu, there were anti-moneylender riots in Mirpur, Kotli, and Rajouri *Talukas,* and eventually the State set up a Grievances Enquiry Commission with some non-official members on 12 November. In July, there was for some days with the *Indian Annual Register* described as 'mob rule'; crowds protesting against new taxes over powered of the police and military, burnt court records, released prisoners from jail, and forced the ruler to Bihar, the Congress leadership stuck to a strongly pro-*zamindar* line but a strong Kisan Sabha Movement was emerging in Gaya district under local leaders like Duggirala Balaranakrishnayya of Krishna District, whose Telegu *ballad*(Karakan) *Gandhi Gita* popularized both agrarian and nationalist agitations. Andhra peasants living in *Zamindari* areas were also being organized for the first time, particularly on the vast *Venkatagiri* estate covering 2117 square miles Nellore. A forest *Satyagraha* began here in 1931, against grazing fees through which the *Zamindar* was curtailing traditional peasant rights to fodder and timber ; leadership was provided by N.V. Rama Naidu and N.G. Ranga. There was a spate of anti *Mahajan* riots in the Districts of Krishna and Guntur in September 1931, involving crowds of upto 4000. In Kerala, with its particularly atrocious forms of caste discrimination, the

Gurvayoor temple *Satyagraha* which was started under the Congress leader Kelappan in November 1931 had a major radicalizing impact on the theory of *'Nam'* or God. Volunteer *jathas* (group) covered on foot large parts of both Malabar and the princely states of Travancore and Cochin, and despite the onset of Civil Disobedience, *Satyagraha* continued in Guruvayour till call off at Gandhi's orders in September 1932. Among the activists at Gurvayoor was a school-teacher named A.K. Gopalan, soon to become Kerala's most popular communist peasant leader[70]. There was a mounting pressure during the Round Table Conferences, the truce months strengthened the tendency in British official attitudes. In official circle a whole sale plan for counter offensive was also made through a pre-emptive strike. D.A. Low has shown in an important article that the shift in British attitudes, usually attributed to Irwin's successor Willington, really had its roots in some official thinking attitude during the first Civil Disobedience Movement and in the strong bureaucratic reaction to the Viceroy's treatment of Gandhi as an equal in February – March 1931. The basic idea of the British officials, as D.A. Low puts in his statement that it was of 'civil martial law' ; empowering civil officials with sweeping, near – military powers, instead of directly calling in the army as at *Amritsar* in 1919[71]. Home Member Emerson emphasized in the Delhi Pact must be 'accompanied by the determination to strike at once and strike hard, if and when the settlement breaks down', and a draft Emergency Powers Ordinance was prepared months before the actual crack-down of January 1932. The hardening of official attitudes in India was helped by a simultaneous shift to the Right in British politics, with the Tory-dominated National Government headed by the Renegade Labour leader Ramsay MacDonald and British business counter-offensive developing as the world economic crisis deepened. The new Tory Secretary of State, Samuel Hoarse, threatened to override the fiscal monetary policy of the Rupee, in this connection autonomy Convention in September, when the

Government of India, in serious financial difficulties as revenue from customs, income tax and railways were all declining due to the economic crisis[72], Dr. B.R. Ambedkar was in London School of Economics and Political Science from 1920 to 1950 was in search out of '*Responsibilities of a Responsible Government of India'* and his 'impressed a future generation of leaders from Africa and Asia as a whole'. It effected in the minds of several other thinkers of his generation of lead the world in new direction by revealing the truth in History. But at that time it was decided to raise the cotton duty from 20 to 25% without imposing politically explosive countervailing excises or Imperial Preference under the Britisher rule. In a pattern which would be often repeated during the year 1930s, the Home authorities eventually agreed to the new tariff despite Lancashire protests in London, but insisted on keeping the Rupee tied to sterling at 1s 6d when Britain went off the gold standard on 21 September 1931. A floating rupee would have devalued considerably 'adversely affecting payment of Home Charges and remittance of profits, metropolitan financial considerations were thus given top priority, even at the cost of some sacrifice for the sectional interests of Lancashire. At the second session of the Round Table Conference September – December, 1931, officials and British business representatives insisted that the Viceroy should retain enormous Reserved Powers in Finance. Birla calculated that under the proposed Federal structure, the supposedly 'Responsible' Indian finance minister would effectively control only Rs. 5 crores out of a total revenue of Rs. 130 crores (Birla to Sapru, 31 October 1931[73]). British business delegates like Benthall also pressed hard for commercial safeguards, guaranteeing foreign capital in India against 'discrimination' by nationalist governments. At the political level, too, there were signs of a return towards 'Simonism'[74]. The Indian Statutory Commission, arrived in India, in early 1928. Dr. B.R. Ambedkar submitted to it a statement on the 29th May, 1928, under the caption "Statement Concerning the Safeguards for the Protection of the Interests of the Depressed Classes as a Minority in the Bombay Presidency, and the Changes in the Composition of and the Guarantees from the Bombay Legislative Council Necessary to Ensure the Same under Provincial Autonomy[75]". Indians at that time were must be 'more and more forced back upon Provincial Autonomy as the first step to be taken' in Indian Constituent Assemblies, Hoare informed Willington on 2 October, 1931[76].

The overall situation made Gandhi at that Round Table Conference singularly futile to his activity participation like a Brahmin do in the politic to make false promise with the public. The session was soon deadlocked on the minorities issue, with 'separate electorates of the Depressed Classes, not only by Muslim, but with Indian Christians, Anglo – Indians, and European, and all these groups, came together in a 'Minorities Pact' for joint action on 13th, November 1931. Benthall in particular cultivated the Muslim delegates, obtaining their support in return for a promise 'that we should not forget their economic plight in Bengal and finally, according to Dr. Eleanor Zelliot, she says'. "One way of explaining the conflict and peace between Ambedkar and Gandhi, perhaps an over-simplication, is to say that Ambedkar say advancement for the *untouchable* in terms of using political means to achieve social and economic equality with the highest classes in a modern society, while Gandhi held to a more traditional concept of a *Varna* system of Brahminical thought, cleansed of untouchablility in which *untouchables* would be *Sudhras* and their unclean work made honorable[77]", but they were pure by thought and used to love work for the society and Brahmin was not in this favour to work for the betterment of life, because his attitude is always socially, morally corrupt to graving the power with false pen, do what we can to find places for them in European firms[78] in the their stand to follow the rules and regulations of the *Sudhras* on scientific method to develop the country for the betterment of the life in different walks of life like social, economic, political;

education ; Gandhi desperately fought against the concerted move to make all Constitutional Progress conditional on a solution of the communal problem. That solution, he argued, would be 'the crown of the *Swaraj* Constitution and not its foundation, and on 5th October Gandhi even offered to accept all Muslim claims provided they supported the Congress demand for *Swaraj.* But the Muslim delegates bluntly rejected the offer, and Gandhi's generosity towards Muslims was certainly not shared by the Maha Sabha delegates, who along with the Sikhs bitterly opposed anything that could give a majority to Muslims in the Punjab. On the Federation question, too, the princes of the various states were now speaking in different voices which gave an impetus boost to the communal understanding and seemed much less enthusiastic than in 1930 during first round of the Round Table Conference, for the threat of an immediate changes in the centre had diminished now that Congress had called off its movement on the protest of Princes and Nawab. A British move to postpone the discussion on the basis of changes because of opposition from the side of Sapru, Jinnah and Dr. B.R. Ambedkar, and MacDonald ended the session on 1 December with a reiteration on his 19 January stand, provinces like North Western Frontier and *Sindhu* or *Vitasta,* the setting up of an Indian Consultative Committee and three expert committees (on Franchise, Finance, and States), and holding out of the prospect, both humiliating and dangerous from the nationalist point of view, of a unilateral British Communal Award if the Indian failed to agree at one point programme of the *'Nam'*; i.e. Dr. B.R. Ambedkar, who was the great domestic saint from Heaven to Earth otherwise division of the Country is there.

In the study, it has been reflected that the whole discussion had been a pointless exercise, inevitably so because Gandhi had given up a call during the Delhi negotiations the demand for majority representation for his party i.e. Congress which had led to the rejection of the Irwin offer in December 1929. The

Congress instead of the above mentioned leaders of the different groups had accepted parity at the Round Table Conference with a variety of sectional interests some of them quite minor or unrepresentative. An obviously out maneuvered Gandhi returned to India on 28 December, to find Pt. Jawaharlal Nehru and Ghaffar Khan in jail on the issue of Communal Award, they were determined for that and situation because tense and large-scale repressive measures already under way in Bengal, U.P., N.W.F.P. Willington rudely turned down Gandhi's request for an interview, leaving the Working Committee with no option, but to resume Civil Disobedience. On 4, January 1932, the long – prepared plans for preemptive strike went into operation, with a battery of Ordinances (Emergency Powers, Unlawful Association, Unlawful Instigation, and Molestation and Boycotting) banning Congress organizations at all levels, arresting leaders, activists and sympathizers, and providing for confiscation of property. There was to be 'no drawn battle this time', declared Hoare : no less than 273 associations were banned on the very first day in Bengal alone[79]. Dr. M.R. Jayakar has to say in this regard : "His (Mahatma Gandhi's) attitude at the Round Table Conference in England drove the minorities to adopt the notorious minorities Pact. He denied to the Depressed Classes even a single seat by Reservation, except through the medium of the Congress[80]". According to James Halliday *alias* D. Symington, retired from the Indian Civil Service and a former Backward Class officer of the Bombay Province[81], outmanouevred and facing repressive measures on an entirely unprecedented scale, the National Movement under the Congress still forgot on valiantly for about a year and a half before admitting defeat[82] of the Congress in the Communal Award in London during the participation of Gandhi in the Round Table Conference with the strong argument of Dr. B.R. Ambedkar in Conference which Britishers accepted and Gandhi as a leader was not ready from the head and heart, he had the jealously on the basis of the caste *Varna Theory* which he could not understand its original meaning i.e. *'Nam'* like the Brahmins, they claim an educate class, but the idea of Divine Power lack in the part and believe on the theory occupation which does not exist to the modern world. Today, we see that everybody is doing their work for the benefit either it is professional field or unprofessional in the context of study, it is equivalent to everybody as nature has granted everything to everyone, but there is a need of *Pure Thought*, which Brahmins of the period are interested in traditions to collecting the money out of their customs as a profession which is difficult for a poor people of *Nam* or God. Therefore, it is essential to establish, again, the rule of *Law* or *Rita* in form of a man as a 'Creator Power.'

So far as, the estimates of the arrests are concerned during the fifteen months between January 1932 to March 1933, of the Civil Disobedience Movement was gone up as high as 12000, though it must be added that this is not a valid indication of relative strength as compared to the figure of 90,000 for 1931-31. Many more arrested to this time because repression had became so much more intense and systematic there was also a significant and quite rapid decline over time. An official break-up of 74,671 convictions up to April 1933 lists 14, 803 for January 1930, 17,818 in February, 6909 in March, and 5254 in April the monthly figures never exceeded 4,000, thereafter, and Willingdon was reporting conditions as 'well under control' by 4th April, 1932 and Civil Disobedience to be 'almost in a moribund condition' on 6th November of the Year[83]. But the provincial break ups for convictions give high percentages relating to the total population for Bombay Presidency during the British ruler in India (14, 101; 0.064%), Bihar and Orissa (14,903 ; 0.040%), U.P. (14,659, 0030%) Bengal (12,791 ; 0.26%) and central province (4014; 0.026%)[84], this is what Professor Edward Thompson wrote to Jawaharlal Nehru, on the 6th December, 1936 : " I never thought Gandhi wrong until the Round Table Conference, when he was both arrogant and irrelevant. Perhaps, he should not have come at all, but having come, he was unjustified in refusing to regard the other Indians[85] as contrasted to only 0.008% in Punjab and 0.007% in Madras. Though Muslim participation remained generally low, the percentage of convictions in N.W.F. P. was the highest for the entire country (6053; 0.25%).Women numbered 3630, and the extent to which the Congress had became a real mass movement is indicated by the fact that it was a destructive movement of the Gandhi that illiterates comprised 759 out of 904 in Madras and 1950 out of 2004 in U.P. in an early 1932 estimate, 1397 out of the U.P. figure were described as tenants or labours[86] lost their life in this movement.

As we have seen that Civil Disobedience Movement in 1932-33 comprised a wide range of activities throughout the nation, in part because so very many things had now become illegal, and civil liberties almost totally suppressed by the Britishers on the activities of the Mahatma Gandhi. Willingdon while finalizing plans for the 4 January attack Confessed that he felt, he was'. (Letter to Hoare, 20 December, 1931). The forms of defiance included picketing of cloth and liquor shops, closing of markets and boycott of white or loyalist business concerns, symbolic hoisting of Congress flags in India, holding in public of illegal Congress sessions (as near the Chandni Chowk Clock Tower in Delhi in April 1932, and on the Calcutta Maidan next year), salt *Satyagrahas'* non-payment of *Chaukidari* taxes, no-rent as well as no-revenue, forest-law violations, and a certain amount of illegal Congress functioning (including even a secret-ration transmitter near Bombay in August 1932) and use of bombs[87] against Dr. B.R. Ambedkar to kill the latter two methods, later strongly condemned by Gandhi. Before we conclude this phase, it may be observed that the prestige of Dr. B.R. Ambedkar began to grow and Brahmin could not like it. After the heartening victory over Hind orthodoxy, at Mahad, the spirit manner in which he presented the case of the Depressed Classes, at the Round Table Conference, had a tremendous effect on the moral of the *'untouchables'.* As we observed by the *Indian Daily Mail* of the 21st July 1931, "Dr. Ambedkar made a tremendous impact at the Round Table

Conference, and his speech at the opening session was of the finest bits of oratory delivered during the whole Conference[88]".

It is no wonder, if the Depressed Classes began to regard Dr. Ambedkar as a 'Fatherly Figure'. Young men in Bombay[89], thus, Ambedkar was far ahead of his time in thinking against Gandhi and on many of the legal and constitutional issues facing India, he solved. His concept of integration of the native princely states and Nawabs could not understand his ideology which was achieved later by Sardar Vallabhai Patel, has indeed been Prophetic[90] at that time to several his idea and thought a worldly hero of the '*Nam*' or *Chamar.*

According to Willington's letter of 4th April 1932 described Bombay city and Bengal as the 'Two Black Spots' on the visit of Dr. B.R. Ambedkar Bombay city to its Governor remained (the keep of Gandhism' therefore, the conspiracy of Gandhi against Dr. B.R. Ambedkar has been detected where the 'Congress have got a deeper hold[91], on the recommendations of Lord Irwin, the English government summoned the Round Table Conference in London in order to through out the problems of India. People from all classes were invited to participate in the Conference; but the Congress boycotted it. Coupland, a prominent scholar has written that although the Round Table Conference was a very significance event as the representative of thirty crore people had never been invited before, but it had no representative of the biggest organization of India, the Congress, but only Dr. B.R. Ambedkar dominated the Conference with his active support ; the Maharaja of Baroda, Sayyaji Rao. This Conference lasted for about nine weeks ; but its decisions were not according to the wishes of the Congress, hence, it was decided by the Congress that the Civil Obedience should continue[92] then anywhere else in India[93].

Moreover, massive participation by the Gujarati business community, and particularly, it seems, of the smaller traders of the '*Nam*' or God, badly disrupted the central *Mulji Jethe* raw cotton market till October 1932, where the government decided by held white firms threatened with ruin by very effective blacklisting and pushed through a law establishing official regulation of the cotton trade. But mill-workers remained aloof, as in 1930, and Muslims at time hostile[94] for communalism means the narrow and fanatic spirit of a particular religion or race for its own existence[95] is not sufficient, but there is need of broad mindedness like Dr. B.R. Ambedkar, who protected the interest of every community not in London in the Round Table Conference, but also certain provision were also made in the Indian Constitution by sharing the power of *'Nam'* or God as a human being on earth. No doubt, there was in fact, a major serious communal riots in Bombay city between May and July, 1932. In the countrywide, whether in Bombay or elsewhere in India, response on the whole seems to have been less than in 1930, for the Congress had spiked its own guns during the 1931 truce[96]. On 23rd March, 1931 A.D., the great revolutionary and patriot, *Bhagat Singh* and *Rajguru* were hanged to death; consequently people condemned Gandhi's activities in the entire country. Communal riots were broke out in Kanpur in which Ganesh Shankar Vidyarathi, the President of the Provisional Congress Committee was killed. Under such circumstances in the last week of March 1931; a session of the Congress condemned the policies of Gandhi. The angry and excited leaders declared that if there had been some other leader in place of Gandhi, like Dr. B.R. Ambedkar, we should have thrown him into the sea by now. But in spite of this severe opposition and condemnation of Gandhi, at last his name was proposed for taking part in the Second Round Table Conference to be held in London. It highlights the significance of Gandhi in the field of Indian politics[97] during his visit in London missed the psychological moment in the history of India for an all – out no-revenue and no-rent movement. Kheda and Bardoli were handicapped at that time by the British success in pressurizing Baroda to close its borders and only 15 villages were with holding revenue in Kheda by February 1932. A village like *Ras*, in Kheda, however, was still refusing revenue in 1933, though its *Patidars* had lost by then 2000 acres of land, and some of then had been stripped naked, publicly wipped, and given electric shocks by the police. A powerful no-tax movement developed in parts of Karnataka particularly in Ankola and Siddapur *talukas* of north Kanara where more than 200 villages with held revenues; and the All India Congress Committee reports refer to scattered outbursts of forest *Satyagraha* of Gandhi in many parts of Central and South India. In Ankola, on 1st may, 1932, for instance, 4000 villagers poured into the *taluka* headquarters carrying freshly cut firewood for auction, and in Betual in Central Province in the same month, forest *Satyagraha* was offered under tribal leaders like Mannu Gond and 'Chaitu Koiku. The Kerala Pradesh Congress Committee also reported forest *Satyagraha* in Kasergod *taluka* of Malabar in August and October 1932[98].

It has been noticed that Civil Disobedience was weaker in Tamil Nadu and Andhra as compare to 1930, though there were some active centres of urban picketing (e.g.) Madras city, *Madura* (Punjab) and Virudhanagar in Tamil Nadu), and the British were seriously alarmed for a while in 1933 by signs of a revival of no-revenue movements in coastal Andhra. In Bihar, there were several mass attacks on police stations in Monghyr and Muzaffarpur districts in February 1932 by crowds of up to 7000, and excise revenues continued to decline till 1933. In U.P., though a secret AICC bulletin of March 1932 reported no-rent movements in a number of districts[99]. Now, Civil Disobedience Movement was now becoming much more of an urban affair. Agra district, for instance, was quite except for an isolated no-rent movement in Barauda village, while 80% of land revenue due from Rae Bareli had been collected by July 1932, two months before the time[100].

March, 1932, in Bengal AICC bulletin reported revival of salt *Satyagraha* in coastal areas, non-payment of *Chowkidar* taxes and Union Board boycott in many Districts and no-rent in Arambagh sub-division of Hooghly and parts of Tippera, Sylhet and Jalpaiguri. The continued failure of the Congress leadership to espouse agrarian radicalism even in Depression conditions however, encouraged Muslim peasant movements to develop increasingly on separatist lines. The Praja movement gathered strength during these years, and in December, 1932, Maulana Bhasani, who throughout his career would combine genuine agrarian populism with communalist appeals, organized a big Praja Sammelan at Sirajagunj which demanded abolition of *Zamindari* and sealing-down of debts. Bengal remained a nightmare for the British, however, because of terrorism remain there for the long period in Indian history, because these people belonged to *Nila-mata Purana*. Though the new governor Anderson was a specialist in repression ever since the Irish civil war days, the number of terrorist cases was the highest ever in 1932 (104), before declining to 33 in 1933 and 17 in 1934. Two more white District magistrates were killed in Midnapur, Governor Jackson was attacked at the University. Convocation by a girl student, and Surjya Sen could be arrested only in February 1933; More than 3000 were detained at concentration Camps in Buxa, Hijli and Deoli, while the Chittagong prisoners were sent to the Andamans[101] and Nicobar.

The second phase of the Civil Disobedience Movement coincided with significant upsurges in two princely states. In Kashmir, the concession offered by the Grievances Enquiry Commission in April 1932 (steps to promote Muslim education, return of government occupied Muslim religions building, partial suspension of a grazing tax, and payments for state-requisitioned labour) failed to stop a growing movement. The Muslim Conference was started in October 1932, and though it would be renamed the National Conference only six years later, its leader Sheikh Abdullah had already started to develop a close contacts with a group of anti-autocratic Jammu Hindus under P.N. Bazaz. In the Rajasthan State of Alwar in early 1933, there was a formidable rising against Maharaja Jai Singh Sawai's revenue enhancement, begar grazing, dues, and reservation of forests for hunting. The Meos, a self-contained semi-tribal peasant community with a large scale. On 12th February, 1933, Willingdon reported the Alwar conditions to be 'getting as bad as they can be', and the *Indian Annual Register* spoke of 80-90,000 Meos participating in what it predictably but mistakenly dubbed "communal trouble" while to Punjab Muslim leader Mohammad Yasin Khan did try to give the anti-Maharaja movement a communal (as well as pro-British) colour, an alternative, consciously radical trend was also developing, associated with Syed Mutalabi Fridabadi, and interestingly, enough, K.M. Ashraf, soon to became one of India's first Marxist historian. Eventually the British decided to pack off the unpopular Maharaja to Europe, and take over Alwar administration for some years[102].

By the second half of 1932, A.D. Civil Disobedience Movement was evidently going down to defeat. It is true that the decline in peasant participation evident for instance in Gujarat, Andhra or U.P. was clearly a submission to overwhelmingly superior force rather than any loss of faith in the Congress, and the had of sacrifice and martyrdom won by the latter during 1930-34 helped decisively in the winning of elections from 1934 onwards. Yet Hardiman has a point when he remains us that 'voting was not the same as agitating[103], the days of the classic Gandhian *Satyagrah* as had passed'. Propertied peasants would go on voting Congress, but were no longer so ready to sacrifice their land, now that Gandhi had failed to get it restored for then in 1931 and in some areas, most notably Gujarat, they would also become more press persons after depression was succeeded by a war boom (when tabacco prices went up 50% in Kheda) and, correspondingly, less militant. Rural capitalism development only a few scattered pockets before 1947, and peasant radicalism retained its potentialities in the greater part of the country, and particularly so in the *zamindar* areas. This was a radicalism, however, which from the mid 1930s would increasingly seek forms of expression outside the Congress proper, through left-leaving *Kisan Sabhas* as well as sometimes through communal organization[104] like Congress, BJP, Leftist, etc. whereas BSP is more secular than that of others because it is the organization of *Sudhra* class.

Business Realignments

In the 1920s *Kisan Sabha* were organized in Bengal, the Punjab and the U.P. In 1928, the Andhra Provincial Ryots Association was formed. However; the first *All Indian Kisan Sabha* was formed at Lucknow on 11 April 1936. The Kisan Sabha explained its objects of "Securing complete freedom from economic exploitation and achievement of full economic and political power for peasants and workers and all other exploited classes". It also demanded a moratorium on debts, abolition of land revenue and rent from uneconomic holdings, reduction of land revenue and rent, licensing of money-lender, minimum wages for agricultural workers, fair prices for sugarcane and commercial crops and irrigation facilities. It also envisaged abolition of *zamindari* and vesting of land in the tiller of the soil. All these objectives were to be achieved by proper organization and active participation in the national struggle for Independence.

The Kisan Sabha launched anti-settlement agitation against *zamindari 'zulum'* in Andhra Pradesh. In U.P. and Bihar heroic struggles were launched against *Bakasht* (self-cultivated land) movement in Bihar. Bakasht was *zamindar's Khas* land which was cultivated by tenants on condition that they would pay a certain portion of the produce as rent to the land owner the *zamindars* sought to bring more and more land under this category in a bid to prevent tenants from claiming occupancy rights. There was largescale eviction of tenants on one or the other plea in 1937. The *Kisan Sabha* organised the evicted tenants and they offered *Satyagraha*, there by preventing others from cultivating land. Violant clashes ocurred resulting in many casullities. The *All Indian Kisan Sabha* organised a Bihar Kisan Day on 18th October 1937 against police repression on *Satyagrahas*. The growth of *Kisan Sabha* also worked as a pressure of the Indian National Congress. The Congress struck a radical posture in agrarian programme at its Karachi and Faizpur sessions. The Faizpur Congress adopted resolutions on the need for reduction of rent and revenue abolition of ensuring dues and levies, fixity of tendure, moratorium on debts and need for statutory provisions for ensuring living wage and suitable working conditions for the agricultural labours[105].

If, we take peasant response was becoming increasing contradictory, urban bourgeo's attitude toward Civil Disobedience Movement also showed considerable ambivalence between the two i.e. rural and urban. Gujarat merchant support throughout 1932 made the Bombay movement formidable, the Indian Merchants Chamber of that city was captured by a nationalist group in early 1932 against the opposition of Thakurdas, and when Civil Disobedience was resumed, the FICCI described to keep away from constitutional discussions for the time being. But G.D. Birla, who had pleasantly surprised Benthall by appearing quite accommodating in private discussions during the 1931 Round Table Conference session, hastened to assure Hoare on 14 March 1932 that the door to co-operation was by no means entirely closed, and that the resolution boycotting the Round Table Conference had been unwillingly taken by the FICCI leaders under great pressure from member-bodies[106]. As the mass movement declined, political *'realism'* plus certain sectional economic calculations pushed some business groups towards collaboration. At the Ottawa Imperial Economic Conference in the summer of 1932, India concerned lower import duty rates for a number of British Commodities in return for preferential treatment in the U.K. for some raw material exports, most of which, like tea or hides and skins, faced little competition in any case. Though strongly denounced by nationalists as well as, in public, by Birla, the Agreement was ratified fairly easily in the Legislative Assembly. Bombay textile magnates in 1932-33 were much more worried by Japanese competition in coarser piece goods than by an evidently weakened Lancashire, and this provided the basis for the notorious Lees-Mody Pact of October 1933, by British textile imports in return for a Lancashire promise to buy more Indian raw-cotton into consideration. Japan had been cutting down its Indian raw cotton purchases as retaliation for high import duties in India, and so a new outlet for Indian cotton was needed if anti-Japanese tariff walls were to be retained. Nationalists were furious at this 'betrayal' through acceptance of lower tariffs for Lancashire, who produced fine cloth in competition with Lancashire and had no desire to see the long-staple cotton it needed flowing away to the U.K. But Bombay mill-owners and *Tatas* (who signed a similar agreement with British steel interests in face of Belgian competition soon afterwards) together represented a formidable combination, and politically, too, Thakurdas was pleading for 'some understanding' by June 1932, and Birla repeatedly tried his hand as mediator between the government and Gandhi during 1932-34[107].

It shows that there was a strong objective compulsions, both economic and political, existed to prevent anything like total sell-out or unqualified collaboration by Indian business groups and agriculture British insistence on retaining the *1st 6d* ratio remained a permanent grievance, for it encouraged imports and required for its maintenance deflationary capitalists world were fighting Depression by greatly extending public expenditure, but in India so-called 'sound finance' remained a dogma, and investments in railways and irrigation were drastically cut down[108]. The massive gold exports which began from 1931, (due to the decline in the gold value of the *Rupee* after sterling had gone off the gold standard) helped the government to meet Home Charges and dept payments at a time when commodity exports were declining catastrophically. They were deeply resented, however, by Indian business and public opinion about the movement, which attributed them to distress sales by Depression- affected peasants, and Congress volunteers tried to picked gold export shops in Bombay Dr. B.R.

Ambedkar though radical nationalists also suspected at that times, because Gandhi was hell bent on the national movement, therefore, there was no other option that the men like Thakurdas and Birla were secretly making 'Lakhs[109] new social forces in the rise the industrial working class and the *Kisan_Sabha's,* their political awakening system and their direct participation in the nationalist movement as independent political unit. These new development which stemmed from India industrialization and moderination were also *Sudhras* and revealed the inner contradictions, which Brahmins could not understand the logic of the movement, and evolving tensions and antagomism. The worker's interests lay in fighting not only foreign imperial and capitalist interests, but also indigenous capitalists and exploiters. However, the Indian National Congress increasingly became the party of the Indian Bourgeoisie[110] from this immoral traffic[111], Lalji Naranji, who had opposed Non-co operation publicity in 1921, warned the liberal leader Jayakar on 27th January, 1932 that 'I in my commercial way of thinking believe more in Gandhi's policy', for Government indifference to us has driven 'we capitalists to work with socialistic organizations like Congress[112], the India industrial bourgeoisie which had gained considerable strength during the First World War started supporting the Indian National Congress by funding against the mobilization of the self interest as the modern politician is working on the false propaganda; the Congress policy of Swadeshism and Boycott of foreign goods was also the same particularly suited it at that time against the poor people of Father i.e. Dr. B.R. Ambedkar, and Congress promoted its own interests[113]. On a purely temporary and limited basis, Naranji hastened to add his more interests in Congress. If the British stopped export of gold, gave protection to Indian textile, modified currency on the name of Gandhi, excise, and fiscal policies[114] of Dr. B.R. Ambedkar as an Economist did a wonderful work for devising '*The Problem of Rupee in India*', and relaxed their near monopoly on banking system, insurance and shipping policies, he felt that Congress would soon withdraw Civil Disobedience Movement of which 'they are not fond '*Thusd'* asserts A.R. Desai" from 1918 the Indian industrial bourgeoisie began to exert a powerful influence in determining the programme, policies, strategies tactices and forms of struggle of the Indian Nationalist Movement led by the Congress of which Gandhi was the leader[115]" at that time particularly Mahatmaji of the present period of the Hindu ideology do not know the reality base function of the *Sudhras*, if Gandhi withdraw his movement, it is sure that we are given what we want[116]', from the Civil Disobedience Movement that is called *Nam-Dana*.

It makes clear from the study that it was difficult by the Dr. B.R.Ambedkar to fight with the Brahminical Ideology which suppressed the thought of *Sudhras* very badly, and it was difficult to talk against then about their 'egoistic' approach towards *Sudhras* as an animal on earth. Gandhi was one of them which could not understand the historical fact, which was lying with Dr. B.R. Ambedkar. The years 1930-34 were marked a wonderful day of Dr. B.R. Ambedkar he defeated the communal forces in The Round Table Conferences and Reserved the Seats of political right of the *'untouchables'* in the long history of man and in India particularly during the Brahminical Ideology was on high peak against the human being only interested for the self-interest not for the welfare of the society, as Gandhi used to believe on *Varna System* as a division maker of the nation and India. His secret policy was checked by Ambedkar in the Civil Disobedience Movement when people were dying with lack of basic need; he was determined to shed their blood in the national war even he could no spare the Ambedkar by ploting *Bombs* against him in Bombay and other parts of the world or Indian territories. No doubt, Bhagat Singh, Rajguru, etc. laid down their life on the inspiration Gandhi's policy against the British to leave India, though they have given a new life to it by creating railway system, telegraph, self-instiuation, education system, etc. Gandhi did not excuse them. He was always busy with creating chaos and disorders in the country.

The ultimate aim of the Congress in this struggle was to re-alignment of the business by graving the power in support of a change in Congress policy, away from mass agitation and their basic needs i.e. food, clothing and shelter. This re-alignment policy of Congress was enabled towards Capitalists to overcome the fairly sharp split between Ambedkar and Gandhi on the issue of 'Separate Electorates' which Ambedkar refused it and with consciously writings, he reserved the seat for *Sudhras* for the political development of India and to give them again, a defeat with writings of papers and articles of the *'Nam'* which Gandhi could not understand his might was his pen not sword, he secured the seats for *Scheduled Castes* and *Scheduled Tribes* in the Constitution of India. After the Round Table Conferences, he became the *Messsiha* of the 'downtrodden' or the *'untouchables'* as a symbol of their life and use to worship his static as a God on Earth. But, it is the blind faith of the man, like such people die, never comes again, it is impossible for those who could not understand the thought of nature i.e. *'Nam'* never dies, He comes in man's form again, but it is difficult to recognize them without poius approach in History to construct a fresh of the same family of the *'Nam'* or *God.*

Notes and References

1. B.G. Ramesh., *Op. Cit.* p. 19.
2. Sumit Sarkar; *Modern India* (1885-1947). New Delhi, 1983. p. 308.
3. K.N. Kadam ; *Op. Cit.* p. 25.
4. J.C. Aggrawal; *Op. Cit.* p. 315.
5. By Four Authors ; *A Simple History of England.* p. 102.
6. R.J. Moore; *Crisis of Indian Unity.* p. 155.
7. Sumit Sarkar ; *Op. Cit.* p. 309.
8. Vasant Moon (Ed). *Dr. Baba Saheb Ambedkar: Writings and Speeches;* Government of Maharashtra Vol. 2. p. 435.
9. Sumit Sarkar; *Op. Cit.* p. 309.

10. K.N. Kadam ; *Op. Cit.* p. 27.
11. C.H. Philips & Wain Wright ; Mary Doreen (Ed). *The Partion of India* ; pp. 61-3.
12. G.S. Chhabra; *Op. Cit.* p. 243.
13. B.R. Ramesh; *Op. Cit.* pp. 19-20.
14. *Ibid.* pp. 20-21.
15. Sumit Sarkar ; *Op. Cit.* p. 328.
16. Robindranath, Tagore, *Boundless Sky;* Kolkata, Reprint, 2006. p. 3.
17. *Ibid.* pp. 13-4.
18. *Ibid.* p.3.1
19. B.R. Ramesh *Op. Cit.* p. 18.
20. Rabindranath Tagore : *Op. Cit.* p. 31.
21. Ibid. pp. 35-6.
22. *Ibid* .pp. 36-7.
23. K.N. Kadam; *Op. Cit.* p. 29.
24. Sumit Sarakar : *Op. Cit.* p 328.
25. K.N. Kadam; *Op Cit.* p. 29
26. Sumit Sarkar; *Op. Cit.* p. 328
27. Daily Excelsior, *New Item Supreme Court Reserves Judgment on OBC Quota.* 11-1-2007.
28. Sumit Sarkar ; *Op. Cit.* p. 328.
29. K.N. Kadam *; Op. Cit.* p. 29.
30. Sumit Sarkar; *Op. Cit.* pp. 328-29.
31. Report of the *Depressed Classes* and *Aboriginal Tribes Committee*, Government of Bombay, March 1930. p. 1.
32. K.N. Kadam ; *Op. Cit.* p. 30.
33. C.R. Khairmoday ; *Op. Cit.* Vol. IV. p. 30
34. Dr. B.R. Ambedkar : *Writings & Speeches*, Vol. 2. p. 593.
35. *Ibid.* p. 595.
36. Vasant Moon (Ed.) ; *Op. Cit.* Vol. 2. p. 529.
37. *Ibid.* p. 653.
38. *Ibid.* pp. 655-56.
39. B.G. Tendulkar ; *Mahatma.* Vol. III. pp. 237-8.
40. Sumit Sarkar; *Op. Cit.* p. 329.

41. B.L. Grover & S. Grover ; *Modern Indian History*, New Delhi. Reprint ; 2005. p. 287.
42. *Ibid.* pp. 287-88. Note. Rameswancy Naicker refers very rightly that in medieval times Indian religious reformers mostly attracted the followers from the lower castes like *Kabir, Namdev, Dhanna, Dryia Sahib, Ravidas, Paltu,* etc.
43. B.R. Tendulkar; *Op. Cit.* Vol. III. p. 344.
44. Dr.B.R. Ambedkar ; *What Congress and Gandhi Have Done to the Untouchables.* p. 82.
45. Sumit Sarkar; *Op. Cit.* p. 311.
46. G.D. Birla; *In the Shadow of the Mahatma*; p. 138.
47. *Jayakar and Thakurdas Papers.* Foot note 42 (vi).
48. Sumit Sarkar*; Op. Cit.* p. 311.
49. Nehru's *Autobiography and Selected Works*, December 1930, Vol IV. pp. 433-51.
50. Sumit Sakar*; Op. Cit.* p. 312.
51. K.N. Kadam. *Op. Cit.* p. 38.
52. Sumit Sarkar; *Op.Cit.* p. 312.
53. *Walchand Hirachand* Paper, F.N 8 (II).
54. Sumit Sarkar, *Op. Cit.* pp. 312-13.
55. D. Hardiman; *Peasant Agitations in Kheda District*_ B.A. low. (Ed) p. 289.
56. Brain Stoddart in *Congress and the Raj.* pp. 121-2.
57. Sumit Sarka; *Op. Cit.* p. 314.
58. K.N. Kadam ; *Op. Cit.* p. 38.
59. Gyan Pandey, *Ascendancy* of different state study by the author on civil disobedience, like Bihar 4. p. etc. p. 41.
60. Sumit Sarkar; *Op. Cit.* pp. 314-15.
61. Gyan Pandey ; *Ascendancy.* p. 160.
62. Sumit Sarkar ; *Op. Cit.* p. 315.
63. ***Note.*** In some places sections of the caste are slowely securing a higher social position by adopting the usual methods employed in *India* or *Chamar.* Those who are well to-do, are making an effort to seclude their women, are prohibiting widow-marriage and are discouraging the more disgusting and heterodox

practices of eating pork, *beaf,* carrion, and the leavings of food of other castes. Such sections are slowly separating themselves from the main caste and from the name "*Chamar*". But, as a whole, the caste still occupies a position in moudling the society on the very outskits of Hindu society. The *Chamar* has a well-organized and influential council, or *Panchayat* not in India, but also in England, they are the followers of *Ravidas Vani* called *'Chamar'* or *'Nam'* or God in our society. It is greatly feared, and exercises a very strong, influence over its constituency. In its simplest form its consist of the whole village or *Mohalla* group, is conterminous with the sub-caste to which the *Chamar* belongs, and consists of all the man under its jurisdiction. The families of a village are represented, or it may be composed of all the old men. Usually the representation is by families. There may be a sub-committee, often composed of five persons, which guides and rules the larger body. (G.W. Briggs ; *The Chamars.* Delhi, Reprint 2004. pp. 47-8.)

64. Sumit Sarkar ; *Op. Cit.* pp. 315-16.
65. K.N. Kadam; *Op. Cit.* p. 38.
66. ***Note.*** S. Gopal gives a good summary of the main political developments in India at that time, and Jawaharlal Nehru, *A Bunch of Old Letters* (Bombay; 1958); includes certain illuminating correspondence of the mid and late – 1930s situation of India. *Home Political* Department 33/24/1931). *Kisan* movement and the issues of the Congress Socialist available at N.M.M.L. along with princely states argument as pertaining to the national movement of India.
67. Sumit Sarkar; *Op. Cit.* p. 316.
68. C.B. Khairmoday ; Dr. B.R. Ambedkar Charitra. Vol. IV, p. 213.
69. Sumit Sarkar ; *Op. Cit.* p. 316.
70. *Ibid.* pp. 317-18. **Note**: According to M.A. Stein note in Kalhana's *Rajatarangini* that Jammu and Kashmir state was ruled by *Sudhra* family called Barawalas, high minded King Maharaja Gulab Singh, used to work with the co-ordination of British-India at that time, because they were both follower of *Ravidas's*

philosophy of the '*Chamar dynasty of Kashmir*' from the heavenly world called paradise on earth. Moreover, they had a *jagir* or *Agrahora* of a *Pirzada* family of *Srinagar*, until it was resumed by Maharaja of Gulab Singh. (R.T. Vol. I. p.23.)

71. D.A. Low; *Congress and the Raj; See Chapter V.*
72. Sumit Sarkar ; *Op. Cit.* p. 318.
73. G.D. Birla, *In the Shadow of the Mahatma* ; p. 46.
74. Sumit Sarkar; *Op. Cit.* p. 319.
75. K.N. Kadam ; *Op. Cit.* p. 27.
76. J.R. Moore; *Crisis of Indian Unity.* p. 232.
77. ***Note :*** Eleanor Zelliot, *Learning the Use of Political Means'.* (In case in Indian Politics, Edited Rajni Kothari, Orient Long mans; India to understand its logic and reasoning *'Nam'* or *Chamar* is very important to the Brahminical Ideology, other wise problems of a developing society are very difficult.
78. See Benthall note, quoted from *Uma Kaure.* p. 77.
79. Sumit Sarkar ; *Op. Cit.* pp. 319-20.
80. C.B. Khairmoday; *Dr. B.R. Ambedkar Charitra;* Vol. IV. p. 217
81. K.N. Kadam ; *Op. Cit.* p. 39.
82. Sumit Sakar *; Op. Cit.* pp. 320-21.
83. **Note**. Study made from the *Templewood Collection* about the arrest of public during Civil Disobedience Movement.
84. Sumit Sarkar ; *Op. Cit.* p. 321.
85. C.B. Khairmoday; *Op. Cit.* Vol IV. p. 218.
86. *Home Political Department.* File No. 3/11/1933-9 in Judith Brown; *Gandhi and Civil Disobedience Movement*; pp. 284-6.
87. Sumit Sarkar ; *Op. Cit.* pp. 321-22.
88. C.B. Khairmoday ; *Dr. Bhimraw Ramji Ambedkar.* (Marathi Magazine).
89. K.N. Kadam; *Op. Cit.* p. 40
90. B.G. Ramesh ; *Op. Cit.* pp. 27-8.
91. Sumit Sarkar; *Op. Cit.* p. 322.
92. K.L. Khurana; *History of Indian*; Agra, Reprint 2007 p. 253.
93. Skyes to Hoare, 6 March, 1932, *Sykesh Collection* Mss. Eur. F.N. 150.

94. Sumit Sarkar ; *Op. Cit.* p. 322.
95. K.L. Khurana, *Op. Cit.* p. 269.
96. Sumir Sarkar ; *Op. Cit.* p. 322.
97. K.L. Khurana; *Op. Cit.* pp. 253-4.
98. *All Indian Congress Committee*, File No. 1/1932).
99. *R.E. Hawkins* Papers in Cambridge South Asian Centre.
100. G. Pandey; *Congress and the Raj*; pp. 177-187.
101. Sumit Sarkar ; *Op. Cit.* p. 323.
102. Chaudhuri Abdul Haye's Article in H. Kauger (Ed.). K.M *Ashraf,* Delhi; 1969).
103. Sumit Sarkar; *Op. Cit.* p. 324.
104. *Ibid.* pp. 324-25.
105. B.L. Grover & S.Grover. *Op. Cit.* pp. 352-3.
106. G.D. Birla; *In the Shadow of the Mahatma.* pp. 54-5.
107. Sumit Sarkar ; *Op.Cit.* pp. 325-6.
108. Amiya Bagchi; *Private Investment.* Delhi 1979, pp. 18, 46-7.
109. Sumit Sarkar ; Op. Cit. p. 326.
110. B.L.Grover & S. Grover; *Op. Cit.* p. 316.
111. Illegal Bombay Congress Bulletin, 17 October 1932, *Thakurdas Papers.* File No. 101).
112. Sumit Sarkar ; Op. Cit. pp. 326-7.
113. B.L. Grover & S. Grover ; Op. Cit. p. 316.
114. Sumit Sarkar ; *Op. Cit.* p. 327.
115. B.L. Grover & S. Grover; *Op. Cit.* p. 316.
116. *M.R. Jayakar Papers* ; No. 456.

4

Self – Respect Movement of Dr. B.R. Ambedkar

(1935 to 1946 A.D.)

Self – Respect movement of Dr. B.R. Ambedkar was quest for a "religion" may be said to have begun when he was still a school boy of six years old. To put it in his own words in his life : "My father was a very religious person, and he brought me up under a strict discipline. Quite early in my career, I found certain contradictions in my father's religious way of life. He was a *Kabirpanthi.* As such, he did not believe in "*Moorti Puja*"(idol-worship). He read the book of his *panth.* At then, he compelled me and my elder brother to read every day, before going to bed, a portion of the *Ramayana* and *Mahabharata,* to my sisters and other person who assembled at my father's house for hearing the *Katha*[1]. Subsequently, when the revered teacher Krishnaji Arjuna *alias Dada Keluskar* presented him with a copy of *Gautam Buddhache Charitra* (life of Gautama, the *Buddha*[2] *or Nam*) written by himself the young lad must have read it called *Sarada* script of the '*Nam*' with profound interest for he said later on, "I read the book with great interest, and was moved by it in Global human society for human feelings are more or less the same as the 'Nam'. The human will also operates largely in similar manner as Kabir's songs and forthright language reflect these conditions on the life of man, exposing the foolish practices of the people of all religions, who do not trust on the philosophy of the *Sudhras.* God indulge in the massacre of thousands, as did by the Sri Ram Chander, the hero of the *Ramayana* who was really a *'Nam'* on Earth. Whereas Sri Krishna advocate the war in the *Bhagavad Gita* which was beyond the three *gunas* or qualities that the shape of the physical Universe, he does not indulge in these kinds of activities. And, Kabir says all this in spite of the fact that these incarnations were worshipped by millions during his time, as they still are today. Kabir goes still further and refutes the belief that the gods Brahma, Vishnu and Shiva, Worshiped by Hindus as the Creator, Preserver and Destroyed of the Universe, are equal to the Lord, and quotes stories from the *Puranas* themselves to prove his stand in new form have new name. The lesser gods and goddesses, he dismisses as of no consequence[3], because, they are wandering in *Brahma,* collecting money becoming Shiva, which is very difficult to express the message of the 'God' as a truth as Dr. B.R. Ambedkar challenged the Brahmins in big opposition. It shows that it was self-respect of the Lord on Earth.

Kabir wanted Hindus and Muslims to live in brotherly love, as Dr. B.R.Ambedkar played the role in the Round Table Conferences to accommodate the every community of India and Gandhi could not favoured his argument on the theory of caste system or *Varna* system, but achieving Hindu – Muslim unity was not the purpose of his life, but to built a *Great India* or *Bharat* though he criticized the elaborate rites and rituals of both the Hindus and Muslims, he did not do so to make it more easily understandable to the masses, nor to meet the challenge of *Islam* with its simple rites during the time of Mohammed Prophet. Some of Kabir's critics faulted him because he was member of *Sudhra* Family could not introduced strong social reform movement in India because of his double standard some says he was Muslim or some says Hindus, but he was nothing as the story the God exist. Saints do not write about their lives because their own personalities, which they identify with the Supreme Lord, do not interest in Hindu and Muslim practice as *Sudhra* do. In the context of the people looking on him as a Muslim, Kabir uses four names for God associated with *Kabir, Akbar, Kubra* and *Kibriya,* associated with Hindu tradition, deliberately provoking both Hindus and Muslim in order to help them to understand that the Nameless One is neither Hindu nor Muslim and can be realized by anyone, regardless of community, profession or religious persuaion[4] is Brahmin or *Mana.*

It has been clearly stated in his (Dr. B.R. Ambedkar) writings a book on the *Annihilation of Caste*[5]. "He must abide by their directions. The Caste and Varna are matters which are dealt with by the *Vadas* and *Smrities* and consequently, appeal to reason can have no effect on a Hindu, it was only on Sudhras" so far as *Caste* and *Varna* are concerned, means that *'Nam'* is *Pure,* it does not permit in the *Sastras* of Hindu, because their philosophy is concerned with these terms. As a strong protagonist of Brahminical doctrine Manu strongly supports the *Varna* system and hence it deals comprehensively with almost every aspect of society during their rule. A large number of commentaries has been written on the Smirit of Manu are indicative of the high esteem in which it was held by law givers[6]. The general attitude towards *Sudhras* is clear in a verse by Manu that "even if freed by his master, a *Sudhra* is not released from servitude, for this servitude, is innate in him[7]". It is further stated that a Brahmana may take possession of goods with perfect peace of mild since nothing at all belong to the *Sudhra* as his own, whatever little he came as his property may be taken away by his master[8].

Sudhras And The Property Rights

According to the injunctions of Manu, three categories of people i.e. wife, son and a slave or *Sudhra* do not own any property ; sons of course inherit the property after the demise of their fathers[9]. The law relating to property right, a general opinion was fact when once fundamental rights are included in the constitution, cannot be amended at all at the level of implementation. Because of the argument, 'the Right to Property' was deleted from the chapter on fundamental right. Similar, there was a strong debate on the *'Right to Work'*. However, today after 60 years of independence still there seems to be a debate on the right to work[10], which Brahmins are not to this favour, therefore, it is the duty of the Father to check them how to control the property which is not lying for you, it is the property of the Father. It was a very difficult task to prepare the Constitution at that time, where were the Brahmins stands at that moment. One who prepares the Constitutions should have a deep knowledge of 'Law', and knowledge of 'History', of the country and he should have a thorough knowledge of the society as he lives. The Constitution is not mere a write up[11], but it has the spirit of Divine Right to work from the distance which Brahmin cannot be understand for this, because they had the *Aerial* message in their life which serve the country for the benefit of the poor which have been degraded by the Brahmins.

Sudhras And The Criminal Law

As law enumerated by Manu expressly deals with offences like adultery, assault, defamation, disrespect, etc. In the present context we will examine it very carefully that various offences of the criminal category with particular references to *Sudhra* class must be analysis the nature of punishment which is up to the Master which would clearly indicate the role of social disorder i.e. caste and *gotra* have been formulated a criminal law. Naturally, the punishment for adultery with a women of superior caste was much more severe than that of women of lower caste unless the women belonged to the lowest (i.e. *Chandala*) caste. It also depended on the consent or non-consent of the girl, but with the *Sudhras,* there is also a caste rigidity, whether she was guarded or unguarded (by her husband or relatives[12]).

It appears from the study the Hindu Law Code Bill is so strong contains various degree of punishment in the absence of the *Sudhra* rule, when they violated the rules of the caste system. However, there punishments are nominal for the Brahmins and stringent for lower castes.

Sudhras and the Payment of Debts and Interests

In the matter of payment of debits also caste system played an important role. Higher castes could pay debt by degrees, but lower castes were to repay by labour or by becoming slaves till debt was rapid in the absence of Father. Citizenship was acquired first by birth during the process of the child. In lawful marriage the child followed the conditions of the Father, and became a citizen, if the Father was so at that time of conception, the status of a person under the Roman Law may or may not be *Civic optimo jure* as mentioned by Dr. B.R. Ambedkar in his writings. It is clearly stated from the study that under the law of Manu, *Sudhra* were very badly effected, because their theory is unscientific and unexplorable, but the theory of the *Sudhra* is scientific and hard one, because there is a need of pious approach toward the *History* of the man.

Philosophical Thought of India, A Comparative *Analysis of Dr. B.R. Ambedkar and Gandhi*

In the scientific history, it has been proved that the philosophy of India has been originated from *'Infinite'* it emerged out of *Nam-Dana,* curiosity for love with him, meditation and intuition to know that 'Reality' as Dr. B.R. Ambedkar realized in his life. Now, we take the example of Gandhi, both known to the mind and existing, as well as, not know to the mind is 'Finite' and the "Reality" (truth) is '*infinite*', means inside the body what the theory of mind display to the public by poster, advertisement, in news paper, T.V. etc. But the theory of *'Nam'* is less in this case as '*Baba Gurinder Singh ji of Beaswale*'. Thus, the Western philosophy originated under the pressure of a practical need as British did, they learned it from the *Sudhras* Family like *Kabir, Ravidas*, arising from the presence of moral and physically evils have been crept in their society, but Brahmins on the names of *Kabir* and *Ravidas*, they hesitate to talk to them called them '*Untouchables*'. The condition which has been imposed upto them is very strong Brahmin cannot understand its wonder and magic spell, who it works secretly against the Brahmins. In India, it was the quest for truth i.e. *'Nam'*. The truth which Indian philosophy is in search is intuitive as well as in the Living Being Deity as we have already mentioned above. It can be distinguished from knowledge, because every knowledge of the world is coming out of it, Brahmin without the knowledge of the *'Nam'* claiming for that. It is logically wrong to say, because their theory believe on mind not God. Accumulation of facts is knowledge. Truth is not accumulated, it serves the society in large-scale. Knowledge can be accumulated with pious approach towards *'Nam'* or God. Truth is like entering into contract with *'Reality'* then it becomes a wonderful reality, as we have seen in the life of Dr. B.R. Ambedkar. A man from the poor family became the world's man with their hard-work and devotion towards *Nam*. Appreciation and assimilation of reality may change one's whole life style as the 'Newton's law of Gravity is the fact which may not impact on everybody life of an individual's personality, on the other side, when we saw the early career of Dr. B.R.Ambedkar and his attachment towards Buddhism displayed a wonderful role in his life.

In the East objective of philosophy is the knowledge of reality. Emphasis has always been laid down on inner experiences of man and it has sought to understand man's inner feeling. In this pursuit, we analysis that Gandhi's philosophy based on Brahmins and Dr. B.R.Ambedkar's philosophy was based on reality or '*infinite*'. It has been seen that good is not to be found in particular events of nature's course, but also in the day to day happenings of life as the life is going to change from bad to good after the scientific process.

Religious Sanctions of Brahmins

According to Dr. B.R. Ambedkar, the religions sanctions have been imposed by Brahmins in the absence of Father's rule, through by making traditions and customs to collect the money from the people for their own benefits, but chanting certain verses of Sanskrit as a common language of the God and the man. But in the absence of the Father, he took the advantage by performing ceremonies at different occasion like marriage, *Sati* system, infanticide systems, untouchables, etc. in the society. Against, these social evils and caste systems, Dr. B.R. Ambedkar written a paper in 1916, during his Columbian days to put-forth his own theory of the origin and growth of the castes in India, from a *'Casteless'* society to the development of the major castes of the *Brahmins*, the *Kshtriyas* and *Vaishyas* ,in the Indo-Aryan society. It was the priests who first isolated or segregated themselves, and built, as if their nature, a caste-wall around themselves, to be thereafter, emulated by the warriors and rulers. Thus, with the formation of the Brahman and the Kashtriya castes, the remainder of the viz. automatically became the Vaishya Caste[14]. The young scholar defined "Caste" as an enclosed class of the Father. He also observed that castes can exist only in the plural society. Thus this system of classification and stratification of the Indo-Aryans were given religions sanction of the *Shastras* composed by Brahmins for their own prestige and power. It was his endeavour "to show the falsity of the attitude that has exacted religions sanction to the position of a scientific exposition[15]". This study of Castes in India led him, as time went by, to make a detailed study of Buddhism; and he observed the vast ideological difference between Hinduism and Buddhism[16]".

Indications of a growth in the volume of interest in Buddhism[17] are noticeable in some sections of Indian people i.e. *Scheduled Castes* and *Scheduled Tribes*. Along with it, the other poor people of the Father is naturally growing demand of the hour to clear the message of the God or *'Nam'* or *Chamar* called Buddhism after the Lord Buddha. It consisted of the teachings of *Buddha* or *Kabir* or *Ravidas*. Anyone who is not a Buddhist but a *Chamar* finds it extremely difficult to present the life and teachings of Buddha in a manner, it presents the present life not the past, but from the past we can construct this history not life, because it is the part of man and material which everybody has to die. Indeed, it would not be an exaggeration to say that of all the founder of Buddhism is the same as presents a problem in other religion, but it is the study of the *'Principal Soul'* who are functioning in this world to mobilized the life and regulates its principles. It is not necessary that these problems should be solved in easy manners, but one must has to pay the compensation of the life which God has to given us with special purpose to serve the society and realize the Father or *'God'*, but transfer policy is there to move in this universe called birth or rebirth.

In the *Varna* oriented Hindu society, *Brahmins, Kshatriyas, Vaisya* were the minorities and unproductive classes, but vested with all the privileges in the absence of the Father. The rules for social discrimination is peculiar and inhuman in the Hindu society on the bases of caste system. As a result, in the sixty years of independence, the Indians gained considerable positions in the government. But alarmingly those positions made available for the Indians were almost grabbed by the Brahmins in the name of Indians.

At the juncture leaders like Bala Gangadar Tilak, Annie Basant, Rabinder Nath Tagore, etc. gave a changed activation to the Indian Movement according to which the educated Brahmins who stood in the forefront of social reform movement during the 20th century A.D. In addition to dominance in

Employment Front, most of the Brahmin intelligentsia also became active either in politics (Indian National Congress or the Home Rule Movement) or in Theosophy and have endeavoured to justify the existing Hindu institutions more particularly the casteism became glorious in the society with all their orthodoxy and social discrimination. This was done on the pretext that the Indian nationalism will be real only by the sustenance and glorification of all that was Hindu and Muslim.

The above circumstances enlightened the non-Brahmin intelligentsia and their discrimination on the bases of casteism as a jealously factor of the development, the fact is that a war of social justice was started in the contemporary society of India, and people of this class are feeling insecure in the main objective of Indian National Congress, when it was founded in 1885, was to gain positions for Indians in the government. They argued that it was the right of the Indians to occupy more offices in different branches of the government that *Sudhra* might be suppress. Magnanimously, this demand of the Indian were not only supported by the English intellectuals at that time like, A.O. Hume, Sir William Wedderburn and others. The purpose of the Congress was different at that time to provide equality before the law, but it could not achieve its objective which were framed at that period, now this party became a party of Brahminical Ideology to suppress the people on the name of 'poverty' and 'social justice' therefore, perhaps in the same line of the Indian National Congress, the south Indian liberal Federation (The Justice Party) was formed in 1916 by non-Brahmin leaders like T.M. Nair, Pitti Theagarayar and C. Natesan. 'The non-Brahmins Menifesto' of the Justice Party declared that their main objective was to achieve for the non-Brahmins the rightful positions in education and government offices, then these will be a check from the side of Father on this earth for the development of the idea in History as a progressive subject. At the sametime, they were not against the Brahmins to get what they justifiably deserve for, because the non-Brahmin Movement was never anti-Brahmins but certainly against the Brahminical domination way back in 1917, in 'Dravidian', the official Tamil Journal of the Justice Party, Sir Pitti Theagarayar wrote an editorial title as "The Education of the Working Classes-Will it cause in convenience to others during the rule of Brahmins, therefore, certain privileges have been made in Indian Constitution". He also wrote that "the genius of Dravidian Civilization does not recognize difference between man and man by birth. The leaders of Dravidian thought, Thiruvalluvar, Awai, Cumber do not claim to be born from the brain of the God-head". This social justice vision of the non-Brahmin leaders can be equated with saying of Alexander Pope. "That true self-love and social justice are the same", as the slaves in medieval India, they used to manage this.

Thus, the non-Brahmin movement had identified the cause for the oppression of the majority and targeted the Brahmins as the Historical exploiters of the Hindu society.

A significant innovation was made in the system of reservation by Sahu Maharaj, the ruler of Kohlapur in 1902 which can be marked as a Royal Benevolence to the *Sudhras.* But a systematic policy of reservation was ordered in 1920s by the British Rule in Madras Presidency. To this effect, the popularly effected non-Brahmin outfit, the Justice Party Government had issued the historical communal G.O. reserving jobs for a different communities. According to which, a unit of 12 positions should be distributed reserving five for non-Brahmins, 2 for Brahmins, 2 for Muslims, 2 for Anglo-Indian including Indian Christians and 1 for *Adi Dravidas.* By this, the Brahmins who constitute 3 percent of the population is getting 16 percent positions, Muslims with 20% populations gets 16% positions. This measures of the Madras Government of the Justice Party, though disproportionate, but it was widely welcomed for the reason that it was a great beginning – the first decisive victory which shatters the corner stone of historic, social despotism in the Hindu society. Therefore, the policy of communal reservation based on the concept of *'Protective*

Discrimination' was conceived and delivered as the social justice to counter the caste exploitations of the Hindu India[18].

It is, in this context that the study of Dr. B.R. Ambedkar *"Struggle for Equality and Self – Respect"* would help those people and communities those work themselves. But in Brahminical society discrimination played a predominant role to suppress the *Sudhras* without reasoning, but only on the basis of the caste system, who are still struggling for self-respect, human rights, in social-set up system by the Brahminical elite class. It has been rightly expressed by Ram Khobragade in the *First World Dalit Convention*, held in Malayasian Capital Kaula Lumpur on 10th & 11th October, 1918, organized by the *Dalit* International Organization and Indian Peoples Front of Malaysia, "I tried to explain this very written aspect of Dr. Ambedkar's '*Struggle for Equality and Self-Respect'* in my article, published in the Souvenir, released on that occasion. This small venture is the modification and enlargement of that article is very difficult to understand. I hope and wish all those communities and groups which were suffered by the Brahminical Ideology, they must struggle all over the world for humanitarian survival and discrimination – free society, would not miss an opportunity to study the life and teachings, of Dr. B.R. Ambedkar[19] which he achieved for the *Sudhras* in the Round Table Conferences.

It is a matter of great pleasures that the book on *Dr. B.R. "Ambedkar and His Writings', A Look For The New Generation"* is coming out in the final shape after the 'Round Table Conferences' in the history of India which was suppressed by the Indian historian without any reasoning, the cause and effective of the '*Round Table Conferences'* in the Indian society. Though, it has been delayed due to certain historical problems in the history of India, but the *Present* volume is decidedly different from the other books of the author which have already published in the context of public welfare in human society as 'Books Rule Over The World'. This volume also represents a broad spectrum of human rights giving substance to the rule of law i.e. was Dr. B.R. Ambedkar at that time from Heaven to

Earth, Brahmin disgraced him on the basis of *'untouchable'* having the ideals of a welfare state in his writings. He expressed in his writings. "A democracy which enslaves the working class, a class which is devoid of education during the time of Brahmins, which devoid means of life, which is devoid of any power of organization, which is devoid of intelligence is no democracy but a mockery of democracy".

• According to him, "A very definite made of political and administrative reservation policy was evolved and incorporated in the Republican Constitution of India 'after an ideological struggle was waged by Dr. B.R. Ambedkar during the freedom movement. His movement focused on different issues connected with the liberation of the oppressed section of the Hindu society. This revolt was not merely to obtain a few privileges for *Sudhras,* but more than that to take their rightful positions in the society[20].

No doubt, Dr. B.R. Ambedkar received letters containing threats of life[21], but he cooled down his head and wrote number of books which now are used for the discovery of the truth. His works, though may be contentions, debatable and controversial, but imperative towards social transformation of the society or to reconstruct it, i.e. to uphold the need for human dignity, equality and liberty, rights and civil facilities for under privileged class i.e. Brahmins, and this may be the gist of his social justice which alone according to him could lead to social harmony and social stability and kindle patriotic feelings of the '*Nam*' or *'God'*. He declared that '*untouchability*' is not only a system of unmitigated economic exploitation, but it is also a system of uncontrolled economic exploitation, i.e. because there is no independent public opinion to condemn it there is no impartial machinery of administration and restraint". Hence, he defined his social ideologies by saying "my social philosophy may be set to be enshrined in three words : Liberty, Equality and Fraternity[22]". It was also the slogan during the French Revolution took place in 1789, after a struggle for war was started in Europe for the *'Self – Respect and Self – Struggle'*;

Ambedkar's concerted debate on justice, equality, and fraternity reminds about the 'Social Justice Trinity' embodied in the Preamble of the Constitution of India in general. In order to remove social inequalities and to achieve the goal of social justice the communal reservation was built up in the constitution so as to permit *'Protective Discrimination'* in favour of certain castes and classes of persons which were subjected to historical injustice[23] called *Sudhras.*

On December 12th, 1935, he received the letter from Mr. Sant Ram, the Secretary of the *Jat Pat-Todal Mandal* (Society for the Breaking of Caste) of Lahore to preside over its Conference. The Presidential Address that Ambedkar wrote for it, has came down to us in the shape of the famous, thought-provoking classic, namely, *Annihilation of Caste.* In the *Annihilation of Caste,* he sought to destroy the very religious sanctity of the *Shastras* that gave religious sanction to the creation of castes and untouchability, but Brahmins were not ready to destroyed it, because they had their personal interest or self governing rule. Therefore, they were not ready to destroy them. Ambedkar's interest was that, he wanted to bring about a radical change in the Hindu society or in Hindu mind, these views were much to extreme to the *Arya Samajist Jat-Pat-Todak Mandal's* Ideology. Dr. Ambedkar, however, was not prepared to after his speech to suit the views of the organization "I have questioned the authority of the Mahatma whom they revere they hate me. To them I am a snake in their garden. The Mandal will, no doubt, be asked by the political-minded Hindus to explain why it was called me to fill this place of honour. It is an act of great daring. I shall not surprised if some political Hindus regard it as an insult like Mahatma Gandhi. This selection of mine stand cancell before the religious minded Hindus[24]", being an '*untouchable*'.

However, Ambedkar, published his work on *Annihilation of Caste,* in 1936. He distinguished the rules of religion and its principles and advocates the annihilation of the religion of rules.

He says, I do not know whether you draw a distinction between principles and rules. But I say that this distinction is real and important. Rules are practical and habitual ways of doing things are different, and the principles are intellectual ; they are useful methods of judging things. Rules seek to tell an agent just what course of action to purse Rules, like cooking recipes, do tell just what to do, and how to do it. A principle such as justice supplies a main trend through head by reference to which he is to consider the bearings of his desires and goal of life". This difference between rules and principles makes the acts done in pursuit of them in different quality and in content, it demonstrate the clear picture of the history and its progress. The principle may be wrong or right, but the act of conscionsness must be responsible for the development of the thought. To permit this responsibility, Religion must come into true form as God exist[25]".

He goes on to say, "Now, the Hindu religion as contained in the *Vedas* and the *Smirits*, is nothing, but a mass of sacrificial, societal, political and sanitary rules and regulations, all mixed up with non-culture of various gradients of the food and crops which does not look in the history of spiritualism, it is simple as human being. Thus, the religion should be truly universal which accommodate all the races of the countries, and classes under one rule that is *'Nam-Dana'* for the development of the life and its objective[26].

In May, 1936, Dr. B.R. Ambedkar addressed and her important Conference, in Bombay, when he delivered his well known speech on *Mukti Kon Pathe*? (Which Way To Emancipation?) In the Course of the speech, he stoutly vindicated his resolve for conversion. Defining the term "religion" as "that which holds the people together[27]", he said that was the real definition of religion" which I have already discussed *'Nam-Dana'* from the Prefect Master not from the Brahmins. Prefect Master comes through historical evidence, not in ordinary ways like the theory of Brahmin. 'Religion' itself is a meaning an obligation imposed on mind from the Father side during the process of the child. Then (perhaps raising his voice) he said, 'The religion which does not recognize the individuality of man, is not acceptable to me[28]".

After the *Mukti* speech, Ambedkar wrote and spoke on several occasions on Buddhism and allied matters. I shall, however, confine myself to only a few of them, to indicate the direction in which his mind was working for the welfare of state as well as for the public. Important among them, to my mind are as under:

1. The article he contributed to the *Maha Bodhi* of May, 1950;
2. The speeches, he delivered at Delhi, in 1950;
3. At Colombo, on the 6th June, 1950;
4. At Worli, Bombay, on the 14th January, 1951;
5. At Delhi, on the 20th May, 1951;
6. At Bombay, on the 27th May, 1953
7. At Rangoon, on the 4th December, 1954.
8. At Dehu Road, on the 25th December, 1954, and
9. At Bombay on 14th January, 1955.

In the course of these speeches, he reiterated the need of religion for human society but on scientific basis. Otherwise society cannot exist without morality and law. He believed that the religion of humanity like *'Radha Soami'*, discussed by Rabindernath, Tagore in his book *"Boundless Sky"* will come to the society as a 'New Religion' or Thought for the welfare of public in the world as a 'Universal Religion'. It must be founded on the principles of Liberty, Equality and Fraternity. Every true religion, if it is going to serve humanity, will have to declare as a 'good religion', disparity always creates problems as Brahmin do. The modern world needs beautiful religion, beautiful race, beautiful thought, because, it came from the poverty stricken society of the polluted Brahmins. Buddhism is the religion of the intellectual *Chamars* and other class of the *Sudhras* which spells out its social, economic and political objectives. Buddhism or *Chamaristic* thought in Sanskrit called *Charmakara* fulfils the need of the modern world[29].

Buddhism or *Chamarist* rejects the Hindu doctrine of *Chatur varnya* which started by Gandhi in India, just as it rejects the belief in *God, soul* and the *Vedas*. Buddhism or *Chamarism*, as the religion of the intellectual, does not believe in idol worship. As the religion of the rationalist, Buddhism gives even individual *Self-Respect* and *Self-Struggle*, but the liberty to examine every thing in the light of reasoning[30], but is the logic of the *Chamar* in History.

The Buddha or *'Nam'*, says to Dr. Ambedkar, was the only founder of a religion who claimed no more *Self-Respect*, but for the generation who developed from Him. Though, he was an ordinary man of his time, but he opened the doors of his religion to all, without irrespective of race, caste, and sex. He did not claim to be God ; he claimed to be only a *'Marga- Data'*(one who should the way). His religion was based on his self-respect, thought and experience of the *'Nam-Dana'* obtaining from his *'Spiritual Guru'*, already mentioned above. He expressly told his followers to believe for the welfare of the society and yourself, but he urged them to examine it for themselves[31].

In 1950, he again said the time had come to decide when people should distinguish Brahminism from Buddhism. The time was getting ripe for conversion. It was, but natural for Dr. B.R. Ambedkar to ask the question : 'What is the object of conversion?" And he replied : Our aim is to gain freedom from the Brahminical thought. We are not interest in anything else, at the moment. If we can gain freedom by conversion from Hinduism to *'Radha Soami'* why should we shoulder the responsibility of reforming the Hindu religion, because the Hindu religion is meant for dogs. The object of our struggle in our liberation from Hinduism, and not reform of Hinduism[32].

Such, in effect of the above study, it shows that Dr. B.R. Ambedkar approach to the problem of conversion to Buddhism or *Chamarist* approach : Pragmatic *ab inttio* in *History* as well as in other social sciences of the society. There was nothing extraterrestrial on this earth, or supre-mundane, or transcendental about it. It was a down-to-earth, healthy, robust, rational, enlightened, scientific, cultured in Brahminical society by defeating them with the stroke of pen. Therefore, pen is mighter than the sword in human approach to overcome the problems in positive manner, who an 'untouchable' of India crushed the Brahmanism not in Round Table Conferences, but also in India, by drafting the Constitution of India as a law for everybody. As, it feels that nobody is above the 'Law' which Ambedkar has given the analysis of the law in scientific way to govern the society and till date Brahmin could not understand the 'Spirit of Law' which never dies. He always lives in Heaven and watch the activities of the man from the distance. Therefore one must have to adopt such type of self-respect and self-governing approach in life to realize the goal of life in human history.

Notes and References

1. Rare Preface, Edited by Bhagwan Das ; *Bheem Patrika* Jalandhar, 1980. pp. 26-7.
2. Reprinted a copy of *Gautam Bhuddache Charita*, Buddhist Welfare Society. Nagpur. 1982.
3. Isaac A. Eekiel : *Kabir, the Great Mystic.* pp. 6,7.
4. *Ibid.* pp. 10,11.
5. Dr. B.R. Ambedkar ; *Annihilation of Caste.* Aurangabad; Reprint; 2003.
6. M. Phil. Dissertation '*Women and Sudhras* under *the Hindu Law.* Anjali Saraf. 1985. University of Jammu.
7. Manu Smriti, VII, 413-414.
8. *Ibid.* IX. – 417
9. *Ibid.* VIII – 416.
10. B.G. Ramesh ; *Op. Cit.* pp. 29-30.
11. *Ibid.* p. 28.
12. Manusmriti XIII ; pp. 354-358.
13. Dr. B.R. Ambedkar; *Who Were the Sudhras?* Aurangabad ; Reprint ; 2003.

14. K.N. Kadani ; Currents & Counter – Currents.
15. B.R. Ambedkar ; *Castes in India.* p. 19.
16. M.F. Ganjre (Ed.); Dr. Babasaheb *Ambedkaranchi Bhashne.* Vol. VI. pp. 132-139. (Marathi)
17. Dr. B.R. Ambedkar ; *The Buddha and His Dhamma.* Nagpur; 1997. *Introduction.*
18. P. Jagdeeshan; *Social Justice and Challenges in Contemporary India.* Bangalore, 2006. Indian Council of Historical Research. pp. 2,3,4,5-6. A Lecture Series.
19. Ram Khobragade ; *Dr. Ambedkar, A symbol of Global Socio-Political Revolution ;* New Delhi, 2005. pp. III. IV My View Point.
20. P. Jagadeeshan ; *Op. Cit.* pp. 6-7.
21. Surendra Ajnat, *Letters of Ambedkar ;* Jalandhar, 1993. p. 8. **Note.** The letters of the threat now became on historical research for the historian as their duty to find out the 'reality' where it stands in human history.
22. P. Jagadeeshan ; *Op. Cit.* p. 7.
23. *Ibid.* p. 8.
24. Dr. B.R. Ambedkar; *Annihilation of Caste* ; Aurangabad; Reprint 2003. p. 19.
25. *Ibid.* pp. 72,73.
26. *Ibid.*
27. Bhagawan Das (Ed.) *Thus Spoke Ambedkar* Vol. IV, p. 25.
28. *Ibid.* p. 26.
29. M.F. Ganjre (Ed) ; Dr. *Babasaheb Ambedkaranchi Bhashane.* Vols. 1 toVI.
30. *Ibid.* Vol. 1. p. 190.
31. *Ibid.* Vol. II. p. 166.
32. Bhagwan Das (Ed.); *Thus Spoke Ambedkar,* Vol. IV. p. 47.

5

A Noble Features of Ambedkar's Scheme in Indian History

(1947 to 1956 A.D.)

Crystallization Methods of the Indian Society After the Death of Dr. B.R. Ambedkar

This chapter deals with noble scheme of Ambedkar's life is, indeed to crystallization of Indian society after his death in 1956 A.D. The culmination and consummation of his experiences in his life, experiments and endeavours during the five hectic decades for his heroic struggle for the upliftment of the poor people from the bad clutches of the *'Brahminical Ideology'*, he emancipated of his people to work for the society for the welfare of the mankind. His socio-political philosophy and activity in writings and speeches, as well as his zeal to reformulate the socio-religious ideology throughout these years, are to our anlaysis, but the two sides of the same coin[1]. In the history, we learn, the struggle for freedom of man is as old as humanity. Man lives to be happy through unrestricted, continuous and creative enfoldment of his personality. He brought society into existence to make a co-operative endeavour for the attainment of this aim. It is not yet established, it was established during the primitive society of the man. We can, however, say that the formation of a tribe was necessary at that time to find out the good and bad in human history. It was necessary at that time that a tribe of man may must face the hostile forces with good manner as Dr. B.R. Ambedkar faced. In primeval human societies the law of the tribe was supreme in human form. All tribes men were brothers, but those outside it, they must be punished with harsh treatment. However, limited in scope, tribal philosophy proved an useful instrument as Dr. B.R. Ambedkar's as an untouchable making man freer than, he was as savage[2].

No doubt, in ancient Greek, a high standard of culture was established and conceived the lofty ideal of democracy for the first-time in the history of human and same is the concept has been launched by Ambedkar in Indian society by establishing the rule of the 'Law' through 'Constitution of India'. But, it was very unfortunate that the Greek society was divided into two parts patricians and plebeians. In the city states of Hellenes very few enjoyed the fruits of democracy, a vast majority suffered the humiliation of slavery as *Scheduled Castes* and *Scheduled Tribes* in Indian society, women like *Sudhras* were also deprived of franchise and given an inferior status[3] in the society.

The human society is a dynamic organization as Ambedkar played a dynamic role in the human society by defeating the Brahmins and 'Reserved' the seats for the *Sudhras* in the Round Table Conferences. Therefore, in course of time when sufficient progress was registered in the philosophy of tribalism or Schedule Caste Status to satisfy advanced individuals or be of value of humanity. Its ideals and principles were not only inadequate for the purpose of the development of the society but to come to aware the race for the rightful purpose to serve the society as a welfare state, in course of time, they also became positive in their thought and behaviour, in which the progress of the man could not be stop. As we have been observed from the spread of Buddhism, Christianity *'Islam*, etc. as it was the religion of the tribal. All religions claims except Hinduism to abolish distinction between man to man without irrespective of nationality, colour or caste, but rigidity is there in fellow-feeling this is the cordial principle i.e. *Nam* or *Chamar* on which they stand the society on the pattern of 'New Thought' as a 'New Society'. The innumerable gods of the vary concept have been born from the *'Nam* or *Chamar*', yielded place to the one supreme authority of monotheism taught by the world religion, after the death of the saint, it became a separate state and its logic stand false. With their inspiration large states were created and a big empire is founded[4] of the S*udhra* Family including all sections of the society as 'One Society of the *Nam or God* on earth.'

No doubt, the discoveries and inventions in different branches of sciences have been made and brought unprecedent economic prosperity to the world as a natural phenomena of the *'Nam'*, whenever it was establish in this kingdom, there is development in the society. After the development of the number of states 'law' destroy it and establish various boundaries between nation to nation. But during the development of the national thought, the boundaries of nations again destroy, and mingled races unknown to each other before this, they talk through the '*Nam'* or God for the establishment of Imperlistic approach in history to unite the man. They are called the friends of *'Nam'* from Heaven to Earth. They just come to fight against the social evils, what is more to say, the sciences of superstitions, and cherished beliefs which are based without reasoning only to show off the man. One after the other orthodox religious States like Pakistan, China and India, no longer able to withstand as a 'One Country' under the new idea of the God, only it was took place during the time of *Sudhra* family, because their idea is based on unity not integrity as Brahmin did. Therefore, there is a crisis in the human mind in this continent. The French Encyclopedists took up this challenge during the time of French Revolution in 1789 beg the labour class against the privilege class and solved it by rejecting the supernatural authority in mundane affairs and by deciding to defect the communal forces of the *'Nam'*, who occupied the throne of French without reasoning and human problem was there. They introduced the secular ideal of the State. "Liberty, Equality and Fraternity" became the symbols of the French Revolution which owned the philosophy of the Encyclopaedists. The modern world was born[5] in Europe.

Tussle Between Religion and Secularism

It has been seen and observed through the study that world is going to conflict between the Religious forces and the Secularism which could not understand by the modern historians about its logic and the blind faith of the religious force have been vigorously resisting. The advancement of the secularism without scientific approach is uncertain in their study. They false forces called *'Brahman Rakashas' or 'Modern Politicians'* governed the society with false propaganda by wearing clothes, hairstyles, and other symbol like black or white caps on the head. A religious state can be created and maintained through Absolute Power of the *'Nam'* or God and the messes of the God. And, the messes of the God must follow and command over the messengers. The ideal of liberty, equality and fraternity, is an anti-thesis of the religious outlook as simple as democracy. Democracy and secularism go hand to hand; one cannot exist without the other, they are inter-independent Brahmin cannot understand it, it is the wonder of the God. In proportion to the element of religious thinking in the political philosophy of a State, it falls short of the ideal of democracy and freedom which still awaiting after 1947, in India. The people have been cursed by the fraud religious groups by identifying self-style symbol of the religion which are based on false propaganda's of the *Brahmin's* or *Molavis.* All those countries which own a state of religion or are influenced by religious principles in the conduct of public affairs virtually live in medieval period under the *Sudhra* rules, like *Akbar, Shah Jahan, Jahangir,* etc. and can not benefit by all the achievements of science and philosophy to the Brahmincial rulers, they were prepared against the *Sudhras* in different forms like Sikh, *Rajputs, Nawab, Peshwas*, etc. and were prepared to kill them to their the lost states. Therefore, with the passage of time, the religious forces of the different states. They suppressed *the Sudhras* as a degraded class of the society called *'untouchables'* and there was the diminishing the concept of *Sudhra* state neither democracy nor justice was establish for theme by the fraudulent saints called Guru, and the result was that the minorities are doomed to live as sub-servant people of the '*Nam*' or God; who can not enjoy the freedom of the independence which was declared in 1947 and they were allowed to live away from majority community[6].

It has also been seen from the early history of the man that these was a sharp struggle between the two forces i.e. reactionary and progressive one and this struggle is still going on in the life of man. In the onward march of humanity, peoples in different parts of the world have been witnessed occasional setbacks but the final victory have been took place of the truth as a new revolutionary force. This is the fundamental principles of the law of evolution in human history. French Revolution which was took place in 1789, having indicated the same idea, as it was based on religious state of politics of the privilege class like Brahmins in India, replaced by secularity in Europe and North America. Those nations which still adhere to the out model theory remain stunted in growth and continued to live in the back waters of history called *Sudhras*. But sooner or later they are bound to undergo an intellectual revolution, abandon they religious outlook and follow the path of progress[7].

Jinnah's Testament on Unscientific Method

In this chapters, it is important to note that *Jinnah's* testament during this period was unscientific, because his idea of dividing the Indian sub-continent was conceived on purely religious ground or 'egoistic' approach in history. The Muslim League leaders were also relentlessly fought for the creation of a Muslim state for over a decade, but when ultimately the long cherished desire of *Mohammed Ali Jinnah*, made a startling declaration about political philosophy which should guide to modern Muslims. Addressing the inaugural session of the Pakistan Constituent Assembly on 14 August, 1947, he observed. "If you work in a spirit of co-operation, forgetting the past and burying the hatchet, I will say that everyone of you no matter to what community you belong, no matter you colour, caste and creed, is first second and last a citizen of the state with equal rights, privileges and obligations.

You are free to go to your temples, and to your places to worship in the state of Pakistan while you belong to any religion, caste or creed, that has nothing to do with the business of the state". (emphasis mine)

He again added:

"We are starting the state with no discrimination, no distinction between one community and another, between caste or creed. We are starting with this fundamental principle that we are all citizens and equal citizens of one state i.e. *Kashmir*. We shall keep that in front of us as our ideal Hindus will cease to be Hindus and Muslim will cases to be Muslims, not in the religious sense because that is a personal faith with which individual like Dr. B.R. Ambedkar has, but in the political sense as citizens of the Nation".

From the propounder of two – nation theory who persistently advocated religion as the basis of nationality these words are revealing. It is the denial of the ideal for the acceptance of which *Jinnah* fought indefatigably through the most active part of his life to create Pakistan. Yet modernist as he was in spirit, he could not help seeing at the end of the struggle that secularism and not religious outlook would make the people of Pakistan happy and prosperous. It is a different matter that these valuable conclusions of the illustrious founder were cast to the winds by his successors. But there is reason to believe that had Jinnah lived longer the story of Pakistan,

Gandhi was the problem created in the human history might have been altogether a different one i.e. Dr. B.R. Ambedkar.

Secularism and Kashmir

A study of the Kashmir chronicles painstaking recorded by indigenous historians which were born for a period of five thousand years[8] before, affords ample evidence to construction the history of Kashmir between the period of progress and reaction, because two forces at that time will be on crucial point as a deciding factor of the authentic history. Broadly speaking, evolutionary processes from savagery to tribalism called *Sudhras* or Scheduled Castes, rule will be establish in Kashmir which they have losted in their own history. During the partition of India, Ambedkar has rightly expressed : "India has lost her freedom only owing to treason of her own people. Raja Dahir of Sindh was defeated by Mohammed Bin Qasim. The only reason for this defeat was that the generals of the Sindh army took bribes from Qasim's men and did not fight for the King. It was Raja Jai Chand of India who invited Mohemmed Ghori to fight against Prithviraj. When Shivaji was fighting for the freedom of the Hindus, other Maratha Leaders and Rajputs were fighting against the Britishers, their leader did nothing. Such things should not happen again, therefore, every one must resolve to fight to the last drop of his blood, to defend the freedom of India[9], then to the establishment of a religious state as an authentic history will be establish and finally the secularization idea of Ambedkar's politic are similar to those that have taken place in other parts of the subcontinent like China and Pakistan. But there have been certain noteworthy trends in the culture of the *Sudhra* history, after the downfall of the *Sudhra,* nobody can dare to establish a peaceful era in all over the world, because *Kashmir* is dear to *Sudhras* and they are the real ruler of the Kashmir. After the downfall of the *Sudhra* dynasty from the Kashmiri thinkers evolved philosophical thinking on the doctrines of Buddha or *'Nam'* or *Chamar* or *Chandala* as mentioned in the Kalhana *Rajatarangini*, it is also known to *Trika* Shastra. Essentially an idealistic philosophy of the world, it does not altogether deny the objective reality of the world as does the *Vedanta* and the *Mayavada* of *Shankara* have expressed in their volume. All writers on *Trika Shastra* have stressed that as a system of philosophy and as an applied science in every concept of the life in all human beings without distinction of creed, colour or sex[10]. Therefore, the philosophy of secularism have been rightly expressed by, Dr. B.R. Ambedkar in the '*Indian Constitution*'. He has given an advance idea in human history to the *Sudhra* section of the society for their development and welfare.

It has been observed from the eighth to the fourteenth century for the last hundred years, as it is reflected in the *Trika Sastra*, that *Trika* guided the Kashmiri's in shaping their personal lives as also the public affairs as Ambedkar did in the Round Table Conference to protect the rights of all human beings in History of India in London on the basis of secularism and caste free society. Election of rulers and disposition of bad monarchs are not unknown to Kashmir history, because forefather of Ambedkar, they used to live in Kashmir as their original home in the shape of *Nam* or God 'Low Caste' or 'Untouchables' have long history in Kashmir even men born out of their race become the wedlock of the '*Nam*' by dint of hard labour as *Cooli* do and intelligence held high office in the state and reached peaks of glory, when they establish their rule in Kashmir in Indian history. No doubt, it was their long struggle against the criminal forces like *Brahmins* or *Molavis*. As stated earlier, women were afforded, opportunity to distinguish themselves in many fields of social activity[11], it has been already discussed in the '*History of the Chamar Dynasty*', written by the same author.

As, it appears that Muslims captured the power in 1339 A.D. during the rule of Sultan Shams'd din in Kashmir and the Hindu Rule came to an end. The Hindu rulers did not lose the country as a result of any foreign invasion[12] of the *'Nam'* or God. The founder of Religious Humanism, *Lal Ded*, was a Brahmin. Her most distinguished disciple or scholar was *Nand Rishi*, a Muslim. He is still a small kid known as Deepit Raj son of Dr. Raj Kumar, the fact is that both of them are equally owned and held in high esteem by Hindus and Muslims and the Chinese should suffice to testify of the non-communal essence of the philosophy i.e. *'Nam'* or God. The two leaders, taught love of all human beings without irrespective of birth, caste or sex and equality of all men and women. As already stated, after the *Nand Rishi* his chief disciples organized an order of religious, humanists known as Rishis of the *'Nam'* not of the Brahmin background but they were the *Sudhras* or *Chandalas.* In his memoirs Jahangir wrote of them that "They possess simplicity and are without pretence. They abuse no one. The restrain the tongue of desire and the foot of the seeking. They eat no flesh, they have no wives, and always, plant fruit bearing trees in fields so that men may benefit by them, themselves desiring no advantage".

Nand Rishi is the patron saint of the Kashmir Valley; his teachings heavily influenced by Trika philosophy exert tremendous authority on the intellectual life of the Kashmiri Muslims.

During the five centuries of Muslim rule, Kashmir Hinduism also went throgh transformation and changed in complexion, because no such *Sudhra* born at that time to balance the new synthesis of Kashmir culture into '*untouchables*', which have been established a broad based concept in history. The rule of *Sudhras* was characterized by respect for the dignity of man, love of all human beings, tolerance for dissent, peaceful pursuit of happiness and hatred for cruelty and bloodshed through natural calamity.

With a few exceptions, the Muslim Sultans generally followed the cardinal principles of Religious Humanism as Dr. B.R. Ambedkar keeps in his memory to accommodate all the religions in one term i.e. called *Buddha* or *'Nam'* in different language to govern the society. Sikandar Sultan of Kashmir, no doubt, attempted to build up a new state of Religion depending on orthodox *Shariat* called *'Nam'* or God, but he was only successful in creating turmoil and disaffection, and the rest of the work done by his son Zain-ul-Abidin, when he obtained the education from the Amir Timur. He was a stunch believer in equality of all human beings before law without irrespective of caste, colour and creed. By implementing the philosophy of Religious Humanism in administrating the state, he ushered in a golden era in the valley of Kashmir and is known as Bud Shah (Great Monarch of the *Nam*[14]).

Secularisation in State Politics

As we know, that Kashmir has a noble cultural heritage, that Buddha was also born there, but Indian scholars could not explore his life properly, the threshold of modern scientific age when the British imperialists sold the Kashmir valley to Maharaja Gulab Singh in 1846. So far as the people were concerned the sale proved to be a mixed blessing i.e. God and Man. Modernism was, no doubt, introduced in education and statecraft but by getting closely associated with the Indian politics, particularly the development in the Punjab, and Kashmiri imperceptibly imbibed some element of religious bigotry, however, alien it was to their nature and temperament. So when the movement for the achievement of freedom and social democracy was launched in the early thirties, it took a communal turn. In 1932, the Kashmir Muslim Conference was founded to end the absolute rule of the Dogras i.e. God and man, and set-up a responsible government of the people in its place. For seven years state politics were deeply coloured by religion and a gulf separated the Muslims from the non-Muslims. Fortunately, the leaders of the movement realized before it was too late that religious approach to politics could not lead the people to their destination. In June 1939, an event of historic significance took place when Muslim Conference was converted into National Conference which was meant to be a representative distinction of creed or sex[15].

Thus, the secularization of state politics was effected by the influential Muslim leaders (173 delegates in the special session of the Muslim Conference out of 176 voting for it) without any outside interference, it was self-style Conference. It is nothworthy to say that there leaders were mostly *Schedule Tribes*, among those who passionately pleaded for the change were Sheikh Mohammed Abdullah, Chowdhari Ghulam Abbas and Mirza Afzal Beg. Induced by their own independent thinking born from the background of the same as Dr. B.R. Ambedkar and personal experience made in the political field for seven years, the leaders felt convinced that to make the religion as a basis in politics, it would hinder the national growth and frustrate the people as we see in the modern politics, most of the rulers they use the religion as an instrument in the politic for their own benefit. What followed proved the freedom forces were strengthened a conflict arosed between the Hindus and the Muslims on the idea of Gandhi and Jinnah and the autocratic rule of the process culminated in the upheaval of 1947, when at the time of independence of the subcontinent the country was divided into two part i.e. India and Pakistan; and Kashmir confronted with the choice of acceding either secularist India or the Islamic state of Pakistan. It was a vexing issue and a choice either ways would be seat with many difficulties[16]. India put this matter of Kashmir before U.N.O. On the request of this organization, India acted as President of supervisory Neutral commission in Korea and Indo-China. She also tried for communist China's membership of U.N.O. India also opposed the aggressive activities of Britain and France and took every step for the establishment of world peace through United Nations Organization. Undoubtedly there were some handicaps before this organization. However, it was achieved success in solving many problems and establishing peace in the world[17]. Yet the

National Conference, under the guidance of its top-most leader, Sheikh Abdulla, after a careful consideration, decided that Kashmir will form a part of India. Backed by the support of the State's premier political organization, the Maharaja ratified through his accredited representative, the instrument of accession as required under the provisions of the Independence Act, of 1947. It however, needed ratification by the state people of Jammu and Kashmir on the Scientific study of the *'Nam'* or *'God'*.

Nineteen Year's Experience of Sheikh Abdulla with Dr. B.R. Ambedkar

Indian leaders frequently asserted the Kashmir issue that it is the symbol of Indian secularism. On 17 September 1953, Jawaharlal Nehru presented a view point in the history of India, "We have always regarded the Kashmir problem as a symbolic for us, as it has far – reaching consequences in India. Kashmir is symbolic as it illustrates that we are a secular state, that Kashmir with a large majority of Muslim, have nevertheless of its own free will wished to be associated with India. Kashmir has consequences both India and Pakistan because if we disposed of Kashmir on the basis of the old two-nation theory obviously millions of people in India and millions in East Pakistan would be powerfully affected. Many of the wounds that had healed might open out again".

An impartial observer can recognize the validity of this statement that Kashmir is a part of India. In fairness, however, it should be conceded that undismayed Brahminical forces partititionized the country and uphold the banner of the secularism, Indian adopted a constitution which is free from sectarian bias and religions prejudice, believes in the sovereignty and dignity of the individual lies in the constitution, has faith in social democracy and affords full opportunities to the Indian people to abandon the medieval outlook of the constitution and enter the modern scientific age. Sheikh Abdullah succincty assessed the value of the Indian Constitution with the company of Dr. B.R. Ambedkar during the national movement, he addressed the Kashmir Constituent Assembly on 5 November, 1951, for the benefit of his followers thus: "The real character of a state is revealed it its Constitution. The Indian Constitution has set before the country the goal of secular democracy based upon justice, freedom and equality for all without distinction. This is the bedrock of modern democracy. This should meet the argument that the Muslims of Kashmir cannot have security in India where the large majority of population are Hindus. Any unnatural cleavage between religions groups is the legacy of imperialism, and no modern state can afford to encourage artificial divisions if it is to achieve progress prosperity. The Indian Constitution has amply and finally repudiated the concept of a religious state, which is a throwback to medievalism, by guaranteeing the equality of rights of all citizens irrespective of their religion, colour, caste and class. The national movement in our state naturally gravitates towards these principles which seems to favour against another. This affinity in political principles as well as in past associations and over common path of suffering in the cause of freedom, must be weighed properly while deciding the future of the state[18] i.e. *Sudhra* Caste.

The Glaring Contrast

It is true in the statement of Indra Gandhi that the Indians have at times failed to live upto the high ideals and grand principles enshrined in the Constitution. In the public speech on 5 February, 1967, she regretted "that despite all the provisions in the Constitution, we have not done all we could for the Muslims and other minorities[19]".

There have been occasion when the Indian Parliament and the Union Government have exhibited strong tendencies of narrow – mindedness and intolerance towards the *Scheduled Castes* and *Scheduled Tribes* by the upper caste Hindus and Muslims against them and towards his leader Dr. B.R. Ambedkar, etc. But, all in all, endeavours are constantly made to be fair to non-Hindu minorities and firm measures taken to control the erring members or sections of the society through constitution which have been made by Baba Sahib Ambedkar, they behave unlawfully or mischieveously in the Parliament House. Whether in the Union Cabinet, the Government of the states or the local administration persons of all the communities are more or less adequately represented and afford opportunity to rise the *Sudhras* in accordance with their talent and capacity of work physically and mentally.

The Vice-President of India, Dr. Zakir Hussain is a Muslim who is a prospective candidate which was not like by the Hindus and likely choice for President-ship when the highest – office falls vacant in May 1967. The Muslims have adorned the offices of Governors of states, Judges of High Courts and the Supreme Court : they have functioned as trusted ambassadors, secretaries, departmental heads and other responsible officers in the centre as well as in different units of the Indian Republic from the background of *Sudhra* family, before that there was no *Sudhra* employ in the centre sectariate.

In striking contrast to this, the Pakistan leaders on the other hand failed for a decade in One; attempted after another to frame a constitution for this country. Ignoring the landable nations expressed by M.A. Jinnah in his opening address to Pakistan Constitution Assembly, 'the men who came to power in Pakistan rejected secularism outrightly and laboured to lay the foundation of a Religious state, till date there is problem in the history of Pakistan'. Religion is conspicuously present in every part of the Constitution and it is not surprising that Muslim Divines have an effective say in the conduct of public affairs[20], now at present there is bloodshed in the country, it proves that their, Religion stands no where, it is problem of 'ego' among themselves, where as the theory of nature stands in '*Infinite*', as we have expressed in the previous chapter of this volume.

Despotism in Azad Kashmir

In the study, we learn that inequality of people is inherent in a Religious state of mind people and non-Muslim can never expect equality from Pakistan and non-Hindu from India. The unfair treatment of minorities is the full evidence, their interest are unsafe in the hands of these communal forces, therefore, there is no other alternative to predict the History of the *Sudhras* which have been based on historical truth that Dr. B.R. Ambedkar was the right man at that time in his opinion in the Indian Round Table Conference of 1940 and declared, "we feel that nobody can remove our grievances as well as we can, and we can not remove them, unless we get political power in our own hands. I am afraid that the Depressed Classes have a waited tool long for the time to work a miracle. It is not sufficiently realized by the communal forces that in the present temper of the country is based on Religious minded people, no constitution will be workable which is not acceptable to the majority of the people, what it has the Spirit of Divine Power of control the system. The time when you were to choose and India was to accept is gone; will return in another from like Baba Gurinder Singh ji. Let the consent of the people and not the accident of logic be the touch stone of your New Constitution, if you desire that it should be worked[21]".

The Constituent Assembly, before coming to the decisive part that Dr. B.R. Ambedkar played a very dynamic role in the making of the Constitution of Republican India, it is imperative to make briefly some observations on the crucial role, he played as an able philosopher, in the political restructuring of India. For, soon after the Government of Indian Act, 1935, came into force, the agonizing problem of partition of India was lurking in the minds of Indian leaders along with M.A. Jinnah. At this juncture, Dr. B.R. Ambedkar, India's frontline scholar and thinker, bent his energies to grapple with the problem. In 1940, he published his *Thoughts on Pakistan*, the most thought provoking book, on the subject. Subsequently, in 1945, he brought out its second revised and enlarged edition under the title '*Pakistan or the Partition of India*. There was no other book to match with Dr. Ambedkar" candid and fearless presentation of facts and argument Even Gandhi and Jinnah cited Dr. Ambedkar's book as an authority on the subject during their crucial talks[22] with the leaders of the Indian society, unfortunately his effort was failed. Finally, Pakistan unabashedly took to the "Free" state of Religion and its protective wings treating it like a dependency ; a joint secretary of the Central Government is functioning as the over lord-ship as Brahmin do in the authorities at his sweet will without ascertaining the wishes of the people. The unceremonious expulsion of K.H. Khurshied from the President-ship of Azad Kashmir in 1964 and his imprisonment for supporting "Independent Kashmir" move bears, testimony to this fact[23] that he was not the real son of the Father, he was the Brahmin by nature. Remarkably, earlier for our two years, the victimized politician in the shape of Dr. Raj Kumar had been boosted by the Father as the head of Azad Kashmir chosen by an elected advisory board of Kashmiri people of the '*Nam*' which use to live in Heaven work from the distance as a Supernatural Force of the Father for the welfare of the *Shudras* which were degraded by the Brahmins during their rule. Now the time has come to settle the score with them as a human being, but as a degraded man on this earth.

The Deciding Factor of the Kashmir

Babasaheb had a strong belief that human society cannot exist without '*LAW*', and without *Dhamma* or *Nam -Dana.* Lawlessness spells anarchy, and anarchy is the negation of the principles of Justice, Liberty, Equality and Fraternity. Again, he believed that *LAW*, if it is to sub-serve human interest, must be founded on reason or science, for a dictotomy between reason and science, on the one hand, and morality, ethics and *Dhamma*, and its implementation must be strong in the life, is, I believe, bound to have disastrous consequences, as any student of the world history would be able to tell Dr. B.R. Ambedkar, therefore, raised his entire *Socio-ethnic-legal-dhammic* structure on rationalism, humanism and science[24].

The work done by Dr. B.R.Ambedkar as the principal architect of the Constitution of the Republic of India, was undoubtedly of first rate importance to the nation as a whole and then to the world. He was the great philosopher of world with the knowledge and wisdom, he defeated the communal forces at that time, when he designed the Constitutional framework on the principles of Justice, Liberty, Equality and Fraternity. He attached considerable importance to these fundamental concepts. "My philosophy", he said, 'may be said to be enshrined in these three words ; Liberty, Equality, and Fraternity. Elaborating these principles, he said that his philosophy had its roots in the teachings of the *Buddha* as we already discussed above. Further, he said that though, in his philosophy, liberty and equality; even he was '*untouchable*' belonged to the *Sudhra* family, and absolute Equality left no room for liberty. Again, he gave the highest place to Fraternity; as the only real safeguard against the denial of Liberty or Equality[25].

It would not be possible, within the narrow compass of this Introduction, to give an exhaustive survey of the Constitution. Let us skip over the letter of the Law; and come to the valedictory address Babasaheb delivered to the Constituent Assembly, on November 17,1949, in the following words; "Will history repeat itself ? It is this thought which fills me with anxiety. This anxiety is deepened by the realization of the fact that in addition to our old enemies i.e. Brahmin in the form of Castes and Creeds, we are going to have many political parties with diverse and opposing political creeds. Will Indians place the country, above their creed as original rulers of the '*Nam*' or will they place creed above country? i.e. '*Nam*' or *Chamar*, I do not know. But this much is certain that if the parties place creed above country, over independence will be put in jeopardy to the Brahmins, a second time and probably be lost for even. This eventually we must all resolutely guard our force against them to protect the interest of the Father. We must be determined to defend our independence with the last drop of our blood". (Shiva Rao '*Word*' The Framing of Indian's Constitution, pp. 935-36).

The Historic Choice of India

Term *India* which has been given by the Britishers during their rule in India, composed of two words In+dia as the dialecte of every language compose in the local language of the man as it was composed by the Britisher called *Nam*. *In* stands for within the body ; and *dia* means *light* which *Brahmins* could not understand the historic meaning of the term *India*. It has been well said by Mrs. Annie Besant that *Sudhras* are the forefather of the Britishers, they learned this idea from the Mughals and became the followers of Ravidas *Chamar* by caste, but actually he was the Prophet of God at that time. People from the same country, they ignore the philosophy of *Sudhras* which is very unfortunate for them and they suppressed them without any reasoning and logic, they did not work for the society. Therefore, the history of the Brahmins and *Molavis* is culprit or inhuman, those work for the welfare of the state, they were suppressed by them and Dr. B.R. Ambedkar was harshed and degraded by them at the crucial movement of the History, partitionization of India was took place and communal forces formed their Government. It is an irony of the history that by a combination of fortuitous circumstances a tying nation of Kashmir has been placed in a position of great importance that whole culture of the world has been reflected from this place either, there was *Ashoka, Kushana, Guptas, Chamars*, etc. developed their philosophy all over the world. The communal forces of the period without reasoning and logic, they marred the future career of so many innocent people of the Father. The Kashmiri ruler have to make a truly historic choice in natural way to evolute the society from one generation to another Civilization. India can help them to make it wisely by trying to understand their feelings, sentiments and aspirations, i.e., '*Nam*', by allaying their fears and suspicious, and, above all, by redeeming the pledges given to the Brahminical society for the time being to develop the history, as it has been clearly mentioned in the Indian Constitution. An awareness of the history choice *Sudhras* before the Kashmiris must have been upper most in the mind of Gandhiji when he said during the trying times following partition : "My sole hope and prayer is that Kashmir should become a beacon light to the benighted subcontinent[27]", i.e., '*Untouchable*' or God.

Problem Cannot be Ignored

It is futile to go on stressing *Kashmir* is a part of India, unless and until the evidence of *'New Kashmir'* like the history of *Sudhra* or *Chamar* does not come to existence in the front the billion Kashmiri. Again, as regards, the argument advanced by defenders of the *Status quo*, saying that, in a secular state, the state has no business to meddle with the personal law of any religions component like Muslims and Hindus. Justice Gajendragadkar says: 'The Hindu code is revolutionary in the sense that it seeks to secularise the personal law of the Hindus[28]", which is not suitable to Dr. B.R. Ambedkar, therefore, he adopted the Buddhism, because Hindu has no history, which we already mentioned in the volume and elsewhere.

Let us now once again turn to the Dr. B.R. Ambedkar's deeper philosophy, *The Buddha and His Dhamma*[29]. We have tried to go as far back as possible to find out the origin of Babasaheb's interest of Buddhism; and we have observed that his interest in the Buddha and his teachings which were similar to *Kabir, Ravidas, Tukarama, Nanak*, etc. and his *Dhamma* means *Nam – Dana*, that every body must have to seek from the Father as a condition imposed by the Father as a maker of life. Ever since them, for years on his end, to the last breath of his life, he was immersed in his studies in Buddhism, which he rightly thought were vital and fundamental to the interest of the nation at that time to get rid from the cycle of birth and rebirth. In an important article, he contributed to the April – May 1950 number of the *Maha-Bodhi* of Calcutta, namely "*The Buddha* or '*Nam*' and the Future of his Religion," in other terms we call it *'Radha Soami'*. The term having the meaning in *'Spiritual Sense'*. He says, "I maintain that society must have either the sanction of law or the sanction of morality to hold it together as the duty of Father. Without Father either, society is sure to go to pieces as did by Gandhi and M.A. Jinnah. In all societies, Law plays a very small part. It is intended to keep the minority within the range of social discipline. The majority is left to sustain its social life by postulates and sanction of morality. Religion, in the sense of morality, must, therefore, remain the governing principle in every society[30] called Brahmins in the absence of the Father. In the course of the same article, he continues to make the following observations about Religion. To quote Dr. B.R. Ambedkar[31].

1. "Religion must be in accord with science. Religion is bound to lose respect, and therefore, become the subject of ridicule ; and thereby not merely lose its force as a governing principle of life, but might in course of time, disintegrate and lapse its original value if it is not in accord with science. In other words, religion, if it is not obligatory, its function must be in accord with reason and logic as the study shows which is merely another name of science', called spiritual science.
2. "Religion, as a code of social morality must recognize the fundamental tenets of Liberty, Equality and Fraternity. Unless a religion recognizes these three fundamentals of social life, religion will be doomed'.

In the same article, viz; *The Buddha and the Future of His Religion*', Dr. B.R. Ambedkar writes about the need of a '*Buddhist Bible*' like the '*History of The Chamar Dynasty*' the other two being to make changes in the organization i.e. *'Encyclopaedia of Untouchables'* and *'Sudharnama'*, in the aims and objectives of the *Bhikshu Sangha*, with a view to setting up a '*World Buddhist Mission*' on the basis of the said Books. Of these, he could achieve the first objective that my society will free from allegation which have been imposed by the Brahmins in the absence of my dear colleague Dr. Raj Kumar the '*Buddhist Bible*' or '*History of the Chamar' Dynasty*' because a monumental works as the book entitle '*The Buddha and His Dhamma*' became after posthumously a monumental work of the same author; like *Constitution of India.* In several places, Dr. B.R. Ambedkar has given evidence of his rational approach, now, we take the various examples from his book published under the title of '*The Buddha and His Dhamma.*'

1. He says, "Buddhism is nothing if not rationalism[32].
2. He maintains that the *Buddha's* path is "the path of reasoning and logic, and his is the way of emancipation for superstition' which could not understood by Brahmins.
3. He says "The Buddha agrued that there must be proof before writing the script of the God can accept a thing to be a reality[34]".
4. He again refers, "He (The Buddha) accepted that reality must rest on proof. Thinking must be based on rationalism[35]', like *Sudhras.*
5. He asserts before the Brahmin, "In his (The Buddh's or 'Nam') opinion nothing was infallible, and no thing could be final. Everything must be open to re-examination and re-consideration, when ever grounds for re-examination and re-consideration, arise[36]".

It appears from his writings that his approach towards Buddhism was essential at that to create a healthy society, on rationalistic and humanistic approach to realize the Truth or '*Nam*' and its importance in the social building measures. He had a '*Universal Thought*' in the welfare of the public which were degraded by the Brahminical forces. The book entitled '*The Buddha and His Dhamma*', he makes a vital distinction between the terms '*Dharma*' or '*Religion*' and '*Dhamma*' as '*Nam*'. He maintains that Buddhism is not a *Dharma* or Religion, but a duly has been imposed on the theory of mind to serve the society and remember the Father, who has given the life to get rid from their birth and rebirth process in history., but without *'Dhamma'* or *Nam-Dana;* one cannot become rationalist in this world because soul is the part of the Father or God, in his absence, she forget the Father and created the Religion by imposing certain identification mark. Thus *Dhamma or 'Nam'* is a way of life as an humantistic approach in life Religion is a personal matter called *'ego'*. According to Buddha, *Dhamma* consists of *Prajnya* and *Karuna*[37], means practise the Father's 'Words' made poor and they used to live on the marcy of Brahmins. Even though, he was not spared by them. Accordingly, on the 14th October, at 9.30. A.M, 1956, he accepted the Buddhism from *Mahasthavira Chandramani* of Burma, in the presence of over 5,00,000 (five lakh) people from various parts of the country as a *Nam* converted to Buddhism as à define state to find out the *'Reality'* where it stands either in *Scheduled Castes* or Hinduism. He also administrated the "Twenty – Two Resolution to the people, to ensure the giving up of the old ways of Hinduism, and the acceptance of the path of the *Buddha*[38] *,i.e., 'Nam or God or Chamar.* His future work remained went to complexion in the process of being built up *History* of his own country and the people. State people with an unprecedented crisis which also provides them with a rare opportunity in the word market like *'cooli'*, they are again in a situation who to get rid from the Brahminical thought which always made the history as a complex subject and the crisis can end in a disaster or a unique triumph depending upon the attitude that is adopted to the situation. Led by demagogues, impatient men or self-seekers who make mountains of mole hills, the state may fall apart and cause the disintegration of the Indian Republic as a living being on Earth.

Now, we come to the conclusion of the book mentioned above, *'The Buddha and His Dhamma, since,* there is no place for God in the Buddha's *Dhamma,* it took the shape for the benefit of poor people as a human being to give a status to those people who have been degraded in the society, in this manner "Morality takes the place of God"[38]. But, it is the essence of *Dhamma* or *Nam-Dana*; who practise it in true spirit and his value become the same. It is for his goodness and to raise the standard of morality than man has to love man[39] in the society.

Kashmir Cut a Sorry Figure During The Partition of India

In the history of the *Sudhras*, Kashmir was at that time, cut a sorry figure in the history of Indian, because communal forces could not understood the idea of Ambedkar, which, he played in his life during the *'Round Table Conferences'* as well as in expressing his idea. Though speeches and writings ; Kashmir became a crucible state, because their rulers were suppressed by the nationalistic people, and they became slave of them in the absence of Father his race made bringing ruin to Asian Democracy in its wake.

If, on the other hand, better counsels prevail with those who guide public opinion in the three regions i.e, India, Pakistan and China, insurmountable obstacle in the way of building a multi-religious, multi-lingual and multi-racial democratic states with goodwill of the God and co-operation making allowances for each others sentiments and respecting the human dignity of all. It will be an unparalleled achievement of which not only the state people, but the people of other part of the world. At that time; every Indian will feel proud, for Kashmir will then have defended the principles enshrined in the Indian Constitution and disproved by the two-nation theory that continues to sap the vitality of democracy in India and Pakistan[40] including China also.

Bold Leadership of Sudhras

Essential things in Kashmir[41] is that we have a great need for a bold leadership like *'Nam* or *Chamar*, who must be bias and wedded with the cause of secularism and social democracy; which he was must vast thinking to teach the Kashmir's new thought of the nature. It should be obvious that a leadership can remain effective as Dr. B.R. Ambedkar, was effective in the 'Round Table Conferences' suppressed the malafide attention of the Communal forces.

Education to Change Outlook of History

The conversion of Muslims[42] and Hindus in valley is not an impossible task, there is a need of purity of thought, high moral, tolerance, self-confidence of positive manners to serve the society as a principle. Having peculiar culture, simple in dress, thinking, eating and un-bias towards man, pacifist by nature. His study should be based on scientific methods, not self-centred the Great Conversion to *Buddhism* or *Chamarization* was, indeed, a unique, historic event bound to make before the people, and to re-think. Though the pages of History that man like Professor Raj Kumar I there during the 21th Century A.D.

In the study, it indicates that during the period from 1947 to 1956, Dr. B.R. Ambedkar worked with compassionate way, he framed the Indian Constitution with wisdom (*prajnya*) and having the fellow-felling (*Karuna*) in it, even though he faced the communal-forces but; with the writings of pen, he defeated them. He had limitedless knowledge and '*Crucible*' from heart like *Ravidas*, *Kabir* or other saints of the world. His philosophy is highly appreciable not in India but in whole of the world. He was a frontline scholar of the period. He was the law-maker of the *Sudhra* society. He struggled for the humanity in rationalistic not like the idiot Brahmin. He played a very constructive role in the Government activities, fought against the social evils like Caste system, Child marriage, etc. It was a moral act of his life that he was born in Hindu society and converted to Buddhism as mind developed from Brahmins to *Sudhras*.

Note and References

1. K.N. Kadam ; Op. Cit. p. 48.
2. Prem Nath Bazaz;. *Kashmir in Crucible*. Srinagar, 2005. p. 129.
3. *Ibid.*

4. *Ibid.* pp.120-30.
5. *Ibid.* p. 130.
6. *Ibid.* pp. 130-31.
7. *Ibid.* p. 131.
8. *Ibid.* pp. 131-32.
9. B.G.Ramesh ; *Op. Cit.* p. 30.
10. Prem Nath Bazaz ; *Op. Cit.* p. 133.
11. For Biographies of Kashmir Queens and Notable women like Didda, Sugandha, *Anga lekha, Suryamatii,* etc. See Again, Prem Nath Bazaz; *Daughters of The Vitasta.* New Delhi, 1957. *'A History of the Sudhra Women'.*
12. P.N. Tikoo ; *Story of Kashmir,* New Delhi; 1979, p. 43.
13. Prem Nath Bazaz; *Op. Cit.* pp. 133-34
14. *Ibid.* p. 134.
15. *Ibid.* pp. 134-35.
16. *Ibid.* p. 135.
17. K.L. Khurana ; *Op. Cit.* p. 364.
18. *Jammu and Kashmir Constituent Assembly*; Opening Addresses p. 18.
19. *Hindustan Times* dated 6, February, 1967. See Prem Nath Bazaz; *Kashmir in Crucible.* p. 137.
20. Prem Nath Bazaz; *Op. Cit.* pp. 137-8
21. B.G. Ramesh, *Op. Cit.* p. 31.
22. K.N. Kadam ; *Op. Cit.* pp. 48-49.
23. Prem Nath Bazaz; *Op. Cit.* p. 139.
24. K.N. Kadam ; *Op. Cit.* p. 49.
25. D.C.Ahir; *Dr. Ambedkar and the Indian Constitution* ; p. 63.
26. M. Rama Jois; *Guruji and Social Harmony* ; p. 57.
27. Pyarelal ; *Mahatma Gandhi; The last Phase.* Vol. II. p. 500.
28. Dr. J.R. Kamble in his *Pursuit of Equality in History.* p. 138.
29. Dr. B.R. Ambedkar : *The Buddh and His Dharma.*
30. Dr. B.R. Ambedkar ; *Buddha and the Future of His Religion* 1950. pp. 11-12.
31. *Ibid.* p. 12.
32. Dr. B.R. Ambedkar ; *The Buddha and His Dharma* ; p. 250.

33. *Ibid.* p. 114.
34. *Ibid.* p. 256.
35. *Ibid.* p. 86.
36. *Ibid*. p. 89.
37. *Ibid.* p. 317.
38. *Ibid.* p. 322.
39. *Ibid.* p. 323.
40. Prem Nath Bazaz; *Kashmir in Crucible ; pp. 153-4.*
41. *Ibid.* p. 153.
42. *Ibid.* p. 156.

Conclusion

From the aforesaid; Dr. B.R. Ambedkar's stormy career in his life-time (1891-1956 A.D.) of barely 65 years, we sum up that his career philosophical the yearnings and aspirations of the weaker sections of the society. It has been seen that every step which he had chosed for his life with a full sense of responsibility. It was a moral act of his life, in the light of his knowledge, he remembered the God on every step of life, God helped him every crucial movement. He played a very constructive and important role in the Government activities as well as in the society as a common human being. He fought against the social evils which were widely spread by the evil minded people with his writings. He enlightened the suffering masses groaning under the dead-weight of the dead-wood of oppressive customs, traditions, of the leading Brahminical society for their own benefit on the basis of Religious tradition as a 'blind faith' of the modern society. The war which he fought against the communal foreces in the 'Round Table Conferences', it is highly appreciable that a man from the background of the *untouchable* society defeated the people with knowledge and arguments like Gandhi and M.A. Jinnah. But the evil minded people could not leave the evil – approach towards society, number of people were killed due to their leadership ideas to show the people that we are the more responsible citizens of the nations. The leader from the background of the poor classes always requested them come to one platform that is humanity, but *satans* was ruling on their mind, and they will bent for the partition of India. A man from the background of Mahar Caste called *untouchables* brought his people out from the dingy dungeon of the past which were badly suppressed by the Brahmins, and led them into the suny, energizing daylight of the knowledge, even after the independence, these people were not allowed to work in the office, Dr. Zakir Hussain, the first Muslim President of India, who took a strong step, and they were encouraged to take part in the government services, even though there are the provisions in the Indian Constitution, the evil-minded called religious – mind, could not allow them to enter in the office. The selfish attitude of the communal forces, slowly and gradually, became weakened, as soon as Dalit freedom from superstition, freedom from tyranny, the power of these forces became decline, but still existing in their mind as we are the leader of the country.

Another significant development which developed in the minds of the *Dalit* due to the Western philosophical thought which was advanced in the world at one time to differinate the idea of Religion and Morality. In fact, the philosophy of India is realistic in approach and has been largely interpreted whereas, else-where it has been a new construction, such as Aristotle and Kant, as we find, had borrwed much from their predecessors, as we took the lesson from the Ambedkar's thought that he was highly impressed with the philosophy of Buddha, Kabir, *Tukarama*, *Ravidas*, many more the great saint of India, whereas Brahmins on the other hand, they are false pretender of the self-style philosophy, which has no scientific base in Indian history as Ambedkar has. Therefore, good always defeat the bad, but there is need of tolerance.

While the inequalities of caste system adversely affected the *Sudhras* in the matter of the criminal law like adultery, the law of the defamation made by Brahmins in the society, he assented over them with the stroke of pen and made certain provisions in the Constitution as a law to crush the evil-minded

Brahminical inspired peoples. Extremely severe penalties including physical and mental torture was there in their thought, he crushed them with slow poison.

He used to believe in the hard-work as we have examined from his career, one side he had to work for the *Sudhras* liberation and on the other side, he was busy with study to defeat the so called priestly class of the Indian society. Every step of his life, has been seen experimental and hardships to face the evil designs things. But he showed us the way to stand erect your self with right way as a positive force, to hold our heads high, and to think and talks the language of free man without malices feelings. No doubt, various kinds of punishments have been prescribed by the Hindu law and Muslim law towards women, so that they might be severe or lenient according to the gravity of offence or in view of the caste consideration like *Shia* and *Sunni* has a great conflict.

The law relating to the property and its inheritance as advocated by Brahmins or Manu is totally based on the rules for marriages which recommended only to the higher castes. But here Dr. B.R. Ambedkar is again has the right suggestions, that everything is related to Father or God, we are here to love to each other for the sake of Father not for the self-interest.

It is clear from the above account that this particularly law is negligible to the *Sudhras* who are twice-born in the *'Nam'* called 'die to live' in the '*Nam*', they become the force of God. Therefore, God needs no much money, He needs love. Love gets love. Bad get bad, what is bad, it is our *mana*, which is a part of the Brahmin.

He took us onto the shoulders of the Buddha or '*Nam*' with practical approach in scientific method on the basis of *Nam-Dana* to realize your *Guru* or Prefect Master. *History* is the only evidence of it, otherwise, we find that there is a majority of fraudlent *Guru* which are wandering in the material life, and became burden on the earth as well as on the society called Brahmins. *Sudhra* has a authority to expel them from their

Kingdom as it has been mentioned in the Hindu Sastras, when *Sudhra* rules Brahmin cannot rule.

It is also come to our knowledge, during the partion of India, when the communal forces were defeated in the 'Round Table Conferences', by Dr. B.R. Ambedkar, the issue of the Kashmir remained there between the two countries, on the issue of Kashmir number of Wars were took place between Indian and Pakistan and number of people became homeless, became rolling stone of society, because the communal interest was there when the two great communal forces that is Muslims and Hindus were fighting there, and *Sudhras* were skated between the two as a third force which has no nation, they used to work for the welfare of society, even they had faced the various challenges of the uncivilized culture of Brahminical Ideology. In the study, it has been visualized by the author that Kashmir was the part of *Sudhra* history, as we have already given a scientific analysis in the Book entitled, *'History of Chamar Dynasty'.* (From 6th century A.D. to 12 century A.D.), that *Sudhras* were real ruler of the *Kashmir.* As we know Kashmir was a great Buddhist learning centre of the world, it was famous in ancient as well as in medieval period of the Indian history that *Chandala, dumas,* ponie driver called *Chak* rulers, they ruled over Kashmir with love and affection an attracted the people from all parts of the world. Kashmir has been seen many Masters, like *Buddha, Asoka, Kushana, Gupta, Karkotas* called *Chamars or Chandalas, Chaks,* etc. All these people belonged the *Sudhra* background family, Ambedkar called them *Scheduled Castes* and *Scheduled Tribes.* As soon as, their spiritual rulers dies and went to Heaven for the rest and this earth was handed over to the philosophers having Brahminical nature, they marred the career of the various *Sudhra* rulers by creating caste, colour and creed. An angle from Heaven to Earth born in India in 1891, again, in the family of *Sudhras* to fight against the Brahminical forces, and now we are observing that his number of Children have been grown up like *Manhor Lal Barawala from*

Gulab Singh Tribe and facing the music of communal forces and some have been absorbed in their thought, they have been forgotten the Father's struggle against the communal people how he fought with them with bold stroke of the pen and realized them. Dr. B.R. Ambedkar was the right man on the earth at the time. Any how score will be settle in the open field of the world community who is right or wrong at time when our projects will be completed.

It appears from the study that *untouchable* is *untouchable* unless and until, he do not wash is heart and head with the power of '*Nam*' called *Chamar* or *Buddha*. No doubt, Buddha or *Chamar* has given us as potential future, either we discuss the philosophy of Ravidas or Dr. B.R. Ambedkar, how a man from the background of the *untouchables* reconstruct the world history as a potential quality in the mind and heart. In the light of this reason, how, Ambedkar forget on the principles of Justice, Liberty, Equality and Fraternity with the writings of various books and articles as a practical approach in scientific way when God's power was there, it never dies and always works constantly, but the people from the background of the money-power, they forget the Father like Jagdish Lal Megh (Mathemeticans) and his friends; they are self-style natural forces like modern Brahmins. They criticized the people, that they have no status in their life. If God has no status, how a man from the background of *Sudhra* as the status, it shows that certain *Sudhras* are also Brahmins.

In Ambedkar's life *Buddha* or *Nam* was a philosophy and a culture of Rationalism as a practical and scientific approach, which loves with Humanism and Morality. It shows the peoples from the background of the money-minded called themselves *Sudhras* for their benefit, but in real sense, they are not *Sudhras*, they are anti-*Sudhras*. They come under the category of Brahmins. Brahmins are always cheater of '*Nam*' or God, because they are self-styled god. But the struggle of the Ambedkar in his life was for the humanity; to make men human in this earth, but one thing is very essential in life that without '*Nam*' one cannot achieve this success in his life. As Nanak says that God-realization is not attained by wandering about. It comes through a true teacher, a *Satguru*, whom one meets through the grace of God. The true master imparts the method for practicing the *Word*, *Shbad*, which enables the disciple to transcend his *mind* and '*ego*' and attain liberation from the wheel of birth and death.

He, again, expresses that God created both reality and illusion, and He can help us to distinguish between the two. We cannot rise above the illusion without the *Nam-dana* to emerge in reality by performing rituals in the absence of God; which are a futile activity. 'Ego' is the root of all ignorance, all evil, as Ambedkar as analysised, it consists in what lies in one heart as Ravidas's picture exposed the reality during the Brahminical rule. The motives of the life with which we see, we hear and we act has to reflect to the others benefit. Nanak again says as that one should not denigrate women. They are conceived and born even as men are conceived and born. Why slanders the sex that gives birth to King's and great men, because to serve that society, and is there anyone living who is no born of women, therefore, every person has to right to live, but in rational and humanistic way as Dr. B.R. Ambedkar has followed the philosophy of *Kabir* and *Ravidas*.

After the Great Conversion into *Buddha* or *Nam* philosophy, Babasaheb, Ambedkar attended the world Buddhist Conference, at Kathmandu, in November, 1956, when he spoke on '*The Buddha and Marx*' having the same philosophy as of *Nanak*, *Ravidas*, Kabir, *Tukaram*, as other great saints express, as *Baba Gurinder Singh Ji Biaswale*, it is the personal judgment of the historian that else stands, no where, because historical truth with them is not existing. If there is a doubt, it is the humble request of the author study the book of the same, '*History of the Brahmans*', a distance communication of the Heavenly world lies in the context for your knowledge and agreement.

Thereafter, on the 6th December, 1956, Ambedkar passed away leaving million of his followers and admires sorrowing under the impact of the sad demise and unexpected event, because such people never dies, they only give a chance to man to think over them. These are worldly people of the *'Nam'* or God', they land on earth, time and again to establish a *'New Story'* to help the poor people. During his death all parties assembled and mourned his death that one of the greatest sons of India passed away as the process of life, but the work which he done for the *'untouchables'* or the weaker sections of the society as well as for other through the Constitution of India, number of people have been absorbed on his pattern of Reservation as well as institutions to practice the law in court ; such kind of work are not realized upto Brahmins, it was approach of a pure *Sudhras* not of money minded or selfish in their motives took the benefit of the Reservation called modern *Sudhra* Brahmin's. Recalling Ambedkar's great services for the society to the nation in Constitution making which Brahmins could not realize the basic idea of it, and abstracting money out of it by discussing various issues in philosophical ways under the Hindu law, Nehru in Lok Sabha, he expressed his view that Dr. B.R. Ambedkar would be remembered mostly as the symbol of revolt against all the oppressing features of the Hindu society, and defeated then with the stroke of pen. His virulent opposition against the Brahmins, had kept people's minds to awake against social evil-designers, thus, his role was, indeed, unique, historic choice, bold, Reserve in speaking, used to speak on appropriate time like in '*Round Table Conferences*', etc. His death became a historic event and bound to make the people to think over his philosophy which carried wait for the common man's thought. His teachings of Buddha or Kabir revolutionized his thought to world community like Britishers, Americans, etc. Now, his thought became the history of world that such race might be love to every body except Brahmins. He displayed his life as Buddha displayed; during his life time to the people of there country. His prophetic thought not less than that of the other saints of world like Christ, Mohammed Prophet, Moses, etc. He always stressed on *Dhamma or Nam-Dana* and says, "Religion is a Religion of rule; while *Dhamma* is a matter of principles, Religion is a matter of rites and rituals, propitiation of depites, and prayers. But *Dhamma or Nam Dama* is to worship the Living Deity which based on Historical evidence, on the other hand "there is no place for prayers, pilgrimages, rituals, ceremonies or sacrifices". It is the work of Brahmin for trade. But in the study of *Dhamma or Nam – Dana*, there is a trade of the Father, which is the ultimate goal of the life to realize the God and get rid from the illusion which is a part of the sorry figure in the life. Life is a precious things for the realization of God and achieve good thing and Live in Heaven as God live.

APPENDICES

Appendix -I

Genealogy of Dr. B.R. Ambedkar's Family

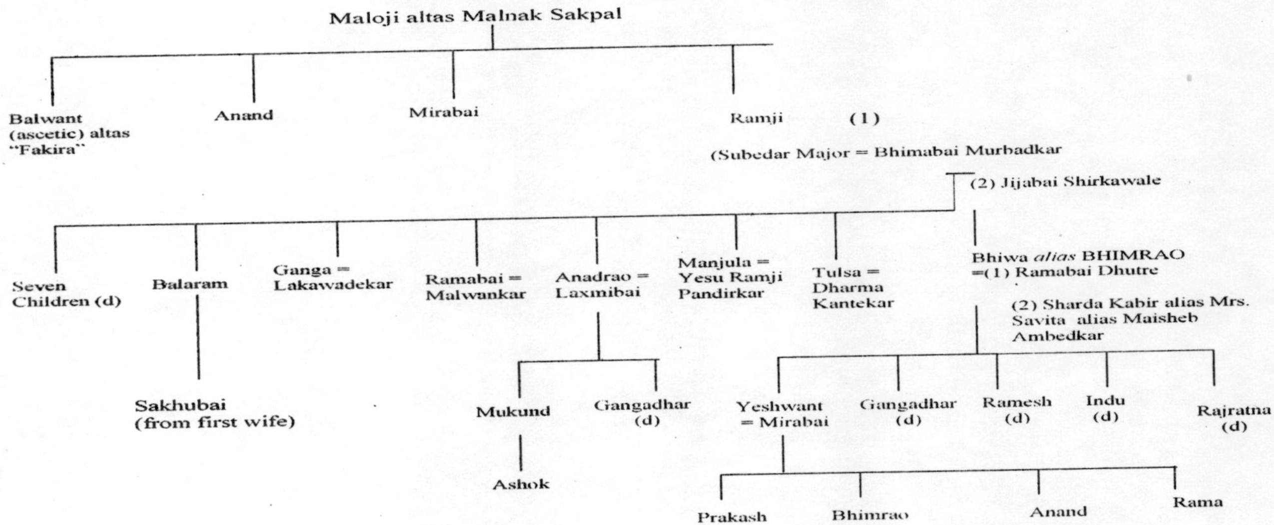

Note : (Means married to 'd' Means young)

Appendix - II

The Educational Career of Bhimrao Ramji Ambedkar

S.No.	*Name of School*	*Date of Admission*	*Standard in in which studying*	*Date of Leaving school*	*Remark*
1.	Primary School Dapoli	1896	Pre-primary CT6moved to	1896	Family
2.	Primary School Satara	1896	Pre-primary	1896	Satara
3.	Government High School Satara (Now Pratap Singh School, Satara)	7-11-1900	I-V	November 1905	Family moved to Bombay
4.	Maratha High Schoo, Parel (Now Shirodkar High school, Parel, Bombay)	1905	V	1905	Joined the Elphinstone High School Bombay.

coutd. Appendix-II

S.No.	*Name of School*	*Date of Admission*	*Standard in in which studying*	*Date of Leaving school*	*Remark*
5.	Elphinstone High School Bombay.	1905	V-VII	1907	Passed the Matricu-lation Exam of the Bombay University

Appendix - III

Post - Matriculation

Educational Career of Dr. B.R. Ambedkar

S. No.	*Year*	*Class Degree*	*College Univ.*	*Dissertation/paper/Thesis*	*Remarks*
1	3-1-1908	Previous Bombay (Bombay University)	Elphinstone College,		
2.	1910	Intermediate in Arts	- do -		
3.	1912	Bachelor of Arts			
4.	July, 1913	Master of Arts	Colombia University	Administration & Finance	(i) The Ph.D. Degree
		(2-5-1915)	New York (U.S.A.)	of the East India Company	was formally
				Caste in India (1916)	Conferred on Dr.
		Doctor of Philosophy		This should be on the line of "Doctor of Philosophy"	Ambedkar on 8-6-1927 though he Was allowed
		(8-6-1927)		Thesis	to use it,
				The National Dividend of India - A Historical &	for all practical purposes, sinc

(Contd.)

(Contd. Appendix- IiI)

S. No.	*Year*	*Class Degree*	*College Univ.*	*Dissertation/paper/Thesis*	*Remarks*
				Analytical Study : A Study in the Provincial Decentralisation of Imperial Finance (1916)	1917. (ii) The thesis was published by S.K. King & Co. London in 1925 under the title The Evolution of Provincial Finance in British India
5	Oct. 1916	Master of Sci. (Econ) 1922	London School of Economic & Political Science (London Unvi.)	Provincial Centralisation	He had to return to of Indian Bombay in 1917. Small Holdings in India & Resumed studies in London in Sept.1920
				Their Remedies	
6	Oct, 1916		Doctor of Sci. (Econ) Oct.1923	Responsibilities of a Responsible Government in India. (Read before the Students' Union) Thesis : The Problem of the	(i) The thesis was

(Contd.)

(Contd.Appendix IIi)

S. No.	*Year*	*Class Degree*	*College Univ.*	*Dissertation/paper/Thesis*	*Remarks*
				Rupee 1922	published by S.P. King Co. in 1923 ii) It was re-issued in May, 1947 under the title of History of Indian Currency & Banking Vol I by Thackers Bombay
7.	11-11-1916		Barrister-at-law 1923		
8.	5-6-1952		Doctor of Laws (Honorary)	Colombia Univ.	
9.	12-1-1953		Doctor of Laws (Honorary)	Osmania Univ.	

Appendix - IV

Writings of Dr. B.R. Ambedkar

1915 Administration and Finance of The East India Company. (His thesis for M.A. Columbia University, 15-5-1915.) Published in Dr. Babasaheb Ambedkar : Writing and Speeches, Vol. 6

1916 "Castes in India : Their Mechanism, Genesis and Development" (A paper read in Professor Goldenweiser's Anthropological Seminar. Later published in the Indian Antiqury, May 1917 now reprinted in Writings and Speeches, Vol. I)

1917 The National Dividend of India : A Historical & Analytical Study. (His thesis for Ph.D. Columbia University. Published in 1925 under the title Evolution of Provincial Finance in British India.)

1918 A Review of Bertrand Russell's "Principles of Social Reconstruction." (Published in the Journal of Indian Economic Society, Vol. I, No.1, of March 1918.)

1918 "Small Holdings in India : Their Remedies." (Published in the Journal of Indian Economic Society, Vol. I-II-III.)

1919 A Statement submitted to the Southborough Committee on Franchise. (See Writings and Speeches, Vol. 1.) Social Conditions During The Regin of Sambhaji.

1923 The Problem of the Rupee. (His thesis for D.Sc (Econ.) of the University of London. Subsequently published, in 1925.

It was subsequently reprinted and published, in 1947, under the title History of Indian Currency and Banking.) (See Writings and Speeches, Vol. 6.)

1923 "Responsibilities of a Responsible Government in India." (A paper read before the Student's Union.)

1925 Evidence before the Hilton Young Commission on Indian Currency.

1928 Statement Concerning the State of Education of the Depressed Classes, in the Bombay Presidency. (Submitted to the Simon Commission. On behalf of The Bahishkrit Hitakarani Sabha.) (See Writings and Speeches, Vol. 2.)

1928 Statement Cornering the Safeguards for Protection of the Interests of the Depressed Classes as a Minority in the Bombay Presidency and Change in the Composition of the Guarantees from the Bombay Legislative Council necessary to Ensure the same, under Provincial Autonomy. (Also submitted along with the previous statement to the Simon Commission.) (See Writings and Speeches, Vol. 2).

1929 "Wanted An Anti-Priestcraft Association." (An article published in the Bombay Chronicle of 8-11-1929.)

1930 Political Rights of the Untouchables (RTC, Vol. III, App. III, Proceedings of the Minorities Sub-Committee No. III (Minorities). 2000 copies got privately printed, in London.)

1930 A Scheme of Political Safeguards for the Protection of the Depressed Classes in the Future Constitution of a Self-Governing India. (RTC-I, App-II, pp. 168-176; Vol, III, Proceedings of the Minorities Sub-Committee.) (See Writing and Speeches, Vol. 2.)

1930 Letter, in "The Second Annual Report of the League of Purity."

1936 Annihilation of Caste. (See Writings and Speeches, Vol. 1).

1937 Mahar Ani Tyanche Vatan (Marathi).

1939 Federation versus Freedom. (See Writings and Speeches, Vol. 1.)

1940 Thoughts on Pakistan.
(Its second revised and enlarged edition was published under the title Pakistan or The Partition of India, in 1945.)
(See Writings & Speeches, Vol. 8.)

1942 "Problems of the Scheduled Castes."
(A paper submitted to the Pacific Relations Conference at Mont Tremblant, Quebec. Subsequently published under the title Mr. Gandhi and The Emancipation of the Untouchables.)

1943 Ranade, Gandhi and Jinnah.

1945 What Congress and Gandhi Have Done to the Untouchables.

1945 The Communal Deadlock; A Way to Solve it.

1946 Who were The Shudras? (See Writings and Speeches, Vol. 7)

1946 The Cabinet Mission and The Untouchables.
(Published privately for the Cabinet Mission.)

1947 States and Minorities.

1948 The Untouchables. (See Writings and Speeches, Vol.7.)

1948 Maharashtra as a Linguistic Province. (See Writings and Speeches, Vol. 1.)

1950 The Buddha and The Future of His Religion.

1950 The Rise and Fall of the Hindu Women.

1952 Baudha Puja – Paatha (Edited in Marathi).

1956 The Buddha & His Dhamma.

1982 The Riddle of Rama. (Jalandhar). (See Writings and Speeches, Vol. 4.)

Other Works

1924 "Studies in History, Economics and Public Law."
(Unpublished)

1924 Hindi Chalan Padhate. (Marathi) (The serial appeared in the Navakal.)

1925 "The Present Problem in Indian Currency." (An article in the Servant of India).

1930 "The Problem of India's Defence." (The problem from the constitutional point of view: Unpublished.)

1931 "Look Before You Leap." (An article in the Morning Post of London.)

1931 India & Communism.

Dr. Babasaheb Ambedkar : Writings and Speeches, Govt. of Maharashtra :

1979 Vol. 1.

1982 Vol. 2.

1987 Vol. 3.

1987 Vol. 4.

1989 Vo. 5.

1989 Vol. 6.

1990 Vol. 7.

1990 Vol. 8.

Source Material On Dr. Ambedkar (Vol.1 Govt. of Maharashtra, 1982.

Note : The above list is not complete. There are still a number of awaiting publications.

Speeches

1936 Mukti Kon Pathe? (Marathi)

1952 Conditions Precedent to the Successful Working of Democracy.

1956 Buddha & Karl Marx (Speech at Khatmandu, 20-11-1956.)

Appendix – V

A Chronological Outline of Ambedkar's Career from 1848 to 1956 A.D.

1848	Birth of Ramji Maloji Sakpal, father of Dr B.R Ambedkar of Ambadave, now in the Mandangad sub-division of the Ratnagiri district, in the Maharashtra State. Jotirao Phooley (b. 1827) started a girls' school in Pune : the first girls' school in Maharashtra.
1850	The first textile mill in Bombay was started. "Untouchables" were not employed in' the weaving departments of such mills until well after 1950.
1851-52	Jotirao Phooley started the first school for "Untouchable" children in Pune.
1854	Birth of Bhimabai, mother of Dr Ambedkar. Narayan Guru was born at Champazendy, Kerala.
19-7-1854	The Court of Directors recommended spread of education' among the masses. This despatch laid the foundation of mass education.
23-7-1856	Birth of Bal Gangadhar Tilak at Ratnagiri.
1856	A Mahar boy of Dharwar petitioned Government protesting against discrimination in admission to schools.

18-4-1858	Birth of Dhondo Keshav Karve.
1858	The British Government issued instructions for throwing open all public schools to children Babasaheb Ambedkar, at Nagpur in 1956.
1878-1880	The Afghan War, in which Mahar soldiers fought successfully under the British flag.
18-2-1879	Birth of Kisan Phaguji Bansod, at Mohapa, near Nagpur.
1879	Subedar Ramji at the Rawalpindi camp. There Bhimabai chanced to meet her ascetic brother-in-law, "Fakira". Ramji met "Fakira" the after quite long.
21-5-1880	Col. Olcott and Madame Blavatsky became Buddhists at Galle. Ceylon (now Sri Lanka).
16-5-1881	Birth of Ramchandra Krishnaji Kadam, of Pune, a colleague of Shivram Janba Kamble, and a close friend and admirer of Dr Ambedkar; a well-known social worker.
28-12-1881	Coronation of Sayajirao Gaikwad, Maharaja of Baroda.
1882	Maharaja Sayajirao Gaikwad started schools for Depressed Class children, at Baroda.
14-3-1883	Karl Marx (b. 5-5-1818) died.
5-6-1883	Birth of John Maynard Keynes. British economist and 'the most influential world figure in economics since Adam Smith, Ricardo and Marx:, author of the widely accla4ned book. *Indian Currency* and *Finance.*
1884	Subedar Ramji was promoted to Naik; 106, Sappers and Miners was closed down and Naik Ramji was transferred to 107. Pioneers (later known as the 7th Bombay Battalion). Subedar-Major Murbadkar retired and returned to Murbad (district Thane) and his six brothers did the same. Olcott started four schools in Madras, exclusively for "Untouchable" children.

1884	Birth of Dr. S.V. Ketkar. (Died 1937)
1885	The Indian National Congress was founded. Allan Octavian Hume took a leading part in founding it.
1886	Gopalbaba Walangkar retired from the army as havaldar, and settled down at Dapoli, in the Ratnagiri district. He vowe to emancipate the "Untouchables" from the thralldom of Hinduism. (It seems that Gopalbaba was born around 1830.)
1886	Vijaya - Dashami, Gopalbaba Walangkar established the "Anarya Dosh – Parihar Samaj", at Dapoli.
1886	Birth of S.M. Mate. (Died 1957)
1887	Birth of M.N. Roy.
29-5-1888	Birth of V.D.Savarkar.
1888	Subedkar Ramji returned to the MHOW camp with the 107. Bombay Infantry.
1-8-1889	Gopalbaba Walangkar published his Vital Vidvansak 'the first volcanic erruption of protest against Brahminism'.
14-11-1889	Birth of Jawaharlal Nehru.
27-11-1890	Death of the great social reformer Jotirao Phooley, at Pune. (He was born on 11-4-1827)
14-4-1891 (dawn)	Birth of Bhimrao Ramji Ambedkar, at MHOW,[1] the fourteenth child of Subedar Ramji Sakpal and Bhimabai.
31-10-1891	An International Buddhist Conference was organised by Anagarika Dharmapal, at Buddha-Gaya.
May,1892	*The Maha-Bodhi* journal was started by Anagarika Dharmapal.
Oct, 1892	Death of G.H. Deshmukh (Lokhitawadi). (He was born on 18-2-1823.)
1892	Lord Kitchener, Commander-in-Chief, decided to reorganise the Indian Army, precluding the

	recruitment of "Untouchables". Subedar Ramji led a protest against the British Government's policy of exclusion of "Untouchables" from the Army.
Feb. 1893	The Mahant of Buddha Gaya made "a murderous attack" on Buddhist monks.
9-4-1893	Birth of Rahul Sankrityayan. (He died in 1963)
Sep. 1893	World Parliament of Religions at Chicago.
1894	Subedar Ramji retired from military service, and returned from central India to Dapoli.
2-4-1894	Shahu Chhatrapati acceded to the throne of Kolhapur.
July 1894	Gopalbaba Walangkar *drew* up a petition addressed to the Commander-in-chief, in consultation with justice M.G.Ranade. (The petition was, however, not issued until 6-3-1895.)
1894	Pandit C. Iyodhi Doss and Swanliar embraced Buddhism).[2]
1895	Gopalbaba Walangkar addressed the Social Conference, at Pune. He was nominated as a member of the Mahad Local Board.
1895	Birth of G.M.Joshi author of *Hindunche Samaj Rachana Shastra* (Died 1937)
1896	Birth of Ramabai, daughter of Bhiku Dhutre of Wanand, near Dapoli. Bhimrao Ramji Ambedkar began schooling at Dapoli. Soon thereafter, Subedar Ramji moved his family to Satara: and he was re-employed in the Public Works Department at Goregaon in the Statara district. Bhimrao's name was then enrolled in the Primary school of Satara. Bhimabai, Bhimrao's mother, died at Satara.
March1897	Death of Savitribai Phooley. (She was born on 3-1-1831.)
1898	Krishnaji Arjun *alias* Dada Keluskar published his *Bhagwan Buddache Charttra* which he later on presented to young Bhimrao Ambedkar.

Subedar Ramji's second marriage Jijabai, widowed sister of Jamadar Shirkawale. Anandro, Bhimrao's brother's name was enrolled in the Satara High School, in Std. I. On the recommendation of the Gatekar Commission, the Indian army was classified classwise into Maratha, Rajput, Sikh, Gurkha, Jat and similar other regiments. *Mahars* and *Chambhars* were discharged from the army, on grounds of 'Untouchability'.

7-11-1900 Bhimrao Ambedkar's name was enrolled in the Government Middle School (later renamed as Pratap singh High School) at Satara, in Std. I. His teacher named Ambedkar changed Bhimrao's surname from "Arnbadavekar" to "Ambedkar.

1900 Pandit Iyodhi Doss started the South India Buddhist Association at Madras.

1900 Gopalbaba Walangkar died at Ravdul, near Mahad, presently in the Raigad district.

16-1-1901 Death of Justice M.G. Ranade. (Bhimrao Ambedkar was then in Std II)

1901 Subedar Ramji moved his family from Satara to Bombay and started living in the Dabak Chawl (B.LT. Chawl No.1, Room Nos. 50-51), Lower Parel. Bhimrao was admitted in the Maratha High School: and soon thereafter in the Elphinstone High School.

26-7-1902 Shahu Chhatrapati of Kolhapur issued orders for reservation of 50% posts in the state services for the Backward Classes.

15-10-1902 B.K. *alias* Dadasaheb Gaikwad was born at Ambe-Dindori, district Nashik.

1902 Kisan Phaguki Bansod started the *Maratha Deen-Bandhu* at Nagpur, a fortnightly.

24-10-1903 Shivram Janba Kamble convened a mammoth meeting of Mahars of 51 villages, at Saswad, near

Pune. Thereupon, he sent a petition to Lord Lamington. Governor of Bombay, containing the following demands: (1) that the Depressed Classes should be admitted freely to the lower grades of the public service: (2) that the restrictions against the attendance of their children at public schools should be removed: (3) that the Depressed Classes should be permitted to join the Police Department; and (4) that they should be allowed to enlist in the Indian Army.

15-7-1904 Birth of Changdeo Bhavanrao Khairmoday, biographer of Dr. B.R. Ambedkar. (He died on 18-11-1971.)

1-8-1904 Shivram Janba Kamble started the "Shri Shankar Prasadik Somavanshiya Hittachintak Mandal", at Centre Street, Pune.

5-1-1905 Birth of Bhadant Dr. Anand Kausalyayan, an eminent Buddhist scholar and author, who helped spread the conversion Movement, after the passing away of Babasaheb; and under whose guidance the cremation of the mortal remains of Babasaheb Ambedkar was done on 7-12-1956. (Bhadant Anand Kaushalyayan passed away on 23-6-1988.)

15-3-1905 Birth of P.N. Rajbhoj. (Died 22-7-1984.)

1905 Maharaja Sayajirao Gaikwad of Baroda commended the work done by Shivram Janba Ramble.

April 1906 Bhimrao Ramji Ambedkar married Ramabal, daughter of Bhiku Dhutre of Wanand, near Dapoll.

18-10-1906 Vithal Ramji Shinde started the Depressed Classes Mission Society of India the first all-India institution of its type.

1907 The Maharaja of Kolhapur started the Miss Clarke Hostel for Depressed Class and Muslim boys, at

	Kolhapur. Earlier he had started the Victoria Hostel for Matatha and Depressed Class boys.
1907	Prof. P. Lakshmi Narasu published his Essence of Buddhism with a preface by Anagarika Dharmapala.
Bhimrao	R Ambedkar passed the Matriculation examination of the University of Bombay. Dada Keluskar presented him with a copy of Bhagwan Buddhache Charitra, in felicitation for Bhimrao's success in the examination. Rao Bahadur S.K. Bole presided over the function.
3-1-1908	B.R Ambedkar joined the Elphinstone College, Bombay.
5-4-1908	Jagjivan Ram was born.
1-7-1908	Shivram Janba Ramble started the *Somavanshiya Mitra* a monthly journal.
11-9-1908	Shivram Janba Kamble was invited as a state guest to Baroda by the Maharaja Sayajirao Gaikwad.
13-9-1908	The Maharaja of Baroda - had talks with Shivram J. Kamble.
1908	Young Bhimrao R Ambedkar was first - attracted to Buddhism.
1909	Shivram Jabba Kamble presented an address to Maharaja Sayajtrao Gaikwad of Baroda, on behalf of the Depressed Classes of Pune, on the occasion of the prize distribution ceremony of the primary school of the Depressed Class Mission Society of Pune.
5-4-1910	Shivram Janba Kamble held the second Mahar conference at Jejuri. (Thereupon he sent a memorandum to the British Government for the amelioration of the lot of the Depressed Classes) Bhimrao Ramji Ambedkar met the Maharaja of Baroda, who thereupon sanctioned a scholarship of Rs. 25 per month for his education.

12-12-1912	Birth of Yeshwant, Dr Ambedkar's eldest son.
Jan.1912	B.R Ambedkar passed the Bachelor of Arts degree-examination of the Bombay University, with Economics and Politics.
Jan.1912	B.R Ambedkar left the Elphinstone College.
23-1-1913	He went to Baroda, and was appointed in the State service, with the rank of Lieutenant. He was there for hardly 11 days, when he received a telegram about his father's serious illness.
2-2-1913	Death of Subedar Ramji, at the age of 65 years.
1913	The Maharaja of Baroda announced his decision to send students for higher education at the Columbia University, U.S.A.
11-2-1913	Birth of Rajaram Ramji Bhole, a trusted lieutenant of Dr. Ambedkar, later a Justice of the High Court, and Chairman of the People's Education Society founded by Dr. Ambedkar.
4-4-1913	The Maharaja of Baroda sanctioned a scholarship of £ 11.50 per month, for a duration of 3 years (15-6-1913 till 14-6-1916), to B.R. Ambedkar.
18-4-1913	B.R. Ambedkar signed an agreement with the Baroda government, for its overseas scholarship.
23-4-1913	Birth of Dhananjay Keer, the well-known biographer of Dr. B.R. Ambedkar.
20-7-1913	B.R. Ambedkar arrived at New York, and joined the Columbia University, in the Faculty of Political Sciences. He stayed at the University Hartley Hall Dormitory. After a week he moved to the Cosmopolitan Club.
1913	Ramesh, B.R. Ambedkar's son, died in infancy.
1914-18	The First World War.
1914	Death of Pandit Iyodhi Doss.
	The Justice Party was founded in south India.
	While B.R. Ambedkar was in the U.S.A. Lala Laljpat Rai invited the former to join the Indian Home Rule League. B.R. Ambedkar told Lajpat

Rai, "If you are going to keep the Untouchables as your slaves, while fighting for Independence, I cannot join hands with you."

19-2-1915 Gopal Krishna Gokhale died.

2-6-1915 B.R. Ambedkar passed the Master of Arts examination of the Columbia University, with Economics as his principal subject, and Sociology, History, Philosophy, Anthropology and Politics as his other subjects.
He submitted his dissertation on "Administration and Finance of the East India Company."

16-11-1915 Booker T. Washington died.

9-5-1916 B.R. Ambedkar read his thought-provoking paper on Castes in India before Professor Goldenweiser's Anthropology Seminar. (It was subsequently published in the Indian Antiquary of May, 1917, before being published in book form. That was the first published work of Dr. Ambedkar.)

May 1916 He left America to join the London School of Economics and Political Science for the degrees of Master of Science (Economics), and Doctor of Science (Economics) and for Barrister-at-Law.

1916 The Columbia University accepted B.R. Ambedkar's thesis for Doctor of Philosophy, on "The National Dividend of India – A Historical and Analytical Study" in the provincial decentralization of imperial finance.[3]

1916 The Lucknow Congress adopted the Tilak-Jinnah agreement on the Congress-League scheme to give representation to Muslims in excess of proportional representation.

6-2-1917 The Government of India lifted the ban on the recruitment of the Depressed Classes in the Army.

1917 The Columbia University accepted Dr. Ambedkar's thesis for Ph.D., and allowed him the use of the degree for all practical purposes.

July 1917	He was appointed Military Secretary to the Maharaja of Baroda, with a view to being groomed for appointment as the State's Finance Minister.
20-8-1917	The Montague Declaration on the progressive Indianization of places of authority.
21-8-1917	Dr. Ambedkar returned to India on termination of the tenure of the Baroda State scholarship.
Sept. 1917	Dr. Ambedkar came to Baroda, accompanied by his elder brother, and stayed in cognate at a Parsee Dharmashala. He joined his appointment in the Government of Baroda; but due to ill-treatment, on grounds of untouchability, he had to return to Bombay.
Nov. 1917	Dr. Ambedkar's step-mother Jijabi died.
	Conference in Bombay, presided over by Sir Narayan Chandavarkar, adopted the move to have representatives of the Depressed Classes, in proportion to their population.
	A meeting was held under the presidency of Sir Narayan Chandavarkar to felicitate Dr. Ambedkar on his success.
	Dr. Ambedkar's brother Anandro died at Gomtigaon, in the Mahad sub-division, at his wife's place.
Dec. 1917	The Depressed Classes submitted their demands to Montagu, Secretary of State for India.
1917	The India National Congress, in its session at Calcutta, for the first time in its history, adopted a resolution for "the justice and righteousness of removing al disabilities imposed by custom upon the Depressed Classes." Dr. Ambedkar calls this "A strange event."
1917	Justice Raman Pillai, a retired judge, led the struggle in Travancore for temple entry.

19-3-1918 The Asprishyata Nivaran Parishad under the guidance of Sayajirao Gaikwad, Maharaja of Baroda and Sir Narayan Chandavarkar, was attended by B.G, Tilak, Khaparde, Bipin Pal, Vithalbhai Patel, M.R. Jayakar, Bhulabhai Desai, and others. It was resolved that untouchability must be abolished immediately.

Mar. 1918 Dr. Ambedkar published his review of Bertrand Russell's principles of Social Reconstruction, in the Journal of Indian Economics, Vol. I, No.1, Mar. 1918.

23&24 The D.C. Society of India held its first all-India Gaikwad, Maharaja of Baroda, on the grounds near the French Bridge, at Bombay.

11-11-1918 Dr. Ambedkar was appointed Professor of Political Economy, in the Sydenham College of Commerce, Bombay. (he held post till 11-2-1920.)

1918 Dr. Ambedkar published his "Small Holdings in India and Their Remedies" in the Journal of the Indian Economic Society, Vol. I, Nos. 2&3.

Gangadhar, Dr. Ambedkar's son, was born. Mahar soldiers were again disbanded.

16-1-1919 Dr, Ambedkar wrote to The Times of India, under the pen-name "A Mahar", He said: "Home Rule is the birth-right as much of the Mahars as that of the Brahmins, The Depressed Classes have first to be elevated."

27-1-1919 He gave evidence before the Southborough Committee on Franchise.

1919 The Maharaja of Kolhapur issued orders that untouchability should not be observed in the matter of education in schools, Offices, wells, Dharmashalas, etc. He also ordered closure of separate schools for "Untouchable" children.

Dec. 1919 The Government of India Act was passed by the British Parliament, accepting the principle of responsible government, and giving a reformed Constitution of India.

31-1-1920 Dr. Ambedkar started the weekly journal Mook-Nayak to champion the cause of the Depressed Classes of India. (Editors : Pandurang Nandram Bhatkar succeeded by Dnyandeo Dhruvanath Gholap.)

In one leading article, Dr. Ambedkar wrote: "It is not enough to have just a politically independent India. What is also needed is to have an Indian nation where every citizen will have religious and political lights, so that every person will have equal opportunity to develop."

D.D. Gholap was nominated on the Bombay Legislative Council, for the three years 1920-23.

15-3-1920 Dr. Ambedkar resigned from the professorship at the Sydenham College to resume studies in London.

20-3-1920 He presided over a conference at Mangaon, in the then Kolhpur state. Shahu Chhatrapati who addressed the conference said : "Depressed Class delegates from my realm, I heartily congratulate you upon your having found your true leader from amongst yourselves. I am confident Dr. Ambedkar will not rest till he achieves your upliftment. And he will not rest there : a time will come when he will lead the entire nation. I feel certain about it."

30-5-1920 Dr. Ambedkar attended the First All-India to Depressed Class Conference at Nagpur.

1-6-1920 presided over by Shahu Maharaj. He criticised the representative character of the Governor -General's council; and thus initiated his political campaign.

5- 7 -1920	Dr. Ambedkar left for London to complete his studies. He stayed at 96. Brook Green. Hammersmith. London.
1-8-1920	Bal Gangadhar Tilak died.
30-9-1920	Dr. Ambedkar rejoined the London School of Economics and Political Science and also Gray's Inn for further studies.
1920	He was invited by Bertrand Russell for discussion on The *Principles of* Social *Reconstruction.*
1-4-1921	The first meeting of the Bombay Legislative Council under the Government of India Act of 1919, was held.
1921	Government of Bombay appointed an Indian as Education Minister. Dr. R.P.Paranjpye held the portfolio from the date the Act came into force, i.e. 3-1-1921, upto December. 1923.
16-4-1921	Shivram Janba Kamble founded the Asprishodharaka Mandal. He led a deputation to Dr. R.P. Paranjpye, Education Minister, and made the following demands : (1) Compulsory education; (2) Increase in the strength of Depressed Class teachers; (3) Scholarships for Depressed Class students in primary schools and high schools; and (4) Hostels for Depressed Class students, in every district.
15-7-1921	Chhatrapati Shahu of Kolhapur abolished the Mahar Vatan slavery.
Mar. 1922	Dr. Ambedkar was called back to London by his teacher Prof. Edwin Cannan, for revision of certain anti-imperialistic portions of his thesis on The Problem of The Rupee, without changing his conclusions.
April 1922	Dr. Ambedkar visited the Bonn University, in Germany, to arrange for his admission in that University, for higher studies. He returned to London in about a month's time.

Nov. 1922	The Government Hostel for Depressed Class boys was started, at Pune. It was the first student's hostel of its type in Maharashtra. Its first Superintendent was Narayanrao Krishnaji Kadam. (The hostel was subsequently renamed as the Sant Dnyaneshwar Vasatigriha, Pune, and continues as such to this day.)
1922	Dr. Ambedkar submitted his thesis for Doctor of Science – The Problem of the Rupee – to the London University, was the old concept of the Sudhra family i.e. called tanner system.
	He read a paper on 'Responsibilities of a Responsible Government in India', before the students' union. Even his teacher Prof. Harold J. Laski thought it to be of a revolutionary nature.
	Dr. Ambedkar left London for further higher studies at the Bonn University.
1923	Dr. Ambedkar was called to the Bar.
3-4-1923	He returned to India.
1923	From Bombay he resubmitted his thesis, The Problem of The Rupee to London University.
5-7-1923	He started legal practice as a Barrister at Bombay.
4-8-1923	The Bombay Legislative Council adopted the resolution moved by S.K. Bole, to the effect that "the untouchable classes be allowed to use all public watering places, wells and *Dharmashalas* (rest houses) which are built and maintained by Government or created by status, as well as public schools courts, offices and dispensaries.[4]
11-9-1923	The Bombay Government issued instructions pursuant to the Bole resolution.
Nov. 1923	Dr. Ambedkar's thesis on *'The Problem of the Rupee'* was accepted by the London University, conferring the degree of Doctor of Science on him.
Dec. 1923	D.D. Gholap and R.S. Nikalje were nominated on the Bombay Legislative Council, for the years 1923 to 1926.

9-3-1924	Dr. Ambedkar convene a meeting at the Damodar Hall, Parel, Bombay, to found the Bahishkrit Hitakarini Sabha, in order to launch his movement for the social uplift of the Depressed Classes.
	Dr. Ambedkar had to sever connection with the Mook-Nayak.
30-3-1924	The Vaikom Satyagraha was started by T.K. Madhavan, Kelappan Nair, E.V. Ramaswami Naikar, and others.
1924	The Second Bombay Provincial Conference of the Depressed Classes, was held at Solapur.
Apr. 1924	Mook-Nayak stopped publication.
15-6-1924	Dr. Ambedkar's son Rajaratna was born.
22-6-1924	Dr. Ambedkar's teacher at the Satara school, Mr. Ambedkar, met his after so long.
20-7-1924	Dr. Ambedkar convened a meeting at the Damodar Hall, when it was formally resolved to found the Bahiskrit Hitakarini Sabha. Its motto was: "Educate, Agitate, Organise". Its aims and objects were : (a) To promote the spread of education among the Depressed Classes by opening Hostels...(b) To promote the spread of culture among the Depressed Classes by opening libraries, social centre and classes or study circles, (c) To advance and improve the economic condition of the Depressed Classes by starting industrial and agricultural Schools, (d) To represent the grievances of the Depressed Classes.
	Among its office-bearers were Sir Chimanlal He. Setalvad, Dr. R.P. Paranjpye, B.G. Kher and S.N. Shivtarkar. Dr. Ambedkar himself was the Chairman of its managing committee.
	The Bahishkrit Hitakarini Sabha functioned upto 1924, concerning itself with social problems.

	Among its trustees was Ramchandra Krishnaji Kadam.
5-10-1924	Dr. Ambekdar wrote in the columns of Ashprishyata Nivaran, in defence of Narayanrao Krishnaji Kadam, Superintendent of the Government Hostel of Pune.
4-12-1924	The Bahishkrit Hitakarini Sabha started a student's hostel at Solapur.
1925	Dr. Ambedkar attended and guided the provincial conference of the Depressed Classes at Nipani.
Jan. 1925	Dr. Ambedkar's article on "Caste & Conversion", was published in the Telagu Samachar, Sankranti Special issues.
10-3-1925	M.K. Gandhi interceded in the Vaikom satyagraha.
10 &11 Apr. 1925	Dr. Ambedkar presided over a conference of The Bombay Presidency Bahishkrit Parishad, at Nipani, district Belgaum. He spoke on the need of social reform prior to political reform ; and he cited the case of the Vaikom satyagraha.
	As a consequence of the Nipani conference, a hostel for students was started at Belgaum, under the supervision of B.H. Varale.
	Dr. Ambedkar's thesis for Doctor of Philosophy (Columbia University) was published Finance in British India : A Study in the Provincial Decentralization of Imperial Finance : publishers P.S. King and Son, Ltd. London. It has a Foreword by his teacher. Prof. Edwin RA. Seligman of the Columbia University. The book was dedicated by the author to "His Highness Shri Sayajirao Gaikwad. Maharaja of Baroda, as a Token of my Gratitude for his help in the matter of my education."

	The Amravati Temple entry satyagraha started under the leadership of Maghoram Govindrao Meshram.
10-6-1925	Dr. Ambedkar was appointed as a part-time lecturer at Batliboi's Accountancy Training Institute. He taught there upto 31-3-1928.
27-8-1925	The Royal Commission on Indian Currency was appointed under the chairmanship of Edward Hilton Young.
15-12-1925	Dr. Ambedkar gave evidence before the Royal Commission on Indian Currency, headed by Hilton Young. He deposed that the gold exchange standard could not be continued with any advantage to India. He recommended to strike a balance at "an average between 1s 4d and 1s 6d, and to see it is nearer to 1s 6d, and away from 1s 4d." He added, "I am therefore strongly opposed to high prices and low exchange: and no righteous Government should be party to such clandestine picking of the pockets of the poorer classes in the country." Dec. 1925 Dr. Ambedkar was nominated as member of the Bombay Legislative Council.
1925	Mahasthavtra Sangharakshita was born in London.
Mar.	1926 The Vaikom temple; entry satyagraha faded away.
1-4-1926	The Bahishkrtt Hitakalini Sabha was registered.
Apr. 1926	Land was demanded at Jejuri, near Pune, for colonisation.
May 1926	The Satara district Mahar Conference was held at Rahimatpur, Koregaon sub-division. Dr. Ambedkar exhorted the people to throw away their inferiority complex, and the chains of their slavery.

19-7-1926 Dr. Ambedkar's son Rajaratna died in infancy.

5-8-1926 A revised Bole resolution was adopted for withholding grants to municipal bodies for not implementing the Bole resolution of 4-8-1923.

Oct. 1926 Dr. Ambedkar won the "Deshache Dushman" law-suit of Pune: *Brahmins of Pune* versus *Bagde, Jedhe* and *Javalkar.* On the opposite side was L. B. Bhopatkar as the lawyer for the Brahmins.

Oct.1926 M.C. Rajah founded the All-India Depressed Classes Association.

The Justice Party burnt the *Manusmrtti.* One seat reserved for the Depressed Classes in the Central Legislature.

Dec. 1926 Dr. Ambedkar and Dr. P.G. Solanki were nominated on the Bombay Legislative Council.

1-1-1927 Dr. Ambedkar, held a meeting at the Koregaon Victory Memorial, 17 miles away from Pune. The Memorial symbolises the defeat of Peshwa forces, and the inauguration of British rule in Pune. The names of the Mahar soldiers who fought on the side of the British, are inscribed on a marble tablet fixed to the Memorial.

5-2-1927 Dr. Ambedkar was felicitated on his nomination to Bombay Legislative Council.

24-2-1927 Dr. Ambedkar delivered his maiden speech in the Legislative Council. He spoke on the Budget. Has the administration progressed to justify the rise in the expenditure? he asked. Only universal education and welfare measures would justify it he said.

10-3-1927 He spoke in the Council on Prohibition.

12-3-1927 He spoke in the Council on Education. He urged that education should be within the reach of everybody. He cited statistics to show how slow was' the progress of education among the Depressed Classes.

16-3-1927	He left Bombay by steamer for the Mahad satyagraha.
19 & 20 Mar. 1927	Dr. Ambedkar led the satyagraha at Mahad to exercise the right of the "Untouchables" to draw water from the Chavadar Tank. (His brother Balaram also was present there.) On the 20th. Dr. Ambedkar dipped his hands into the lake, took some water and drank it, to demonstrate that everybody, including the Depressed Classes had a right to it. (The Mahad conference was held under the auspices of the Kolaba District Bahishkrit Parishad.) A riot broke out in the, Mahad town, when caste-Hindus spread the rumour that Dr. Ambedkar and his followers wanted next to enter the Veereshwar temple.
21-3-1927	The Brahmins of Mahad ceremoniously drew 1,000 pots of water from the Chavadar Tank "polluted" by Dr. Ambedkar and his followers: and the Brahmins performed religious rites to "purify" the water tank.
23-3-1927	Dr. Ambedkar returned to Bombay after completing his enquiry into the riot at Mahad.
3-4-1927	Dr. Ambedkar started, his fortnightly Bahishkrit Bharat, with himself as its editor.
3-5-1927	He presided over the Shivajayanti Celebrations at Badlapur, near Kalyan.
6-6-1927	Five caste- Hindus were convicted for the Mahad riots.
8-6-1927	The Doctor of Philosophy degree was conferred on Dr. Ambedkar by the Columbia University, on his thesis *The Evolution of Provincial Finance in British India.*
June 1927	The Thakurdwar incident. It had been announced that the new temple in Thakurdwar was open to all Hindus. Dr. Ambedkar, therefore, fixed up an

	appointment with the authorities of the temple, and went there with Shivtarkar. Dr. Ambdkar was mobbed and heckled. The temple authorities went back on their word, cancelled the appointment with Dr. Ambedkar, and ritually purified the temple "defined" by the presence of Dr. Ambedkar!
June 1927	Dr. Ambedkar wrote to Dr. Balkrishna, Principal, Rajaram College, Kolhapur, in connection with making M. K. Jadhav a fellow of the College. Dr. Ambedkar also took up M.K. Jadhav's case with the Governor of Bombay; and Jadhav was soon appointed Deputy Collector.
June 1927 to August 1928	Dr. Ambedkarwas appointed on the Editorial Committee of the *Bombay Law Journal,* along with S.R Davar, and M.C. Chagla.
3-7-1927	Under the auspices of the Bahishkrit Hitakararini Sabha, a public meeting of the Depressed Classes was held at the Cowasji Jehangir Hall, to protest against the hardships inflicted on the 'Untouchables' of Mahad. Dr. Ambedkar presided. It was decided at the meeting that a Conference would be held at Mahad after Diwali, to decide whether a Satyagraha should be offered at Mahad. Another resolution was passed urging the Government to establish a separate department to deal with the grievances of the Depressed Classes, as was done in the Madras Presidency. (This issue was taken up by Dr Ambedkar in the Starte Committee. In course of time the existing Social Welfare Department of Bombay Presidency was established.)
26-7-1927	The Depressed Classes of Amaravati gave an ultimatum to the temple authorities for temple entry.

27-7-1927	Dr. Ambedkar spoke in the Bombay Legislative Council on the Bombay University Bill. He represented the interests of the Depressed Classes and demanded their representation in the Senate.
4-8-1927	The Mahad Municipality revoked its earlier resolution of 5-1-1924, and closed the Chavadar Tank to the Depressed Classes.
21-8-1927	The management of the Ambadevi temple of Amaravati, replied it was not possible for them to break old traditions and customs and allow temple entry to the Depressed Classes.
4-9-1927	The Samata Sainaj Sangh (League for Equality) was founded. Its creed was: "All human beings are equal, and they are entitled to equal opportunities for the realization of their personality and enrichment of their life."
11-9-1927	At a meeting held in the Damodar Hall, the Mahad satyagraha committee was fonned. 15-9-1927 The Mahad satyagraha committee announced the 25th and 26th December as the dates for the satyagraha.
Sept. 1927	C.B. Khatrmoday, the noted biographer, and his associates first suggested the use of the sobriquets "Babasaheb" for Dr. Ambedkar, and "Aisaheb" for Mrs Ramabai Ambedkar. (These sobriquets, however, became current from 1930.)
26-10-1927	Babasaheb presided over a conference of Depressed Class students at the Ahilyashram, Pune.
9-10-1927	He presided over a function in honour of Dr. Harold H. Mann, Director of Agriculture and a friend of the Depressed Classes. The function was held at the Government Hostel for Depressed Class Boys, 381 Padamjee Bungalow, Bhavani

	Peth, Pune. The Mahar community of Pune presented an Address to Dr. Mann, on the eva of his retirement.
10-10-1927	Dr. Ambedkar spoke in the Legislative Council on small land-holdings.
4-11-1927	He presided over a meeting at the Damador Hall when Mardy Jones, a Labour M.P. from the U.K., addressed the gathering.
5-11-1927	A meeting was held at the Kamathipura, Bombay. Babasaheb spoke on the need to repeal the Watan Act.
12-11-1927	Death of Balasaheb, Babasaheb's elder brother, at the age of 56 years. The sad news was communicated to Babasaheb at Amravati by telegram.
13 & 14 Nov. 1927	A conference was held at the Indra Bhuvan Theatre, of Amaravati, under the presidency of Dr. Ambedkar, to take a final decision on the Amaravati temple entry issue.
17-11-1927	Opponents of Dr. Ambedkar held a meeting at the Veereshwar temple of Mahad, to foil the satyagraha move of Dr. Ambedkar. The meeting ended in a pandemonium.
7-12-1927	The District Magistrate of Kolaba visited Mahad, and discussed the law and order situation with both parties in the ensuring satyagraha. He refused to issue an order prohibiting the Depressed Classes to draw water from the Chavadar Tank.
12-12-1927	Caste – Hindus of Mahad filed a suit against Dr. Ambedkar and others, in the civil court of Mahad, for an injunction against the claim of the Depressed Classes to draw water from the Chavdar Tank (Pandurang Raghunath Dharap and others versus Dr.Ambedkar and others.)

14-12-1927 The Civil Court of Mahad issued the injunction.

19-12-1927 Principal government officials camped at Mahad, and the police stood guard around the Chavdar Tank.

21-12-1927 Depressed Class delegates began to gather at Mahad, for the satyagraha.

24-12-1927 Dr. Ambedkar arid his colleagues left Bombay by sea. for the conference at Mahad.

25-12-1927 The Mahad conference started at 4 P.M., after seeing the District Magistrate who pressed for postponement of the satyagraha.

Addressing the conference. Babasaheb said: "Ours is a movement which aims at not only removing our own disabilities. but also at bringing about a social revolution that will remove all man-made barriers of caste by providing equal opportunities to all to rise to the highest position and making no distinction between man and man so far as civic rights are concerned. They are upto the Master.

The Manusmriti was publicly burnt, at the Mahad conference, at 7.30 pm. at the hands of "Untouchable" ascetics. (Prior to this. about a year before, the *Manusmrtti* had been also publicly burnt. at a non-Brahmin conference. in the Madras Presidency.(This was stated by Dr. Ambedkar himself, in the course of the evidence given by him in the Chavdar Tank case. in the Mahad civil court. on 2-4-1930.)[5]

26-12-1927 The second day of the Mahad Conference. Dr. Ambedkar read out the letter received from the Collector saying that it was the desire of Government that the Depressed Classes abide by the injunction of the civil court, and defer the proposed satyagraha. In the evening, at 5-30,

	Hood, the Collector, addressed the meeting, assuring the Depressed Classes that Government was on their side, and advised them to abide by the court's injunction order.
27-12-1927	The Mahad conference reassembled at 10 a.m. It was resolved to postpone the satyagraha till the decision of the civil court. In the evening, Dr. Ambedkar addressed a meeting of the Chambhar community of Mahad, and asked them to take an active part in the struggle for rights. On conclusion of the conference, Dr.Ambedkar addressed a meeting of about 3,000 women of the Depressed Classes, advising them to reorient their day-to-day lives.
28-12-1927	Dr. Ambedkar and his party visited the Buddhist caves, near Mahad; and then proceeded to Raigad, the capital of Shivaji.
29-12-1927	Dr. Ambedkar and his party climbed the Raigad mountain, and halted at the Fort. The Depressed Class people of the Raigad region had sensed a plot endangering the life of Dr. Ambedkar. They organised themselves and kept a vigilant watch throughout the night.
Dec. 1927	During the days of the Mahad satyagraha, Dr. Ambedkar said that, if social revolution failed to remove untouchability, we shall have to bring about a religious revolution. [6]
1927	Appadurai, an associate of Pandit Iyodhi Doss, founded the South India Buddhist Association, at the Kolar Gold Fields. He spread the message of Dr. Ambedkar in South India and helped start the Scheduled Castes Federation there, later on.
2-1-1928	Dr. Ambedkar returned from the Mahad conference to Bombay. He left for Pune and Kolhapur by the night train.

3-2-1928 The Simon Commission arrived in Bombay.

March1928 M.K. Jadhav was felicitated at Baramati, on his appointment as District Deputy Collector. (He was the first Deputy Collector from the Depressed Classes.)

A Conference of the Dhangar caste was held at Baramati to discuss the marriage of Tukoji, Holkar Chief of Indore, with Miss Miller.

An all-parties conference appointed the Motilal Nehru Committee to draft a Swaraj Constitution for India.

19-3-1928 Dr. Ambedkar introduced a Bill to amend the Hereditary Offices Act of 1874.

3-5-1928 He spoke in the Bombay Legislative Assembly. on the Bombay Municipal Act.

29-5-1928 He sent a printed memorandum to the Simon Commission. on behalf of the Bahishkrit Hitakarini Sabha.

The topics discussed in it related to education, employment and political problems of the Depressed Classes.

21-6-1928 Dr. Ambedkar was appointed as a Professor at the Government Law College. Bombay.

29-6-1928 The *Samata* monthly was started, with Deorao Vishnu Naik as editor.

24-7-1928 Dr. Ambedkar withdrew the Bill he had introduced in the Assembly on 19-3-1928.

28-7-1928 He spoke in the Assembly on maternity leave faculties to women workers.

3-8-1928 He moved a Bill in the Assembly for the abolition of Mahar Watans: and suggested that the Bill be referred to a Select Committee. He gave a separate statement to the Simon Commission.

5-8-1928 The Bombay Legislative Assembly elected Dr. Ambedkar to work on the Simon Commission. 8-

8-1928 Dr. P.G. Solanki moved a resolution in the Assembly to appoint a committee for the Depressed Classes and Aboriginal Tribes.

10-8-1928 The Moti Lal Nehru Committee's Report on the Swaraj Constitution for India, was published. It says, "We have not made any special provision for the representation of the depressed classes in legislatures. This could be done by way of special electorates or by nomination. We are not prepared to extend this unsound and harmful principle, if we can help it: nor do we think that we will do any good to these classes by ensuring some seats for them in this way. We are still more opposed to nomination."

21-9-1928 Narayan Guru, an "Untouchable" philosopher, died.

26-9-1928 Caste-men impose a social boycott on S.N. Shivtarkar.

Oct.1928 Textile mill-workers' first strike involving 1,50,000 workers, Depressed Class workers were hardest hit. Dr. Ambedkar did not favour the strike. Depressed Class workers were not allowed to work in the weaving departments of the mills: and no labour organisation had till then cared to remove this disability. Trade unions were using the weapon of strike rather for political ends than for the welfare of the workers. Dr. Ambedkar was thinking of having two textile mills set apart for Depressed Class workers.[7]

8-10-1928 The Government of Bombay approved the Depressed Class students' hostel scheme, and gave sanction to the opening of five such hostels.

23-10-1928 Dr. Ambedkar gave evidence before the Simon Commission, at Pune. He asserted that the "Untouchables" were distinctly apart from the

	Savama-Hindus, and demanded 22 seats in the Bombay Legislative Assembly for them.[8]
5-11-1928	A Committee of nine persons was constituted under O.B.H. Starte, by the Government of Bombay, "to enquire into the educational, economic and social condition of the Depressed Classes (Untouchables) and of the Aboriginal Tribes, in the Presidency, and to recommend measures for their advancement." Dr. Ambedkar and Dr. P.G. Solanki were nominated by Government on the committee. (The committee submitted its Report to Government in March 1930.)
Dec.1928	Dr. Ambedkar and Dr. Solanki were deputed by Government to visit the Sakkar Darn.
March1929	Dr. Ambedkar's term of professorship at the Government Law College expired.
13-4-1929	Death of Tulsa, Dr. Ambedkar's elder sister.
April 1929	Dr. Ambedkar presided over the Chiplun conference when "sacred threads" were distributed to Depressed Class men.
17-5-1929	Dr. Ambedkar submitted a separate report to the Simon Commission, emphasisingon the political rights of the Depressed Classes.[9]
29-5-1929	A resolution was passed at a meeting at Jamod (Vidarbha), on the need to convert to another religion.
2-6-1929	Twelve Mahars embraced Islam.[10]
13-6-1929	The law court gave a verdict in favour of the *Depressed* Classes, in the Mahad satyagraha case.
9-7-1929	Satyagraha at Khulna (Bengal) by "Untouchables", before the temple of Kali.
24-7-1929	Dr. Ambedkar withdrew the Bill to amend the Hereditary Offices Act.
Ganapati Festival,	Organisers of the Dadar Sarvajanik Ganapati Festival had to concede the demands of the

1929	Depressed Classes.
22-9-1929	At Pune, the Parvati Temple Satyagraha Committee was formed, with Shivram Janba Kamble as chairman, and P.N. Rajbhoj as secretary.
2-10-1929	Shivram Janba Kamble sent a notice to the trustees of the Parvati temple, Pune, regarding the proposed temple entry satyagraha.
6-10-1929	The Parvati temple trustees gave a reply to Shivram Janba Kamble's notice in the negative.
13-10-1929 (Vijaya-dashami)	The Parvati temple satyagraha began.
16-10-1929	Dr. Ambedkar supported the Parvati temple satyagraha.
22-10-1929	In a conference of the Depressed Classes' at Madras, N. Shivraj supported the Parvati temple satyagraha of Pune.
24-10-1929	The Collector of Pune declared the steps leading to the Parvati temple, open to all, irrespective of caste.
8-11-1929	Dr. Ambedkar wrote an article in the *Bombay Chronicle* under the title 'Wanted an Anti-Priestcraft Association."[11]
1929	The Belgaum students' hostel was shifted to Dharwar.
15-11-1929	The last issue of Bahishkrit Bharat.
30-11-1929	The *Janata* fortnightly was started.
2-3-1930	The Nashik Kalaram temple satyagraha started under B.K. (Dadasaheb) Gaikwad's direction.
3-3-1930	Dr. Ambedkar at Nashik to support the Kalaram temple entry satyagraha. A procession was taken out, and Dr. Ambedkar addressed the conference.
4-3-1930	Shivram Janba Kamble, R.S. Ghatge, Patade and others "waylaid" M.K. Gandhi, during the celebrated Dandi March. *The Times of India*

appears to have written an editorial on the offensive slogans shouted during the Dandi March: "Who will go to the Assembly?"

28-3-1930 Dr. Ambedkar cautioned Dadasaheb Gaikwad of Nashik not to precipitate matters relating to the Kalaram temple satyagraha. Dr. Ambedkar had written to the Governor of Bombay, protesting against the attitude of the Collector.

2-4-1930 Dr. Ambedkar gave evidence in the case *No.* 405 of the Mahad Chavdar Tank.

9-4-1930 In the chariot procession of the Nashik Kalaram temple, caste-Hindus played foul.

May,1930 The Simon Commission's Report was published.

8- 7 -1930 Dr. Ambedkar was appointed on the Select Committee on the Bombay University (Amendment) Bill.

8-8-1930 &
9-8-1930 Dr. Ambedkar presided over the all-India Depressed Class Conference (First Session), at Nagpur-Kamptee.

His speech was important, for it outlined the ground-plan for future action. He demanded: (1) Adequate representation in all the Legislatures of the country, Central and Provincial; (2) Reservation in adequate proportion in the Public Services of the country.

The Conference accepted the Round Table Conference as the best means of solving the constitutional problem.[12] of Indian society.

9-9-1930 Dr. Ambedkar received an invitation to the Round Table Conference (1930-1932)

11-9-1930 Names of delegates to the Round Table Conference, were announced.

25-9-1930 The Chirnar firing incident. (Chirnar near Panwel) (3 accused defended by Dr Ambedkar.)

Sept. 1930	The foundations of "Rajgriha" and "Charminar", were laid.
2-10-1930	A reception was given to Dr. Ambedkar, on the eve of his departure to London, for the RT.C. Dr. P.G. Solanki presided. An address was presented to Dr. Ambedkar.
4-10-1930	Dr. Ambedkar left for London for the R.T.C., by S.S. "Viceroy of India".
18-10-1930	Dr. Ambedkar and Srinivasan, the other Depressed Class delegate, arrived at London.
12-11-1930	The Round Table Conference was inaugurated by King George V.
24-11-1930	Janata was started in place of Bahishkrit Bharat, (Deorao Naik was its first editor.)
Dec.1930	Dr. Ambedkar prepared two Memoranda, in London: (1) Political demands of the Untouchables, and (2) Recruitment in the Army. He got 2,000 copies of the Memoranda printed privately.
Dec.1930	Mrs Ramabai Ambedkar, son Yeshwant, Mrs Laxmibai (sister-in-law), and Laxmibai's son Mukund, went for a change of air to Dharwad, along with R.H. Varale.
19-1-1931	The First Round Table Conference ended. The Maharaja of Baroda, Dr. Ambedkar's benefactor, was very much impressed by Dr. Ambedkar's performance at the R.T.C.
13-2-1931	Dr. Ambedkar left London for India. 27-2-1931 He arrived at Bombay.
5-3-1931	The Irwin-Gandhi Pact was signed. It paved the way for Congress participation in the next R.T.C.
10-3-1931	Dr. Ambedkar addressed a conference at Nashik, exhorting the people to keep up the struggle for social freedom by lawful and constitutional means.
15-3-1931	The Depressed Class people of Nashik took out a procession. Caste-Hindus threw stones at it. The

Depressed Class people of Nashik resented the atrocity, and thought it better to convert to another religion. Dr. Ambedkar advised them restraint.

16-3-1931 Dr. Ambedkar defended the patriots (Accused Nos. 8, 9. and 10) in the Chirnar firing case.

March1931 Government threw open the Police Department, for recruitment of the Depressed Classes.

April1931 M.N. Roy (under the pseudonym Dr. Mohamud), met Dr. Ambedkar at his office, in Bombay. Dr. Ambedkar found that Roy had not given thought to the problem of the Untouchables. (It seems that during the interview. Dr. Ambedkar saw through Dr. Mohamud's disguise)[13]

19-4-1931 Dr. Ambedkar convened a meeting of Depressed Class leaders from all over India, at Loveji castle, Parel, Bombay. (Gokhale Education Society's High School).

8-6-1931 In the matter of the Chavdar Tank case, the caste-Hindus of Mahad went in appeal to the higher court.

July 1931 Names of delegates to the Second Round Table Conference were announced. Dr. Ambedkar's name included.

2-7-1931 The Chirnar case hearing ended.

14-8-1931 Dr. Ambedkar met M.K. Gandhi at "Mani Bhavan", Malbar Hill. Bombay. That was his first encounter with Gandhi. He was accompanied by Shivtarkar, Naik, Pradhan. B.K.Gaekwad and Kadrekar.

Gandhi maintained that the 'Untouchables' were an integral part of the Hindus; so they cannot be politically alienated from the Hindus.

Dr. Ambedkar replied: Congressmen oppose our movement. It was Congressmen who opposed us in our Mahad and Nashik satyagrahas. The president of the Nashik District Congress Committee was himself the chainnan of the orthodox group that opposed our satyagraha. Congress wants to divide and rule (in our case); but Congress is, eager to reconcile with Muslims, and Sikhs: not with us.

The Times of India of 15-8-1931 reports: "He (Dr. Ambedkar) tried to impress on Mr Gandhi his point that the Congress had not so far done anything tangible for the depressed classes, and that Mr Gandhi was under a delusion in imagining that the Depressed Classes were solidly behind him ... Dr. Ambedkar eventually left without convincing Mr Gandhi or being convinced by him ...

15-8-1931 Dr. Ambedkar left for London, for the Second R.T.C.

29-8-1931 He arrived in London.

M.K.Gandhi left Bombay for London.

7-9-1931 The Second RTC starts: (7-9-1931 to 1-12-1931).

12-9-1931 M.K.Gandhi arrived in London for the Second R.T.C.

28-9-1931 The Minorities Committee of the R.T.C met. (It met subsequently on 1-10-1931.8-10-1931 & 13-11-1931.)

6-10-1931 Gandhi-Muslim secret pact to scuttle the Depressed class demand for separate electorates.[15]

8-10-1931 Dr. Ambedkar signed the Minorities Pact.

5-11-1931 The Nashik Kalaram temple entry satyagraha was resumed.

Delegates to the R.T.C. were invited by King George V to tea.

10-11-1931 Dr. Ambedkar addressed the Institute of International Affairs at London.

Nov.1931 Dr. Ambedkar's Appeal on behalf of the D.C. Institute, was issued.

21-11-1931	Kalappan launched the Guruvayur temple satyagraha. It lasted for one year.
1-12-1931	The Second R.T.C. was adjourned.
5-12-1931	On conclusion of the Second R.T.C. Dr. Ambedkar left London for New York to meet his old teachers.
27-12-1931	The Indian Franchise Committee was constituted under Lord Lothian, with Dr. Ambedkar as a member of it.
28-12-1931	M.K. Gandhi returned to Bombay from the R.T.C. Depressed Class people staged a black- flag demonstration against him.
31-12-1931	The Ratnagiri District Bahishkrti Parish ad was convened at Chiplun. A "charge-sheet" against M.K. Gandhi was placed before the people.
1-1-1932	The Nashik Kalaram temple satyagraha was resumed.
4-1-1932	Dr. Ambedkar returned from New York to London. M.K. Gandhi and Vallabhbhai Patel were arrested and interned in the Yeravada Jail.
15-1-1932	Dr. Ambedkar left London and embarked at Marseilles.
29-1-1932	He arrived at Bombay along with British members of the Franchise Committee and Shaukat All. Dr. Ambedkar and Shaukat Ali were enthusiastically received by Depressed Class people: and they were taken out in a procession to Byculla. In the evening, a huge meeting was held at Parel. In the address presented to Dr. Ambedkar, on the occasion, it was said. "You have, indeed, proved to the hilt our claims for equality of status and treatment; and but for the valiant fight you put up on our behalf, our claims would have been ignored." [16] Dr. P.G. Solanki presided over the meeting.

31-1-1932	At the Bhusawal railway station, on his way to Delhi. Dr. Ambedkar was presented an address by his followers.
Feb to Apr. 1932	Dr. Ambedkar travelled with the Franchise Committee in Bihar to Calcutta and other places.
28-2-1932	He was given a thunderous reception at Madras.
Feb. 1932	The Samaj Samata Sangh published S.D. Nadkami's *On Ram-Rajya And Slave Mentality.*
1-3-1932	The Raja-Moonje Pact was made at Delhi. It stood for joint -electorates and reserved seats for the Depressed Classes in proportion to their population.
March 1932	The Government of Bombay constituted a committee with D. Symington, ICS, to enquire into the condition of the Depressed Classes in the Nashik district.
11-3-1932	M.K. Gandhi wrote to Sir Samuel Hoare, from the Yeravada Jail, against separate electorates for the Depressed Classes: and announced his determination to fast unto death, if the decision regarding separate electorates for the Depressed Classes was not revoked.
14-4-1932	The Naspik Kalaram temple satyagraha-entered into its third stage. Dadasaheb Gaekwad and Amritrao Ranakhambe were arrested. (The situation worried Dr. Ambedkar: he considered the struggle for political rights to be more important than the problem of temple entry.)
1-5-1932	Dr. Ambedkar submitted his note of dissent to the Franchise Committee. [17]
4-5-1932	He returned from Simla to Bombay.
7th & 8th May 1932	Dr. Ambedkar attended the All-India Depressed Classes Congress. at Nagpur-Kamptee, under the presidency of Muniswami

	Pillay. The conference repudiated the Raja-Moonje Pact: and it declared the Minorities Pact as the irreducible minimum of the demands of the Depressed Classes.
22-5-1932	Dr. Ambedkar was given a hero's welcome at Pune, and was taken in a procession through the principal streets of the Cantonment to the "Ahilyashram" where a meeting was held under the presidency of A.B. Latthe. A welcome address was presented to Dr. Ambedkar, In reply. Dr. Ambedkar said: "When after some days the dust settles down and a review of the proceedings of the Round Table Conference is dispassionately taken by future historians, the future generations of the Hindus will acclaim my services to the nation as a 'Nam' on earth.[18] It is my solemn vow to die in the service and cause of those down-trodden people among whom I was born. I was brought up and I am living."[19]
24-5-1932	Dr. Ambedkar was presented an address. (Belgaum) Dewan Bahadur Latthe presided. Latthe introduced Dr. Ambedkar as "a strong nationalist at heart."[20].
26-5-1932	Dr. Ambedkar left for England "in secret" to interview the Premier and Cabitlet Ministers.
7-6-1932	He arrived at London; and presented a memorandum of 22 typed pages to the British Premier.
June-July 1932	Dr. Ambedkar stayed for about a month, in a German Sanatorium conducted by Dr. Moller at Dresden.
4-8-1932	The Communal Award was announced by the British Premier, giving separate electorates to the Depressed Classes.

17-8-1932	Dr. Ambedkar returned from England.
18-8-1932	M.K. Gandhi decided to fast unto death, as a protest against the Communal Award.
19-9-1932	Hindu leaders met at Bombay, On the eve of Gandhi's fast, at the Indian' Merchants' Chamber, under the presidency of Madan Mohan Malviya. Dr. Ambedkar issued a press communique on the subject of Gandhi's decision to fast unto death. [21] Dr. Ambedkar and Hindu leaders came to Pune to meet M.K. Gandhi.
20-9-1832	M.K. Gandhi commenced his fast unto death at noon. He wrote to P.N. Rajbhoj, "so far as Hinduism is concerned. separate electorates would simply vivisect and disrupt it." Dr. Ambedkar met Gandhi.
21-9-1932	Gandhi wrote to 'Rajbhoj. "Nothing will satisfy me till the last vestige of untouchability is eradicated." Dr. Ambedkar, Malviya, and M.C. Rajah met Gandhi in the Yeravada Jail, to discuss terms for ending Gandhi's fast.
22-9-1932	Dr. Ambedkar met Gandhi again, accompanied by M.R. Jayakar, Birla, Chunilal Mehta, and C.Rajagopalachari.
24-9-1932	Gandhi agreed to accept the terms of settlement reached at a conference of the leaders. The conference had resolved: "Hence-forward among Hindus, no one shall be regarded as an untouchable by reason of his birth."
24-9-1932	To Dr. Ambedkar who was present, Gandhi said, "I am here today to ask you for a reprieve for my caste-Hindu brethren."
At 5 p.m.	Dr. Ambedkar signed with Gandhi the Poona Pact, giving up the demand for separate electorates, and making it possible for Gandhi to end his fast.

25-9-1932 (Sunday)	Hindu leaders met in a conference, at the Indian Merchants' Chamber hall, to confirm the Poona Pact.
25-9-1932	Dr. Ambedkar spoke at Wadala, Bombay, on the occasion of the Ganapati Festival, expressing his disgust with Hinduism.
26-9-1932	The Poona Pact was ratified by the British Premier.
28-9-1932	Dr. Ambedkar addressed a mammoth meeting at Worli, Bombay, and cautioned the Depressed Classes not to fall a prey to the religious wiles of the Hindus.
30-9-1932	The Anti-Untouchability League was founded. (It was later renamed as 'Servants of the Untouchables Society', and thereafter as 'Harijan Sevak Sangh.)
1-10-1932	M.K. Gandhi sent a telegram to Kelappan to end his fast started on 21-9-1932 for the Guruvayur temple entry.
6-10-1932	Dr. Ambedkar spoke in the Bombay Legislative Assembly on a Bill to amend the Village Panchayats Act. He opposed the Bill, asking the question: "Are the Depressed Classes represented in the Gram Panchayats?"
19-10-1932	Dr. Ambedkar met Gandhi in the Yeravada Jail and suggested that more Depressed Class men be taken on the Committee of the Anti-Untouchability League.
28-10-1932	Dr. Ambedkar addressed a meeting at the Cowasjee Jehangir Hall, Bombay, organised by the Rushi Samaj. He warned the people not to get lost in the temple entry movement, and in inter-dining programmes. That would not solve their bread problem. He also gave expression to his thoughts on fate, poverty, and human misery. He said.:

"The sooner you remove the foolish belief that your miseries were pre-ordained, the better, The, thought that your poverty is an inevitability, and is inborn and inseparable, is entirely erroneous[22]

4-11-1932 On the eve of Dr. Ambedkar's departure for the Third R.T.C., the Meghwal community presented an address to him.

7-11-1932 He left Bombay for London to participate in the Third R.T.C.

14-11-1932 On the way to London from Port Said, Dr. Ambedkar wrote to A.V. Thakkar, General Secretaty. Anti-Untouchability League, saying. 'Want a change of heart in the savarna-Hindus *'Nam'*. not for helping a few individuals at random, or a few selected boys belonging to the Depressed Classes, but for raising the whole class to a higher level"

(Dr. Ambedkar records that Thakkar Bapa did not even care to acknowledge its receipt)

17-11-1932 The Third R.T.C. commenced its deliberations. Dr. Ambedkar was appointed on the Communal Safeguards Committee and on the Joint Select Committee of both Houses of Parliament.

24-12-1932 The Third R.T.C concluded its work.

Dec.1932 In the Central Assembly, Ranga Iyer presented his Untouchability Abolition Bill.

24-1-1933 Dr. Ambedkar returned from England to Bombay.

30-1-1933 Dr. Ambedkar met the Viceroy at Delhi, in response to an invitation from the Viceroy to all delegates to the Round Table Conference. The savama-Hindus appeal in the Thane court, regarding the Chavadar Tank case (Appeal No. 32), was rejected. They decided to appeal to the High Court.

4-2-1933	In response to a telegram from M.K. Gandhi, Dr. Ambedkar met Gandhi in the Yeravada Jail. Dr. Stanley Jones too was present during the interview for some time. Dr. Ambedkar made it clear to M.K. Gandhi that the Depressed Classes would not be satisfied with mere temple entry. Moral and social uplift and education were of far more importance. The entire caste system must be annihilated. Gandhi, it seems, was not prepared to give Dr. Ambedkar encouragement to that extent. Untouchability was a sin, Gandhi said; but the caste system was only social distinction.[23] Dr. Ambedkar's message to Gandhi's Harijan was: "So long as there are castes, untouchability will remain. There can be no uplift of the untouchables without annihilation of caste."
12-2-1933	Dr. Ambedkar spoke in the Bombay Legislative Council, on the Village Panchayat Bill He issued an important statement on Temple Entry Bills. "If the Hindu religion is to be a religion of social equality, then an amendment of its code to provide temple entry is not enough. What is required is to purge it of the doctrine of *Chaturvarnya.* This is the root cause of all inequality, and is also the parent of the caste system and untouchability which are merely other forms of inequality. Unless it is done, the Depressed Classes will reject not only temple entry but also the Hindu faith. To accept temple entry and be content with it, is to compromise with evil, and to barter away the sacredness of human personality as a tanner system of Indo-Aryan society called Chamar an old concept of *'Ravidas Culture*[24]
18-2-1933	He spoke in the Bombay Legislative Council on the Whipping Act.

February 1933	At a meeting in Mazgaon. Bombay. Dr. Ambedkar said: "The mission of our movement is to fight against tyranny, injustice and false traditions, undo all privileges and release the harassed people from bondage."
Mar. 1933	A White Paper on Indian Constitutional Reforms was released by the British Government.
22-3-1933	Maharaja Sayajirao Gaekwad of Baroda spoke highly of Dr. Ambedkar at the "Ahilyashram", Pune.
24-3-1933	Ranga Iyer presented his Temple Entry Bill the Central Legislature.
April1933	Dr. Ambedkar had talks with M.K. Gandhi for revision of the Poona Pact.
	Death of Anagarika Dharmapala.
	Death of Professor P. Lakshmi Narasu, the author of The Essence of Buddhism.
14-4-1933	Dr. Ambedkar's Birth Anniversary first publicly celebrated in Bombay, and Nashik, and Pune.[25]
24-4-1933	Dr. Ambedkar left: for London.
6-5-1933	He arrived in London.
11-7-1933 to 28-7-1933 and 3-10-1933 to 7-11-1933	Dr. Ambedkar participated in the transactions of the Joint Parliamentary Committee on Indian Constitutional Reforms, under the Chairmanship of Lord Linlithgow.
23-10-1933	Dr. Ambedkar interviewed Winston Churchill.
	While in England, Dr. Ambedkar was busy collecting material for a book on the Indian Army.
1933	Construction of Dr. Ambedkar's "Rajgriha" was completed.
1933-1950	Dr. Ambedkar was Fellow of the University of Bombay, Faculties of Arts and Law.

8-1-1934	Dr. Ambedkar arrived from London to Bombay.
3-3-1934	Dr. Ambedkar wrote to Dadasaheb Gaekwad to abandon the Nashik Kalaram temple entry satyagraha.
June1934	Dr. Ambedkar was appointed part-time professor at the Government Law College, Bombay.
	The Bombay Legislative Council rejected RR Bakhale's Removal of Hartjan Disabilities Bill.
14-10-1934	Dada Keluskar died.
24-12-1934	Dr. Ambedkar and his colleagues went to see to the Daulatabad Fort. They were insulted by an
30-12-1934	old Mohammedan when they drew water from a tank to wash themselves with. (The party consisted of Dr. Ambedkar, Shivtarkar, Pradhan, Kawli, Madkebuwa, Diwakar. Pagare, Deoji Dolas, Amritrao Ranakhambe. Raoba Thenge and his sons Krishnarao and Bhagwat.)
27-5-1935	Death of RarnabaiAmbedkar.
1-6-1935	Dr. Ambedkar was appointed Principal of the Government Law College, Bombay, & Perry Professor of Jurisprudence.
	He was there for over two years, during which time he did much to improve the institution.
July 1935	He was contemplating to renounce public life, due to the death of Ramabai Ambedkar.
13-10-1935	In the morning, the Yeola Municipality (district Nashik) presented an address to Dr. Ambedkar.
	At the Yeola conference, Dr. Ambedkar made the epoch-making announcement of his determination to leave Hinduism for another religion. "It is the inequality in Hinduism," he said, "that compels me to quit Hinduism." And he added, "I had the misfortune of being born with the stigma of untouchability; that is not my fault.

But, I will not die as a Hindu; this is within my power. "[26]

25-10-1935 Dr. Kurtakoti, Shankaracharya, deputed his representatives to meet Dr. Ambedkar. Dr. Ambedkar assured them that he would not do anything that might harm the interests of the nation by his conversion. "But why do you try to hide the hideous face of Hinduism in practice?" he asked them. "My only intention", he said, "is that Untouchables should adopt such a religion as will promote their progress. We have Buddhism, Sikhism, and the Arya Samaj religions before our eyes."

27-10-1935 Prof Dharmanand Kosambi met Dr. Ambedkar at "Rajgriha".

10-11-1935 A conference of the Depressed Classes was held at Nashik Road. It resolved to renounce Hindu gods, scriptures, priests, pilgrimages, and to stop propaganda for temple entry. It seems that some people of Nashik consigned their family deities and religious books to the flames.

12-12-1935 Dr. Ambedkar was invited by the Jat-Pat--Todak Mandal of Lahore to preside over its conference.

1935 Death of Professor Cannan. Dr. Ambedkar's teacher at the London School of Economics and Political Science.

Principal Dr. Ambedkar contributed an article on 'Thoughts on the Reform of Legal Education in the Bombay Presidency: to the magazine of the Government Law College, Bombay.

1935-1937 Dr. Ambedkar was a member of the Academic Council and the Syndicate of the University of Bombay.

11th &12th Jan. 1936 Dr. Ambedkar reiterated his resolve to quit Hinduism, and added, "I have come to the conclusion that the best way out, is complete severance from Hinduism." He was speaking at a conference, at the "Ahilyashram", Pune, under the presidency of N. Shivraj.

29-2-1936 The *Chambhar* community of East Khandesh (district Jalgaon) supported the conversion resolution.

5-4-1936 Dr. Ambedkar, Madkebuwa. Deorao Naik and others came to Kaivalyadham, Lonavala, for rest and recoupement of health.

On his return from Lonavala, son Yeshwantrao left for Kerala with his uncle, Shankarmama, for medical treatment for rheumatism.

Apr.1936 Dr. Ambedkar attended a conference of the Sikh Mission.

27-4-1936 He informed the *Jat-Pat-Todak Mandal* he would not preside over their conference, as he was not prepared to alter his presidential address.

15-5-1936 The Annihilation of Caste speech prepared for the Jat-Pat-Todak Mandal's conference, was released by Dr. Ambedkar.

30-5-1936 Dr. Ambedkar held a conference of Mahars at to Dadar (Nagaum) to sound their reaction to his

2-6-1936 call at Yeola for conversion. B. Venkatrao of Andhra presided. In the pandal, in the morning, was held a conference of ascetics. They shaved their heads, beards and moustaches and discarded the symbols· of Hinduism. and made a bonfire of them all. On the 31st May, Dr. Ambedkar delivered his famous *'Mukti Kon Pathe?'*(Which Way to Emancipation?) Speech.

The burden of his speech was:

If you must gain Self-Respect, change your religion;

If you desire Independence, change your religion;

If you want Equality, change your religion;

If you wish to create a Society that ensures Co-operation and Brotherhood, change your religion; If you want Power, change your religion; and If you wish to make Happy the world in which you live, change your religion.

June 1936 The Italian Buddhist monk Lokanatha met Dr. Ambedkar, in Bombay, "with the object of persuading him to become a *Buddhist*".

16-6-1936 A largely attended meeting of Devadasis, Potrajas, Bhutes, Aradhls, and Jogtis, was held at the Damodar Hall, to support the mass conversion movement inaugurated at Yeola. Dr. Ambedkar made a fervent appeal, especially to the women, most of whom had come from the "red-light" zone of Kamathipura: "... I insist that if you want to be with us, you must give up your disgraceful life. The Mahar women of Kamathipura are a shame to the community ... There are only two ways open to you: either you remain where you are and continue to be despised and shunned; or you give up your disgusting profession and come with us."

18-6-1936 Ambedkar-Moonje talks at Bombay on the question of the conversion of the Depressed Classes. Dr. Moonje favoured conversion to Sikhism.

28-6-1936 Anti-conversion Matang parishad, in the Bhokarwadi (now Rajewadi) locality of Pune. Dr. Kurtakoti, Shankaracharya, was honoured at the Conference. Dr. Ambedkar was understandably annoyed on reading a news report on it.

July1936 Dr. Ambedkar sent his son Yeshwantrao and his nephew· Mukundrao to the Sikh Gurudwara at Amritsar, to get to understand Sikhism.

15-8-1936	Dr. Ambedkar founded the Independent Labour party to contest the general elections under the Government of India Act, 1935.
15-9-1936	He deputed sixteen men (mostly bairagis) to the Sikh Mission at Amritsar to study Sikhism. They became Sikh converts.
17-9-1936	He introduced his Khati Abolition Bill, in the Bombay Legislative Council.
Sept. 1936	He sold his "Charminar" to pay for books purchased.
11-11-1936	He left for London via Geneva. He was on a mission to discuss with constitutional experts the situation that would arise on the conversion of the Depressed Classes to another religion. He was also in search of a publisher for his Military Problem of India written from the point of view of the constitutional law of India.
12-12-1936	Temple entry proclamation in favour of the Depressed Classes, made by the Maharaja of Travancore the first of its kind in modern India.
30-12-1936	At the 17th convention of the Hindu Mahasabha. Pandit Madan Mohan Malaviya vetoed Dr. Jayakar's resolution for inter-caste marriages and inter-caste dinners.
14-1-1937	Dr. Ambedkar returned from England to Bombay.
17-2-1937	General Elections under the Government of India Act of 1935. (Total seats 175; reserved seats 15; ILP candidates 17.) Among the ILP candidates elected were: Dr B.R. Ambedkar. B.K. Gaikwad, RR Bhole, D.G. Jadhav, B.H. Varale, Sawadkar, G.G. Bhatankar, K.S. Sawant, J.S. Aidale & P.J. Roham.
17-3-1937	The Mahad Chavadar Tank case was decided in favour of the Depressed Classes, by Justice Broomfield and Justice N.J. Wadia.

19-3-1937 Elected Congress leaders took oath of office, at Bombay, and formed a ministry under the Premiership of B.G. Kher.

June 1937 The Khalsa College was started at Bombay. Dr. Ambedkar was associated with the College.

27-7-1937 Death of Ramchandra Krishnaji Kadam of Pune

23-8-1937 Dr. Ambedkar spoke in the Bombay Legislative Assembly on the Bill for ministers' salaries. The principle he underlined was that offices in a free country should not be put beyond the reach of men of moderate fortune.

11-9-1937 Dr. Ambedkar spoke on the abolition of the Khoti system, in the Bombay Legislative Assembly; and also on another Bill to abolish Mahar Vatans.

31-12-1937 Dr. Ambedkar addressed a conference convened by the Sholapur District Depressed Classes Conference, at Pandharpur.

1-1-1938 He addressed a conference of the Mangs of Sholapur.

4-1-1938 The Sholapur Municipality presented an address to Dr. Ambedkar.

18-1-1938 During the course of a debate in the Bombay Legislative Assembly, on a Bill for amendment of the Local Boards Act, B.K. Gaikwad objected to the definition of the term 'Scheduled Caste' as 'Hanjan: Dr. Ambedkar rose to support Gaikwad. When the ruling party forced the appellation 'Harijan' down the throats of the Scheduled Castes, Dr. Ambedkar and his partymen walked out in protest.

20-1-1938 Dr. Ambedkar spoke in the Legislative Assembly on Probation of Offenders Bill.

23-1-1938 He addressed a conference of peasants at Ahmednagar.

12th&13th He presided over a conference of the G. I. P.

Feb.1938	Railway Depressed Class workers, at Mamnad, (district Nashik), He spoke on the need to organise against the twin enemies, namely Brahminism and Capitalism.
2-3-1938	He spoke in the Legislature on the Budget.
27-4-1938	He spoke in the Legislature on the Bill to amend the Police Act. He said he would resist the exploitation of the Scheduled Castes to the last drop of his blood.
April 1938	In the national interest he opposed the creation of a separate Karnatak Province.
May 1938	He resigned from the Principalship of the Government Law College, Bombay.
13th to 21st May 1938	He went on a tour of the Konkan districts: Kankavli (14-5-38). Deorukh, Aravali, Chiplun (16-5-38). Guhagar. Khed, Dapoli, and Mahad. He was determined to abolish the notorious Khati system.
13th to 15th May 1938	The Konkan Panchmahal Parish ad at Kankavli.
20-6-1938	The Khalsa College was started in Bombay. Aug. 1938 A meeting was held in the R.M. Bhat High School, Bombay, for exposing M.K. Gandhi's attitude in opposing the inclusion of a Scheduled Caste man, Agnibhoj, in the Central Provinces Ministry.
11-9-1938	Dr. Ambedkar addressed the 11th Annual Depressed Class Students' Gathering at the "Ahilyashram", Pune.
Sept. 1938	He spoke on the Industrial Disputes Bill, in the Bombay Legislature and bitterly opposed the Bill for its attempt to curtail the rights and liberty of industrial workers.
6-11-1938	Sixty unions of industrial workers met under the Chairmanship of Jamnadas Mehta. Dr. Ambedkar, S.A.Dange. Shamrao Parulekar, and others were present. Dr. Ambedkar summoned

	his' party MLAs, to make the ensuing strike a success.
	A Labour rally was held at the Kamgar maidan, Jamnadas Mehta presiding.
7-11-1938	The workers' strike. Dr. Ambedkar spoke at the workers' rally.
10-11-1938	As directed by Dr. Ambedkar, his partyman, P.J. Roham, moved a resolution in the Legislature for adopting measures for birth control.
11-12-1938	The Vatandar MaharVethi Parish ad was held at Srirampur (district Ahmednagar) to change 'judi" (tax) into full assessment on payment of a monthly salary.
Dec.1938	Dr. Ambedkar addressed the first Depressed Class Conference in the Nizam's dominion at Hyderabad.
18-1-1939	Dr. Ambedkar flew to Rajkot, as a state guest, to study the problems of the Scheduled Castes. He interviewed the Thakore Saheb.
19-1-1939	Dr. Ambedkar saw M.K. Gandhi. The problem before pr Ambedkar was the non-inclusion of Depressed Class Representative on the State's Reforms Committee. But as Gandhi suddenly got fever, Dr. Ambedkar could not fully discuss the matter with him.
29-1-1939	Dr. Arobedkar spoke on Federation versus Freedom, at the Gokhale Hall, Pune.
6-2-1939	Death of Maharaja Sayajirao Gaikwad of Baroda, at his Jai Mahal Palace, in Bombay.
17 -3-1939	Dr. Ambedkar raised in the Bombay Legislative Assembly, the issue relating to the police firing on mill-workers of Bombay.
July 1939	Dr. Ambedkar addressed a meeting of the '*Rohidas Shikshan Samaj*', at the R.M. Bhat High School, Bombay. He said that it was regrettable

	that there should be difference of opinion among the different sections of the depressed classes; his work was not meant for any particular section, but for the benefit of the whole community.
1939-1945	World War II.
11-9-1939	The Viceroy announced the suspension of the Federation.
25-10-1939	Dr. Ambedkar spoke in the Legislature on Premier Kher's resolution regarding India's involvement in the World War II.
Oct. 1939	Lord Linlithgow interviewed Indian leaders.
(1st Fort night)	Dr. Ambedkar was interviewed on the 9th.
Oct.1939 -(3rd week)	Jawaharlal Nehru, Chairman of the War-sub committee of the Congress held talks for two days with Dr. Ambedkar, in Bombay. (This was their first meeting, face to face.)
	Discussions were held between Congress leaders and Dr. Ambedkar for a couple of days. The talks were confined to the resignation of Congress ministry of Bombay. Dr. Ambedkar said that the Scheduled Castes would not accept the status of political Shudras.
Nov. 1939	Congress ministries in India resigned.
16-12-1939	Dr. Ambedkar presided over a conference of Vatandar Mahars, at Haregaon, Srirampur sub-division, district Ahmednagar, to protest against the rise in 'Judi" assessment. (Judi -land revenue levied on service or vatan lands; it is less than the usual assessment.)
27-12-1939	He was presented with an address by the Beigaum Municipality.
	Death of Professor Edwin R.A. Seligman, Dr. Ambedkar's teacher at the Columbia University.
26-3-1940	The Muslim League passed the Pakistan Resolution. in its conference at Lahore.

May 1940	Dr. Ambedkar founded the Mahar Panchayat.
22-7-1940	Subhas Chandra Bose met Dr. Ambedkar, at Bombay. After a talk on the proposed Federation. Dr. Ambedkar asked Bose his attitude to the problem of the Scheduled Castes. Bose, it seems, did not have a convincing reply to give.
11-1-1941	Shivram Janba Kamble died.
Jan.1941	Dr. Ambedkar pursued the question of recruitment of Scheduled Castes in the Army. Mahar Battalions were formed after a lapse of 49 years.
7-5-1941	Dr. Ambedkar wrote an editorial on the political significance of Buddha Jayanti, and said, "Brahminism is denial of democracy; Brahminism is inconsistent with democracy. If you want democracy, you must put an end to *Chaturvarnya.*"
14-7-1941	He submitted a memorial to Sir Roger Lumley, Governor of Bombay, regarding Maharvatans.
July 1941	He was appointed on the Defence Advisory Committee of the Government of India.
Aug.1941	Conference at Sinnar (district Nashik) to agitate against the tax on Mahar vatans. Dr. Ambedkar launched a no-tax campaign. He saw the Governor; and the tax was abolished.
30-3-1942	Dr. Ambedkar held (consultations with Sir Stafford Cripps.
April 1942	He founded the All-India Scheduled Castes Federation with N. Shivraj as its President, and P.N. Rajbhoj as its General Secretary.
17th-20th	Dr. Ambedkar addressed the All-India July 1942 Scheduled Castes Conference at Nagpur. The political demands of the conference were then incorporated in the paper he submitted to the Pacific Relations Conference, at Mont Tremblant,

	Quebec. (It was subsequently published under the title of Mr. *Gandhi and the Emancipation of the Untouchables.)*
20-7-1942	Dr. Ambedkar was inducted into the Viceroy's Executive Council, as Labour Member, which position he held upto June 1946.
1942	He took steps to have scholarships sanctioned to Scheduled Caste students for studies abroad. (The scheme was discontinued by the Congress in 1946).
9-8-1942	The historic 'Quit India' resolution was passed by the Indian National Congress, at Bombay.
13-11-1942	Dr. Ambedkar spoke on the All-India Radio, Bombay, on 'Indian Labour and The War'.
18-1-1943	He delivered an address at the Gokhale Hall, Pune, on the occasion of the 101st Birth Anniversary of Mahadev Govind Ranade. (Later. in April, it was published in book form. under the title of Ranade. Gandhi and Jinnah.)
Oct. 1943	Lord Wavell was appointed as Viceroy.
	The Central Assembly passed a resolution for removal of restrictions on recruitment of Scheduled Castes in the defence services.
	Dr. Ambedkar delivered a talk on Labour and Parliamentary Democracy.
11-11-1943	The Government of India nominated R.R. Bhole as its representative for propaganda overseas. He left for Britain.
1943	Dr. Ambedkar met Mahasthavtra Chandramani at Kushinara.
2-1-1944	Vithal Ramji Shinde died at Pune.
26-1-1944	Scheduled Castes Federation Conference at Kanpur.
3-4-1944 to 31-7-1944	R.R. Bhole in the United States of America.

1944	The Bombay Scheduled Castes Improvement Trust was founded, at Bombay.
Feb.1945	Dr. Ambedkar's *Pakistan* or *The Partition of India,* was published by Thacker & Co., Bombay. (It was the second and enlarged edition of *Thoughts* On *Pakistan.)*
8-5-1945	The Scheduled Castes Federation's annual conference was held at Parel, Bombay. Dr Ambedkar delivered his address on "The Communal Deadlock: A Way To Solve It".
June 1945	Dr. Ambedkar's *What Congress' and Gandhi Have Done to the Untouchables* was published.
	The Simla Conference: N. Shivraj, President, SCF, cabled to Churchill and Amery for adequate representation.
26-6-1945	The Charter of the United Nations was signed at San Francisco.
July1945	Dr. Ambedkar founded the People's Education Society of Bombay.
Aug. 1945	He spoke at the inauguration of the School of Politics, Pune.[27]
10-1-1946	He gave evidence before the British Parliamentary delegation
3-3-1946	He addressed an election meeting of the SCF at Nare Park, Bombay.
12-3-1946	*Jai Bheem* of Madras published Dr. Ambedkar's article on "Congress Attempts to Bypass Untouchables."
23-3-1946	The British Cabinet Mission arrived in Delhi.
30-3-1946	Black-flag demonstration by Scheduled Caste and people before M.K.Gandhi halting at Worli,
31-3-1946	Bombay.
3-4-1946	Congress governments formed in the provinces.
5-4-1946	Dr. Ambedkar gave his proposals to the British Cabinet Mission.

May 1946	The Bharat Bhushan Printing press set up by Dr. Ambedkar was burnt down in the clashes between his followers and caste-Hindus.
16-5-1946	The British Cabinet Mission announced its proposals. Dr. Ambedkar was greatly annoyed at claims of the Scheduled Castes being ignored.
28-5-1946	World War II ends.
17-6-1946	Dr. Ambedkar cabled to the British Premier asking for adequate representation for Scheduled Castes. He also sent to the Premier "A Critique of The Proposals of The Cabinet Mission." The Cabinet Mission announced setting up a Constituent Assembly.
20-6-1946	The Siddharth College was started by Dr. Ambedkar, in Bombay.
30-6-1946	The Cabinet Mission returned to London.
June 1946	Dr. Ambedkar resigned from the Viceroy's, Executive Council.
21-7-1946	He addressed a meeting of the SCF at Pune. Satyagraha at Pune against Congress.
24-8-1946	The interim Central Ministry was announced.
10- 1946	Death of Kisan Phaguji Bansod at Nagpur.
13-10-1946	Dr. Ambedkar's Who *Were* The *Shudras?* was published.
4-11-1946	Dr. Ambedkar met Winston Churchill, at Westerham, Kent, Churchill's country home. He also met premier Atlee at London.
5-11-1946	He addressed a meeting of the Conservative India Committee in the House of Commons. He demanded the abrogation of the Poona Pact and restoration of MacDonald's Communal Award.
Nov. 1946	He was elected to the Constituent Assembly from Bengal.
15-11-1946	He returned from London.

15-12-1946	His first speech in the Constituent Assembly was immensely applauded.
1946	The eminent economist J.M. Keynes died.
27-3-1947	Lord Mountbatten, the new Viceroy of India arrives in Delhi.
	March 1947 Dr Ambedkar's States and 'Minorities published.
29-4-1947	Article 17 of the Constitution, abolishing the practice of "Untouchability" in any form, was passed.
7-5-1947	Dr. Ambedkar released the Second Edition of The Problem of the Rupee under the new title of History of Indian Currency and Banking. Publishers: Thacker & Co., Ltd., Bombay.
14-7-1947	Lord Mountbatten inaugurates the Constituent Assembly.
22-7-1947	Dr. Ambedkar was re-elected to the Constituent Assembly in the vacancy caused by Dr. M.R. Jayakar's resignation
3-8-1947	Names of Cabinet Ministers were announced with Dr. Ambedkar as Minister for Law.
14/15-8-47	India achieved Independence, and simultaneously Pakistan was formed.
29-8-1947	The Drafting Committee of the Constituent Assembly was set up with Dr. Ambedkar as its Chairman.
1947	Prof. Dhannanand Kosambi died.
12-1-1948	M.K. Gandhi went on a fast for the release of Rs. 55 crores to Pakistan.
15-1-1948	India released Rs. 55 crores to Pakistan, in deference to the wishes of M.K.Gandhi.
18-1-1948	M.K. Gandhi broke his fast.
25-1-1948	Dr. Ambedkar convened a conference of the SC Federation at Lucknow.
30-1-1948	M.K. Gandhi was assassinated by Nathuram Godse.

Feb. 1948	Dr. Ambedkar completed the Draft Constitution.
10-3-1948	Dr. Ambedkar wrote his Preface to the Third Edition of Professor P. Lakshmi Narasu's The Essence of Buddhism. He considered Narasu's book to be 'the best book on Buddhism that has appeared so far".
9-4-1948	A Select Committee was constituted under the Chairmanship of Dr. Ambedkar to study the Hindu Code Bill.
15-4-1948	Dr. Ambedkar's second marriage with Dr (Miss) Sharada Kabir.
21-7-1948	Dr. Rajendra Prasad, President of the Constituent Assembly objected to the Hindu Code Bill.
22-7-1948	Prime Minister Jawaharlal Nehru wrote in reply to Dr. Rajendra Prasad of his full support to the Hindu Code Bill.
11-9-1948	Death of M.A. Jinnah, President of Pakistan, at Karachi.
14-10-1948	Dr. Ambedkar submitted his Memorandum on 'Maharashtra as a Linguistic State to the Dhar Committee.
18-10-1948	Dr. Ambedkar's The Untouchables was published by Amrit Book Co., New Delhi.
4-11-1948	Dr. Ambedkar presented the Draft Constitution to the Constituent Assembly.
28-11-1948	Prime Minister Nehru said in Parliament that his Government was committed to having the Hindu Code Bill passed.
17-11-1949	The third reading of the Constitution Bill began.
25-11-1949	Dr. Ambedkar's valedictory address in the Constituent Assembly received a thunderous applause.
26-11-1949	The Constitution was adopted.
19-12-1949	Prime Minister Nehru reiterated his commitment to the Hindu Code Bill.
2-5-1950	Dr. Ambedkar delivered his first public talk on

Buddha	Buddhism.
	Jayanti Dr. Ambedkar spoke on 'The Merits of 1950 Buddhism", in Delhi.
May 1950	Dr. Ambedkar contributed an article "The Buddha & The Future of His Religion", to the Maha-Bodhi of Calcutta, for its April-May 1950 number.
26-5-1950	Dr. Ambedkar visited Kandy, Sri Lanka, to see for himself 'to what extent the religion (Buddhism) is observed in its pristine purity and to what extent its people had been encrusted with beliefs incongruous with the doctrine.' He also wanted to see Buddhist ceremonials and rituals 'which the people of India had no means of witnessing'.
6-6-1950	He visited Colombo, Sri Lanka, and addressed the Young Men's Buddhist Association. He spoke on The Rise and Fall of Buddhism in India'. He was collecting material on the subject. According to him, the rise of Vaishnavism and Shaivism, and the onslaught of Islam under Allaudin, were the causes of the eclipse of Buddhism in India.
June 1950	The Milind College of the People's Education Society, was started at Aurangabad.
19-1-1951	Death of A.V. Thakkar *alias* Thakkar Bapa.
5-2-1951	Dr. Ambedkar introduced his Hindu Code Bill in Parliament, on behalf of the Government.
Feb. 1951	He contributed to the *Maha-Bodhi* of Calcutta, an article on The Rise & Fall of the Hindu Woman.
April 1951	He laid the foundation stone of Ambedkar Bhavan, in Delhi.
	May 1951 He introduced in Parliament his Representation of the People Bill.
11-6-1951	He addressed the Siddharth College Students Parliament on the Hindu Code Bill.
July 1951	He founded the Bharatiya Baudha Jana Sangha.

10-8-1951	Prime Minister Nehru let down Dr. Ambedkar in the matter of the Hindu Code Bill.
Sept. 1951 (1st week)	The foundation stone of the Milind Mahavidyalaya Aurangabad was laid by President Dr. Rajendra Prasad.
15-9-1951	President Rajendra Prasad reserved the right to sign the Hindu Code Bill, even if it was passed by Parliament.
19-9-1951	The Marriage and Divorce Bill was debated in Parliament.
11-10-1951	Dr. Ambedkar, utterly disappointed, resigned from the Nehru Cabinet.
26-11-1951	The Hindu Code Bill was killed without a tear being shed over it.
5-1-1952	Dr. Ambedkar (S.C. Federation) was defeated in the General Election by N.S. Kajrolkar (Congress).
9-3-1952	He was elected to the Parliament on the Council of States, from Bombay state.
2-6-1952	He left Bombay by air for New York to receive the honorary degree of Doctor of Laws from the Columbia University.
5-6-1952	The Columbia University conferred the honorary degree of Doctor of Laws & Letters on Dr. Ambedkar. The Columbia University hailed him as "One of India's leading citizens, a great social reformer and a valiant upholder of human rights".[28]
15-6-1952	Dr. Ambedkar returned from New York to Bombay.
22-12-1952	Dr. Ambedkar delivered a talk on "Conditions Precedent to the Successful' Working of Democracy" at a meeting of the Pune Bar.
1952	Death of Professor John Dewey, the eminent American philosopher and educationist, and Dr. Ambedkar's teacher at the Columbia of University.

1952	Babasaheh met Mahasthavir Sangharakshita, at the "Rajgriha", for the first time.
24-12-1952	Dr. Ambedkar addressed the annual gathering of the students of the Rajaram College, Kolhapur. Women of Kolhapur presented an address to him. He said that none of the prominent Indian women was genuinely interested in the social progress of women. The Hindu Code Bill was like spoilt milk.
12-1-1953	The Osmania University conferred on Dr. Ambedkar the honorary degree of Doctor of Laws.
April1953	The Untouchability (Offences) Bill was introduced h. Parliament.
May 1953 (27-5-1953)	Dr. Ambedkar spoke at Bombay on the need of Buddhism for the world.
June 1953	Opening of the Siddharth College of Commerce, Bombay.
2-9-1953	While speaking in the Council of States, on the Bill for the creation of the Andhra State. Dr. Ambedkar criticized the Government for its vacillating policy on the formation of linguistic States.
Jan.1954	Periar E.V. Ramaswami, an associate of Appadurai, convened a Buddhist conference, at Erode, to intensify Buddhist propaganda in south India.
4-1-1954	Dr. Ambedkar performed the inaugural ceremony of the Atre Pictures' film on Jotirao Phooley.
24-1-1954	While inaugurating the All-India Sat Devotees' Convention, in Bombay, Dr. Ambedkar observed that people in India had not only gone wrong on the concept of religion, but it had become a profession to collect money in the name of religion, and then waste it on sadhus, or on purposes for which there could be no moral justification. [29]

Apr.1954	He contested the reserved seat in the Loksabha from Bhandara.
May 1954	Dr. Ambedkar visited Rangoon, on the occasion of the Buddha Jayanti celebrations. He was defeated in the by-election from the Bhandara constituency. He read the news about it at Rangoon.
12-9-1954	He spoke in the Rajya Sabha on the Untouchability (Offences) Bill. He suggested that the Bill should be entitled as The Untouchables' Civil Rights Bill.
3-10-1954	He spoke on the All-India Radio on "My Personal Philosophy." He said. "I reject the Hindu social philosophy propounded in the *Bhagvadgita*, based as it is on the Triguna of the Sankhya philosophy which is, in my judgement, a cruel perversion of the philosophy of Kapila, and which had made the caste system and the system of graded inequality the law of Hindu social life."[30]
1954	When he visited Madras. Dr. Ambedkar collected the manuscript of Professor Narasu's 'The Religion of a Modern Buddhist", for publication.
Dec. 1954	He visited Rangoon for the 3rd World Buddhis Conference.
14-1-1955	Dr. Ambedkar spoke at Bombay on what he saw of Buddhism in Burma.
24-5-1955	He declared at Bombay his intention to convert to Buddhism, in October 1956.
4th May 1955	The Bharatiya Baudha Mahasabha founded by Babasahab in 1954 was registered.
25-12-1955	He installed an image of the Buddha, at Dehu Road.
29-12-1955	His Thoughts on Linguistic States was published.
1955	Prabuddha Bharat started with Yeshwantrao B. Ambedkar as its editor. (The Janata renamed as Prabuddha Bharat.)

1955	R.R Bhole was appointed as a District Judge. (Subsequently, in 1967, he was elevated to the position of High Court Judge.)
Dec.1955	Babasaheb met Mahasthavir Sangharakshita, at the Siddharth College, Bombay. (That was their second meeting.)
Feb.1956	Dr. Ambedkar completed his works The Buddha and His Dhamma. Revolution and Counter-Revolution in Ancient India, Buddha and Marx.
15-3-1956	He wrote and dictated his Preface to The Buddha and His Dhamma.
1-5-1956	He spoke in the Council of States on the problem of linguistic states.
May 1956	He spoke on the BBC on 'Why I Like Buddhism". He asserted that Buddhism was a complete answer to Marxism. He also spoke on the VOA, and dealt with the prospects of Democracy in India. "Democracy," he observed, "is a mode of associated living. The roots of Democracy are to be searched for in the social relationship, in terms of the associated life among the people who form the society."[31]
10-6-1956	He spoke in Delhi, and compared the Dhammapada with the Gita; and referred to Caste in the Dhammapada.
June 1956	The People's Education Society started the Siddharth College of Law, at Bombay.
23-9-1956	Dr. Ambedkar issued a statement on the ensuing conversion to Buddhism.
30-9-1956	He declared his intention to start the Republican Party of India.
14-10-1956	THE GREAT CONVERSION TO BUDDHISM AT NAGPUR. Dr. Ambedkar took the Buddhist vows administered to him and to Mrs Ambedkar, by Mahasthavira Chandramani, at 9:30 a.m. Dr.

	Ambedkar then administered the Buddhist vows, and the 22-Precepts to the vast concourse of the people.
Nov. 1956	Babasaheb and Mahasthavir Sangharakshita met for the third and last time, at Babasaheb's Alipore Road residence, New Delhi.
15-11-1956	Dr. Ambedkar went to Kathmandu, as a delegate to the World Buddhist Conference. He spoke on 'The Buddha & Marx'.
6-12-1956	The great Babasaheb Ambedkar passed away at Delhi.
7-12-1956	His mortal remains were cremated on the Dadar sea-shore in Bombay amid thousands of his grief-stricken followers and admirers.

Notes and References

1. The initials M.H.O.W. represents 'Military Headquarters of War' near *Satara*.
2. Pandit Doss was a native doctor, a reputed Tamil Scholar and crusader against untouchability. Krishna Swamiar was a school-teacher. Olcott took them to Ceylon, and there they became Buddhists. During the life time of Dr. B.R. Ambedkar
3. **Note :** The Historical analytical study of Dr. B.R. Ambedkar based on scientific truth i.e. call *'Nam'* or *'God'*.
4. Quoted by James Halliday alias D. Symington, Retd. I.C.S. (1926- 1947), in his A Special India, p. 126. **Note :** It was difficult to understand the Brahmins where stands the thought of *'Untouchables'* i.e. *God* or *Chamar*
5. C.B. Khairmoday, Dr. Bhimaroo Ramji Ambedkar Charitra, (Marathi), Vol. III, p. 277. **Note:** His declared were against the Brahminical pollution i.e. false Religious practice of man made not God made as a blind faith of the Brahmins.
6. Bhalchandra Phadke, Dr. Babasaheb Ambedkar (Marathi), p. 184. **Note** : War against the evil designer to brought a new concept of society i.e. class-struggle based on have and have nots.

7. Dhananjay Keer, Dr. Ambedkar : *Life & Mission*, pp. 119-120.
8. Dr. B.R. Ambedkar, Speeches & Writings, Vol. II, pp. 459-489.
9. *Ibid.*, pp. 313-478.
10. Ratnakar Ganvir (Ed), *Dr. Babasaheb Ambedkaranchi Bhashane* (Marathi).
11. B.G. Kunte (Ed), *Source Material on Babasaheb Ambedkar*, p. 36.
12. *Ibid.*, p 39.
13. Dhananjay Keer, Dr. Ambedkar : *Life & Mission*, p. 162.
14. B.G. Kunte (Ed), Source Material on Dr. Babasaheb Ambedkar, Vol. I, p. 52.
15. B.R.Ambedkar, *What Congress and Gandhi Have Done to the Untouchables*, pp. 72-73.
16. Dhanajay Keer, Dr. Ambedkar : *Life & Mission*, p. 194.
17. Dr. Ambedkar, *Speeches & Writings*, Vol. II, pp. 491 – 500.
18. B.G. Kunte (Ed), Source Materials, Vol. I, p. 79.
19. Dhananjay Keer, Dr. Ambedkar : Life & Mission, pp. 201-202.
20. B.G. Kunte (Ed), Source Material, Vol. I, p. 80.
21. *Ibid.*, p. 85,
22. Dhananjay Keer, Dr. Ambedkar : *Life & Mission*, p. 219.
23. B.G. Kunte (Ed), *Source Material*, Vol. I, pp. 106-107.
24. Dhananjay Keer, Dr. Ambedkar : *Life & Mission*, p. 230.
25. B.G. Kunte (Ed), *Source Material*, Vol. I, p. 116.
26. See C.B. Khairmoday, *Dr. Bhimrao Ramji Ambedkar*, Vol. VI, p. 96.
27. See B.G. Kunte (Ed), *Source Material* on Dr. Babasaheb Ambedkar, Vol. 1, pp. 303-304. **Note**. Dr. Ambedkar said, "I do not propose to found a school or creed of my own." He appealed to the students to follow his lead, only if they were satisfied in their minds that he was right. He commended, however, the object of the institution which was the study of politics. He differentiate the academic and politics from the intelligentsia which mar the career to the student.
28. B.G. Kunte (Ed), *Source Material*, Vol. I, p. 399.

29. *Ibid.*, p. 417.
30. D. Keer, Dr. Ambedkar : *Life & Mission*, p. 459.
31. *Ibid.*, p. 490.

Glossary

Adosa	– Loving - Kindness
Akasa	– Space
Akusala Kamma	– Bad Deeds and Bad Thoughts like Brahmins do
Ambedkar	– Policy of tolerance for future result and to work for other like labour class.
Aloka	– Circle of Light
Adharma	- Uprighteousness i.e. One.
Amritsar	- Pool of Nectar
Bhikkus	- Monks
Barawala	- Aboriginal race of Maharaja Gulab Singh of Jammu and Kashmir State
Bahishkrit Bharat	– Outcaste India, *Sudhras.*
Baba	- Father, God.
Buddha –e–Nama	- Go for the Natural thought with the practice of the '*Nam'.*
Buddha or Buddho	- Wisdom, Light, Power, Nam, God, Spiritually awakened
Brahmin	- Black power, Priestly class of tradition Self-Style God, 'Ego'.
Bhagat	- Devote.
Chamar	- God, Nam, Untouchable
Culture	- True Religion, Called 'Nam or Truth'
Chaturvarny	- Cleaverness of the mind, not above the God, but dangerous for others on *Manmukha*

Chanda	-	Will
Caste	-	Latinized word means *Pure*
Dhamma	-	Nam-Dana, Spread virtue to realize God, Reality
Dharma	-	Religion
Dukkha	-	Sorrow-Misery
Dana	-	Giving, generosity
Dyarchy	-	Duel system of Government that is God and Man, A Greek word.
Devata	-	Deity.
Dharma Rai	-	Lord of Justice or Lord of the Judgment.
Dhyan	-	Inner contemplation
Dharama shala	-	Religion House
Gurmukh	-	Face turn to Guru, Prefect Master based on historical fact not self-style.
Gandhi	-	Bad thought, Krishna, Black Power like Brahmin of India, believe on 'sexual union'
Gunas	-	Three attributions of Prakriti
Hansa	-	'Swan'
Ishwara	-	God
Janata	-	Public
Jat	-	Mouth
Jataya	-	Bird
Janam-sakhi	-	Birth – story
Kalma	-	Word, Shbad
Kabir	-	Thought of the God.
Karma	-	Action and Reaction of deeds
Kusala Kama	-	Good Deeds and thoughts
Kasthriya	-	Serve the society, Protect the people study the Veda
Khalsa	-	Pure one with obtain Living Deity called *'Nam'* or *'God'*.
Karuna	-	Fellow –feeling
Katha	-	Story

Mrityu	-	Death
Mook – Nayak of	-	The Leader of the Dumb or the 'Voice the Damb'
Macca	-	God or Nam is the Bold of the mind.
Mahabharata	-	Great Story.
Manmukh	-	Devotee of the mind like Gandhi and Jinnah, a destructive power.
Maha-Bodhi	-	Spiritualism.
Maya	-	Illusion, Unreality.
Marga – Data	-	God or Light
Murti-Puja	-	Idol-worship, Black – Power.
Nam	-	Path of purity, Path of virtue for self-realization. Creative power in man form.
Namaskara	-	To obtain the Bliss of Father realize with the practice of the 'Nam'.
Nawab	-	Governor in India under the Moghul Empire.
Narad Rishi	-	Ancient Indian sage.
Periyar	-	Great Soul.
Pingula or Pingala	-	Current column of the finer body called 'Nam'
Purusha	-	Creator 'Primal Being'
Patar	-	Letter
Prajapatis	-	Lords of creatures
Prabuddha Bharat	-	India of the Self-Enlightened soul
Pat	-	Love of the father Buddha or God
Prajnya	-	Wisdom
Panth	-	Way
Parivraja	-	Renunciation
Rama	-	Way of the mind for Salvation Called *Nam* in living Deity in Idol – form for others
Rajput	-	Race of the slave women
Shastras	-	Application of Brahmins.

Sahib - *Nam, God, Chamar, Untouchable*
Sabdavidya - The treatise of the Heavenly Bodies and thought
Sudhra - Pure thought
Sikh - To learn, disciple
Samma Satti - Mindfulness
Sattva - Pleasure of Light
Samma Vyayamo - Right Endeavour
Sila - Morality
Samma Vacca - Right speech
Samma Ditti - Self Practice of the *Nam.* Right Views
Tantu - Strand
Tantric Creed - Practice of *Tantra*, came into the tradition of Brahmins to fear the man and to collect the money
Tulsi - Holy Basil
Tattwa - 'Element' The entire world is made up five tattwas : Earth (prithiv), Water (Jal), Fire (Agni), Air (Vayu) and ether (akash).
Tilak - A mark on forehead, Brahminical out worldly thought to symbolize as 'ego'.
Udasi - Detached from the world life with the practice of *Nam.*
Var - Heroic Balled in Spiritual form
Vyas - Without desire i.e. God.
Vital-Vidhavansak - Destroyer of Brahminical or Ceremonial Pollution
Vidyas - Treatise of blessed God
Verna - Word or 'Nam', Akshar
Vaishya - Race of mind or mana, viz, with trade. 'Husbandman'
Vaishnavite - Worshipper for the lust of money not for the purification of soul.
Visvamitra - God, *Nam, Chamar*
Vedas - 'Knowledge', Rig-veda Knowledge of the

		'Nam' as a real centre of knowledge.
Yama	-	God of Death
Yuga	-	Age of Cycle of time
Yana	-	Vehicle, the path

Bibliography

(A) Primary Sources

1. *Manusmirit*, VII, VIII, XIII.
2. *Paingala Upanisad* by R.N. Kanlsk Aggarwal.
3. Rig Veda.
4. *Rajatarangini*, Kalhana, Tr. By M. A. Stein, 1-2 Vols. Delhi Reprint; 1989.
5. Srimad Bhagavad gita : Tr. By. S.C. Vaishya, Revised by R.N. Kaul & K. Aggarwal.
6. Satpatya Brahman – VII.
7. *Vishnu Purana.*

(B) Modern Works

8. Ambedkar, B.R. *Annihilation of Caste* ; Aurangabad, Reprint. 2003.
9. Ambedkar, B.R. *Who Were The Sudhras* ?; Reprint ; Aurangabad ; 2003.
10. Ambedkar, B.R. *Writings and Speeches. Vol. I & II.*
11. Ambedkar B.R. *What Congress and Gandhi have Done To the Untouchables.*
12. Ambedkar B.R. *Caste in India.*
13. Ambedkar B.R. *The Buddh and His Dhamma* ; Nagpur; 1997.
14. Azad, A.K. *Indian Wins Freedom.*
15. Aggarwal, J.C. *Modern Indian History*; New Delhi; Reprint; 2004.

16. Ahir, D.C. *Dr. Ambedkar and the Indian Constitution.*

17. Ambedkar B.R. *Buddha and the Future of his Religion* ; 1950.

18. Ajnat, Surendra ; *Letters of Ambedkar*: Jalandhar; 1993.

19. Basham, A.L. *The Wonder That Was India* ; Delhi Reprint

20. Bagchi, Amiya ; *Private Investment,* Delhi 1979.

21. Besant, Annie ; *India That Shall be;* New Delhi 1914.

22. Besant, Annie ; *India Bonnd or Free, 1926.*

23. Besant, Annie ; *The Future of Indian Politics.*

24. Besant, Annie ; *India and The Empire, 1914.*

25. Bose ; A.C. *The Call of Vedas ;* Bombay; 1970.

26. Bazaz, Prem Nath ; *Kashmir in Crucible* ; Srinagar ; 2005.

27. Bazaz, Prem Nath ; *Daughters of Vatasta* ; New Delhi; 1959.

28. Birla, G.D. *In the Shadow of the Mahatma.*

29. Briggs ; G.W. *The Chamars ;* Delhi ; Reprint. 2004.

30. Chhabra, G.S. *Advance Study in the Constitutional History of India, Jalandhar. 3 Vols.*

31. Carr, E.H. *What is History ?* New York; Reprint : 1984.

32. -do- *The New Society* ; London ; Reprint ; 1960.

33. Chand, Tara ; *History of Freedom Movement in India;* 2 Vols.

34. Choral, V. *Indian Unrest.*

35. Chinta Mani, C. Y. *Indian Politics Since Mutiny.*

36. Das, Bhagwan ; *Bheem Patrika.* Jalandhar ; 1980.

37. Das, Bhagwan ; *Thus spoke Ambedkar,* Vol. I-IV.

38. Dude, S.C. (ed) *Tribal Hesitage of India,* New Delhi, 1977 – Vol. I.

39. Ezekiel, Isacc A. *Kabir, The Great Mystic ;* Beas ; Reprint, 2003.

40. *Encyclopaedia Britannica,* Fifteenth edition ; Chicago ; 1978.

41. *Encyclopaedia of Religion and Ethics* Vol. X.

42. Four Authors ; *A Simple History of England.*

43. Gamom, George ; *The Creation of the Universe* ; New York ; 1952.

44. Gunther, John; *Inside Asia.*

45. Grover, B.L. & Grover ; S. *Modern Indian History ; New Delhi ;* Reprint. 2005.

46. Ganvir, Ratnakar; *Bahishkrit Bharatated Agralekh*; Bhusawal 1976.

47. Ganjre ; M.F. Dr *Babasaheb Ambedkar Karanchi Bhashana 1 to VI. Vols.*

48. Halliday, James, retd. I.C.S. (1926, 1947) A Special India 1925.

49. Hugel, B.C. *Kashmir and the Punjab*, Jammu 1972.

50. Hoyland, J.S. Gopal Krishan Gokhale; *His Life and Speeches,* Calcutta 1930.

51. Hardiman, *Peasant Agitation in Kheda District.*

52. Jagadeeshan, P. *Social Justice and Challeges in Contemporary India.* Bangalore ; 2006.

53. Jois, M.Rama ; *Guruji and Social Harmony ;* Karnataka, 2006.

54. Kumar Raj. *History of The Chamar Dynasty*; Delhi ; 2008; 2 Vols.

55. Kumar, Raj, *History of the Brahmans.* Delhi ; 2006.

56. Kumar, Raj. *Paintings and Lifestyles of Jammu Region*; Delhi ; 2006.

57. Kumar, Raj, Encyclopaedia *of Untouchables,* Ancient, Medieval and Modern. Delhi 2008.

58. Kane, P.V. *History of Dharmasastra* 3 Vols. Poona, 1968.

59. Kadam, K.N. *Dr. Babasaheb Ambedkar and the Significance of His Movement*; Bombay 1993.

60. Kadam ; K.N. *Currents and Counter – Currents.*

61. Kapoor, M.L. *History of Jammu and Kashmir State ;* 3 Vols.

62. Khairmoday, C.B. *Dr. B.R. Ambedkar Charitra.* Vols. I to IV.

63. Khairmoday, C.B. *Dr. B.R. Ambedkar.* Vol. 1. Bombay.

64. Kunte, B.G. (ed) *Source Material on Dr. B.R. Ambedkar* Vol. I.

65. Khurana ; K.L. *History of India ;* Agra ; Reprint ; 2007.
66. Kamble, J.R. *Pursuit of Equality in History.*
67. Khobragade ; Ram; *Dr. Ambedkar, A Symbol of Global Socio-Political Revolution.* New Delhi, 2005.
68. Keer, Dhananjay ; Dr. B.R. Ambedkar : *Life and Mission* ; Bombay ; Reprint; 1981.
69. Kundra & Baba ; *Modern Europe since 1789* ; Delhi ; Reprint; 2006.
70. Kundra & Baba ; *Modern History of India* – Delhi, Reprint, 2006.
71. Kunte, B.G. (Ed). *Source Material on Baba Saheb Ambedkar.*
72. Limbala, Sharan Kumar; Tr. *Towards and Aesthetic of Dalit literature,* New Delhi 2004.
73. Lawrence W.A. *Provincial Gazetter of Kashmir,* New Delhi; Reprint 1985.
74. Low, B. A. (ed) *Congress and the Raj.*
75. Luniya ; B.N. *Evolution of Indian Culture* ; Agra Reprint, 2005.
76. Mehta. D.D.; *Positive Sciences in The Vedas* New Delhi.
77. Moore, J.R. *Crisis of Indian Unity.*
78. Mehta, Rohit, *The call of the Upanishads* ; Delhi 1984.
79. Moon, Vasant (ed). *Dr. B.R. Ambedkar Writings and Speeches,* Maharashtra 2 Vols.
80. Moqsood, R. Islam, U.S.A 1975.
81. Masani, R.P. *Dadabhai Naoroji.*
82. Naik, J.V. *The Reformer and the Quest for Social Justice in Indian History,* Karala ; 2007.
83. Nehru's Pt. J.L. *Autobiography and Selected Works,* 1930, 4 vols.
84. Puri; J.R. *Guru Nanak, His Mystic Teachings ;* Beas, 2004.
85. Pyarelal ; *Mahatma Gandhi The last Phase* Vol. II.
86. Philips, C.H.& Wain Wright ; *The Partition of India.*
87. Pandey, Gyan ; *Ascendancy.*
88. Radha Krishna, S. *Indian Philosophy,* London ; 1929.
89. Romesh, B.G. *Biography Series ; Dr. B.R. Ambedkar ; Bangalore ;* 2005.

90. Russell, Bertrand ; *History of Western Philosophy ;* London ; 1946.
91. Rajshekar, V.T. *Brahminism.* Reprint. 2003.
92. Rao; K.S. *John Maynard Keynes, an Article in Mirror* ; Bombay ; 1983.
93. Rose, H.A. *A Glossary of the Tribes and Castes ;* Language Department Punjab, Reprint ; 1990. 3 Vols.
94. Rush, J. H. *The Dawn of life.* Bulter and Tanner, 1958.
95. Singh, Sampuran ; *Dynamic Interplay Between Science and Religion ;* Jodhpur ; 1978.
96. Sumit Sarkar ; *Modern India (1885-1947)* Delhi Reprint ; 2005.
97. Srivastva, A.N & Majundar, R.K. *History of Modern India,* Delhi 1986.
98. Saraf, Anjali ; *Women and Shudras Under the Hindu Law. M. Phil Dissertation ;* University of Jammu ; 1985.
99. Spencher, Herbet, The study of sociology London.
100. Sheering, M.A. *Hindu Tribes and Castes ;* 1881. Vol. 1.
101. Singh, Sohan ; *The Ballad of God and Man*; Amritsar ; 1982.
102. Sharma, Vasdev, *Cosmic View of Life in Guru Nanak Bani;* Language Dept. of Punjab (Patiala) 1996.
103. Sethi, V.K. *Kabir, The weaver of God's Name* ; Beas.
104. Sharma, L.P. *Indian National Movement and Constitutional Development.* Agra ; Reprint, 2003.
105. Singh, Taran *Guru Nanak and Indian Religious Thought,* Patiala ; 1970.
106. Tale of the Mystic East, Beas ; Reprint, 2006.
107. Tagore, Rabindranath ; *Boundless Sky*; Kolkata ; Reprint. 2006.
108. Tendulkar, B.C. Mahatma ; 3 Vols.
109. Townsend ; P.N. *Dimension of Islam*; London ; 1969.
110. Tahar, Mohammed (ed), *Islam The Religion of Submission.* New Delhi, 1998.
111 Upadhyaya; K.N.Guru Ravidas, *The Philosopher's Stone*; Beas ; Reprint, 2005.

112. Vittie, G.C. M.C. *Cosmological Theory*, London ; 1952.
113. Yadav, Ramakant; Gopal Baba Walangkar in Siddha; 1982.
114. Zelliot, Eleanor ; *Learning the Use of Political Means* ; 1973.
115. Zakaria, Rafiq ; *Muhammad and the Quran* ; New Delhi, 1991.

(C) Papers, Magazine, Newspapers and Files

116. Jayakar and Thakurdas Papers.
117. Walchand Hira Chand Papers. File No. 8(11).
118. A Bunch of Old Letters, Bombay, 1958. S. Gopal for Political development of India. *Home Political* Department 33/24/1931.
119. Temple wood Collection about the arrest of Public *Benthall* & *Uina* Kaure's papers.
120. R.E. Hawkins Papers in Cambridge South Asian Centre.
121. Chaudhari Abdul Hey's Article in H. Kanger (ed) K.M. Ashraf Delhi, 1969.
122. Illegal Bombay Congress Bulletin, 17 Oct. 1932, Thakardas Papers F.N. 101.
123. M.K. Jayakar Papers ; F.N. 456.
124. Home Political Dept. F.N. 3/11/1933-9 in Judith Brown ; *Gandhi and Civil Disobedience Movement.*
125. Shyes to Hoare, 6 March; 1932, *Shyles Collections* MSS; Eur. F.N. 150.
126. *Daily Excelsior*, Nov. 1, 2007.
127. *Hindustan Times.* 6-2-1967.
128. *Dalit Voice*, Magazine, Bangalore,, 6-15-2005.
129. A Copy of Gautam Buddhache Chanita Buddhist Welfare Society. Nagpur, 1982.
130. A.S. *Alias* Appa Ranapise ; *Dalitanchi Vrithia.* Patre.

Index